Software Failure Risk

Measurement and Management

APPLICATIONS OF MODERN TECHNOLOGY IN BUSINESS

Series Editor: **Eric Clemons**
University of Pennsylvania

Founding Editor: **Howard L. Morgan**
University of Pennsylvania

COMPUTERS AND BANKING: Electronic Funds Transfer Systems and Public Policy
Edited by Kent W. Colton and Kenneth L. Kraemer

DATA BASE ADMINISTRATION
Jay-Louise Weldon

DATA COMMUNICATIONS: An Introduction to Concepts and Design
Robert Techo

DECISION ANALYSIS
Geoffrey Gregory

OFFICE AUTOMATION: A User-Driven Method
Don Tapscott

OPERATIONS MANAGEMENT OF DISTRIBUTED SERVICE NETWORKS: A Practical Quantitative Approach
Niv Ahituv and Oded Berman

SOFTWARE FAILURE RISK: Measurement and Management
Susan A. Sherer

Software Failure Risk

Measurement and Management

Susan A. Sherer
College of Business and Economics
Lehigh University
Bethlehem, Pennsylvania

Springer Science+Business Media, LLC

Library of Congress Cataloging-in-Publication Data

Sherer, Susan A.
Software failure risk : measurement and management / Susan A. Sherer.
p. cm. -- (Applications of modern technology in business)
Includes bibliographical references and index.
ISBN 978-1-4613-6316-3 ISBN 978-1-4615-3020-6 (eBook)
DOI 10.1007/978-1-4615-3020-6
1. Computer software--Reliability. 2. Risk management.
I. Title. II. Series.
QA76.76.R44S54 1992
005.1'068'1--dc20 92-29736
CIP

ISBN 978-1-4613-6316-3

Originally published by Plenum Press, New York in 1992
Softcover reprint of the hardcover 1st edition 1992

To my husband,
Howard,
and my children,
Jeffrey and Ilana

Acknowledgments

I am most appreciative of the people whose efforts have contributed to the publication of this book.

Professor Eric K. Clemons, Wharton School, University of Pennsylvania, provided many ideas and suggestions that helped launch this research. His advice and thought-provoking comments have strengthened the quality of my work.

At each of the case study sites, there were a number of individuals, both users and systems developers, who not only provided access to their data but also devoted their time to describing the applications and environments and critically evaluating the methodology. Although the identity of the case study sites remains confidential, I would be remiss if I did not collectively thank these individuals.

I also thank James B. Hobbs, Professor Emeritus, Lehigh University, for his painstaking editing of the original manuscript. In addition, Anneliese von Mayrhauser, Colorado State University, provided excellent and practical suggestions that improved the content of this book.

Finally, a special thanks to my family—to my parents, Shirley and Herbert Tilchen, who provided my educational foundation; to my children, Jeffrey and Ilana, for understanding the time commitments of my work; and most of all to my husband, Howard, who not only provided the environment for me to achieve my goals for this project but also wholeheartedly continues to support all my efforts.

Contents

Part I. Understanding Software Failure Risk

Part III. Software Failure Risk Management

Appendixes

Part I

Understanding Software Failure Risk

Chapter 1

Introduction

Modern society depends on automated systems to process, manipulate, and store vast amounts of critical information—information that controls functions crucial to the viability of many organizations. "An increasing portion of our GNP is devoted to the collection, analysis, packaging, movement of information." Information has become a commodity and it resides in computers (D. Jenkins, quoted in Burgess, 1988).

Computer software contains the instructions that manipulate this critical information. Failure of that software can lead to faulty information processing and subsequently to losses that may threaten economic survival or human life. *Software failure risk* is the expected economic loss that can result if software fails to operate correctly. The ability to identify and measure software failure risk can be used to manage this risk.

This book provides an understanding of software failure risk and its relationship to other risks associated with software development and use. It provides methodology along with applications describing how this risk can be identified and measured. Finally, the book illustrates how software failure risk can be managed during software development and use.

1.1. WHY IS SOFTWARE FAILURE SIGNIFICANT?

The past decade has shown an increasing reliance on computer software by government, corporations, and individuals. Evidence suggests that this reliance on software will increase even more rapidly. Many functions previously performed manually are being computerized; few functions, once automated, lose computer support. The increasing computerization of society is creating more dependence on software, even for such critical functions as air traffic control, nuclear power plant control, and operating medical equipment. In the business community, everything from supermarkets to stock exchanges is computerized. And a growing number of systems operate in real time, thereby decreasing or eliminating the opportunity for human intervention, further contributing to our reliance on software.

Difficult and unsolved problems regarding the failure of software have been recognized:

> During the past five years, software defects have killed sailors, maimed patients, wounded corporations and threatened to cause the government securities market to collapse. Such problems are likely to grow as industry and the military increasingly rely on software to run systems of phenomenal complexity. (Davis, 1987)

Peter Neumann, editor of *Software Engineering Notes*, advises that "if something you really care about (such as lives, money, resources, just plain data, or even the survival of the world) is to be entrusted to a computer system, you should all be very suspicious." He suggests, in fact, that when the real risks become too great, we had better rethink the use of computers in those applications (Neumann, 1985, 1989).

Corresponding to the greater dependence on computers has been the development of increasingly reliable hardware. These hardware improvements have increased the likelihood of software as a source of failure. Software has contributed to some of the most widely publicized computer disasters in the past decade:

- A software error in the Patriot missile's radar system allowed an Iraqi Scud to penetrate air defenses and slam into an American military barracks in Saudi Arabia, killing 28 people during the gulf war (Schmitt, 1991).
- A software error in the programs that route calls through the AT&T network was blamed for the nine-hour breakdown in 1990 of the long-distance telephone network, dramatizing the vulnerability of complex computer systems everywhere (Elmer-DeWitt, 1990).
- A software error involving the operation of a switch on the Therac-25, a computer-controlled radiation machine, delivered excessive amounts of radiation, killing at least four people (Jacky, 1989).

- A software design error in the Bank of New York's government securities system resulted in the bank's failure to deliver more than $20 billion in securities to purchasers (Juris, 1986).

Even when only economic loss is involved, it is difficult to estimate the total amount of damage caused to society by software failure. Many failures are probably not even reported. A study commissioned by Great Britain's Department of Trade and Industry conservatively estimated the direct cost of Britain's software failures at $900 million per year for software produced domestically and sold in the open market. If imported and inhouse software costs as well as indirect costs are included, failure costs are considerably higher (Woolnough, 1988).

Software failure can result in direct losses to an organization when information is missing or invalid. Indirect losses such as lost business from lack of customer trust may also result from software failure. Additional costs may be incurred to install manual backup systems and to recoup customer loyalty. Several examples of the repercussions of reported failures within the last five years illustrate the impact of software failure.

- The Bank of New York had to pay $5 million interest on more than $20 billion it was forced to borrow from the Federal Reserve Bank in order to repay sellers for the securities it had been receiving when its software failed to process incoming credits from those transfers. Moreover, when government securities trading was disrupted, metal traders, believing that a financial crisis had hit the Treasury bond market, bid up the price of platinum futures from $12.40 to $351.20 per ounce—a 29-year record (Juris, 1986).
- A computer error cost American Airlines $50 million in lost ticket sales when its reservation system mistakenly restricted sales of discount tickets, driving price-conscious travelers to American's competitors (Andrews, 1988).
- A computer error understated the British Retail Price Index by 1% from February 1986 to October 1987, costing the British government £121 million in compensation to pension and benefit holders, donations to charities, and related administrative costs (*Software Engineering Notes*, 1991).
- A software error allowed winning lottery tickets to be sold after the winning number had been drawn in the Tri-State Megabucks game for Vermont, New Hampshire, and Maine, resulting in several belated winners collecting up to $5000 (*Software Engineering Notes*, 1991).
- A software error in Washington's Rainier Bank Teller machines permitted unlimited amounts of money to be withdrawn in excess of customer balances. The bank then had to incur the cost of trying to recover the overages (*Software Engineering Notes*, 1985).

- After the failure of its long distance network in January 1990, AT&T's damage-control effort to regain customer confidence involved a day of discounts that averaged 33% below the regular tolls. Most analysts projected a loss of market share for AT&T when corporate customers added a backup long distance carrier. After AT&T had spent millions of dollars in advertising, the software failure left its corporate image sounding rather hollow, a fact capitalized on by Sprint when it provided its access code in full-page ads two days after the mishap (Mabry, 1990).
- When the American Airlines SABRE system shut down for twelve hours, business was lost because operators in 14,000 travel agencies could not immediately confirm reservations on American without the network. In addition, airline reservations had to be written and confirmed later, increasing the cost of business (*Los Angeles Times*, May 1989; *San Jose Mercury News*, 1989).
- When a hospital bookkeeping system's software failed, at least one hundred hospitals had to incur costs involved in switching to manual bookkeeping functions. While permanent data was not lost and no threat to patient treatment occurred, the installation of manual procedures posed additional operational costs (*Los Angeles Times*, September 1989).

1.2. WHY CAN'T SOFTWARE FAILURE RISK BE ELIMINATED?

If software failure can be so disastrous, why can't the potential for failure be completely eliminated? The main reason is that software can never be guaranteed to be 100% reliable. Software systems are discrete-state systems that do not have repetitive structures. The mathematical functions that describe the behavior of software systems are not continuous, and traditional engineering mathematics does not help in their verification (Parnas, 1985). Nor are correctness proofs possible for large software systems. The number of states in software systems can be infinite, prohibiting exhaustive testing. While testing can show the presence of errors, it can not prove that software is free of errors.

So what can be done? Improved software engineering techniques are developed and used. Prototyping and the use of formal verification methods can minimize the introduction of errors when requirements are being developed. Modular designs that incorporate information hiding, data abstraction, and structured programming can minimize system errors. And new software development practices such as the cleanroom approach (Selby *et al.*, 1987), are advocated when reliability is critical. But none of these methods can guarantee the reliability of software.

So how do we gain confidence in the software we develop? We test and test and test:

> Programming is a trial and error craft. People write programs without any expectation that they will be right the first time. They spend at least as much time testing and correcting errors as they spent writing the initial program. Large concerns have separate groups of testers to do quality assurance. (Parnas, 1985)

But testing and implementing improved methods for evaluating and controlling reliability in software add to the time and money spent to develop and release a new system. Reliability requirements conflict with the need to introduce new software quickly. As organizations become increasingly aware of the possibilities provided by information technology and the advantages to be gained from using software to perform critical functions, the demand for new software systems increases.

Studies have shown that the demand for new software is increasing faster than the ability to develop it (Boehm, 1981). The U.S. Department of Defense alone estimates that it is short one million programmers and analysts (Davis, 1987). Moreover, the supply of skilled programmers is decreasing even as demand continues to grow. Between 1980 and 1987 enrollment in university computer science curricula fell from 8.6 percent to 3.2 percent of the student population of the United States; half are foreign nationals, most of whom intend to return home upon graduation. The vast majority of people who entered the profession in the mid-1960s with the advent of the IBM System/360 are going to retire by the end of this century (Williamson, 1990).

Meanwhile, the rate of software growth is considerably greater than that of the economy in general. This growing software backlog provides impetus for the early release of software. Since testing comes at the end of the development project and is usually the most mis-scheduled part of the programming effort (Brooks, 1982), the need to meet deadlines contributes to the release of improperly tested systems. Moreover, competitive advantage can sometimes be obtained by early release of software. This creates a situation which produces a great deal of bad software (Boehm and Papaccio, 1988). Recent examples abound.

- The Bank of America brought its new trust accounting and reporting system on line before it was fully debugged in order to replace an aging system. The system crashed for days at a time, resulting in costly delays in trading securities in pension and trust funds valued at more than $38 million for more than 800 corporations, unions, and government agencies (Zonana, 1987).
- A Minneapolis public relations firm switched to a new accounting and billing system, hoping to save staff time by dismantling the old system before installing the new one. When the new system failed to work, customers could not be billed for months, and even then manual methods had to be used. This led to a substantial cash flow crunch, causing the firm to depend on interest-bearing loans until the situation was corrected (*Software Engineering Notes*, 1988).

1.3. HOW CAN WE MANAGE SOFTWARE FAILURE RISK?

Thus, because of the limitations of verification technology, exacerbated by development pressures that often encourage the early release of software, we cannot guarantee that software will never fail. So how do we deal with the risk that software *may* fail? By managing software failure risk during both development and use. Development, testing, and project management research have focused on ways to improve quality and reliability. Special procedures have been developed to evaluate the safety of critical applications. Vulnerability is reduced by installing controls on the use of the software. Recovery procedures have become important components of most software systems. Even software error and omission insurance has become available.

However, none of the traditional methods of managing software failure risk actually identifies and measures the risk of software failure. The expected loss due to failure of a software system varies tremendously with the application of the system and the environment in which it operates. The loss will be very different if software fails in a financial planning system as compared to an air traffic control system. Even in the same air traffic control system, the potential loss varies widely between operations at O'Hare and Altoona airports.

Within a system the failure risk may also vary greatly. Some modules or components of a system may provide more critical functions than others, with the expected loss due to failure in these modules proving much greater than in other modules. Moreover, reliability among modules may differ. Risk can be managed more cost effectively by identifying those portions of a system that provide the greatest risk of failure. Measurement of the risk of failure of specific components of a system can guide the management of risk both during development and use of a software system, minimizing software backlogs while still reducing risk.

1.4. HOW CAN SOFTWARE FAILURE RISK BE MEASURED?

Software failure risk is the expected loss from software faults in a system. It can be estimated from the likelihood of failure multiplied by the *software exposure*, the expected economic significance of failure. This estimate combines the significance of software failure with the more traditional reliability measure, failure likelihood.

The economic significance of software failure can be estimated from environmental considerations almost independently of the details of the software. The economic consequences of the loss of an aircraft do not depend on the nature of the air traffic control system in use. However, the likelihood that a software failure will produce a loss does depend on environmental considerations, such as manual back-up, training, and the quality of personnel and procedures.

Estimating the probability that a failure might occur is more complicated. This estimate is composed of

- The number of faults, and
- The probability that a fault will produce a failure

The former can be estimated using Bayesian analysis. The model presented in this book assumes that characteristics of similar programs, written by similar personnel, can be analyzed to determine a rough estimate of the number of faults and that this estimate can be improved as experience with the system is gained.

Analyzing the second component is too complex to be treated by studying the entire system as a single unit, primarily because individual components of a system have different failure probabilities, which contribute differently to loss. The probability that a fault will produce a failure is best computed by analyzing individual modules. This requires examining the following:

- The probability that a given module contains one or more faults, again estimated using Bayesian analysis based on experience with similar modules
- The probability that a fault will produce a failure, largely based on the structure and use of the module

Actually computing *module exposure*, the expected consequence of failure due to faults in one specific module, is performed by relating individual modules and their potential faults to failure modes and their economic consequences.

Finally, the *software failure risk* is computed by combining the exposure due to individual modules with the probability that these modules contain faults that can produce failure, using

- Module exposure, and
- The expected number of failures due to faults in that module

1.5. HOW CAN SOFTWARE FAILURE RISK MEASUREMENT GUIDE RISK MANAGEMENT?

Software failure risk measurement can be used to guide the development, testing, maintenance, and use of a software system. First, knowledge of the operational risks due to software failure can be used when making critical decisions about the system's design. The high-risk functions of the system are identified and the system designed to minimize the probability of failure of the software performing these functions. More experienced personnel, for example, can be assigned to functions with the highest risk.

Generally, it is not possible to test a software system until perfection is assured, due to the possible existence of an infinite number of combinations of inputs and paths. Trade-offs must be made concerning allocation of test resources: although all portions will be tested, some may be tested more intensively than others. Software failure risk assessment can direct and guide this testing process. Instead of randomly testing until the likelihood of failure is judged small enough, testing continues until the consequences of failure no longer justify the cost of testing.

Trade-offs concerning the allocation of effort are becoming increasingly prevalent during software maintenance, as the amount of software that must be maintained grows. Software failure risk assessment can provide a theoretical basis for these tradeoffs.

The growing number of product liability claims against software manufacturers is expected to continue, according to experts on computer law (*Business Insurance*, 1987). Increasing litigation by customers, some of it successful, is driving an awareness that service contracts, license agreements, and sales contracts are no longer satisfactory means of avoiding responsibility for damages due to software failure (Haack, 1984; Fass, 1984). Insurers are offering "errors and omissions" policies for software as one step in the management of software risk (*Business Insurance*, 1987). To set rates for these policies, underwriters use general information regarding the company and the data processed. Measurement of the differential risk of software failure could supplement this information to determine how to insure software products properly.

Evaluation of software failure risk can enable users to choose among competing software products. Software failure risk assessment can be integrated into decisions regarding the purchase and installation of software.

In addition, internal auditors are faced with the task of designing and implementing controls in the computing environment. Software failure risk assessment can evaluate the effectiveness of these controls and suggest where additional controls may be warranted.

1.6. OVERVIEW OF THIS BOOK

The first section of this book provides background for understanding risk—what it is and how it is manifested in information systems. The objective of Part I is to provide a framework for understanding how to deal with risk and to specifically describe what software failure risk measures.

Chapter 2 defines risk and discusses the process of analyzing and managing all types of risk, including new techniques developed to analyze risk in complex engineered systems.

Chapter 3 focuses on software risks, introducing and describing the components of risk in software development. The objective here is to develop an understanding of what software failure risk is and what it is not.

Part II provides and explains the methodology for measuring software failure risk. Chapter 4 develops procedures and mathematical models for assessing software failure risk. Both the magnitude and likelihood of loss are estimated. First, procedures are identified to assess the magnitude of loss caused by factors that operate in the environment external to the software. Second, a methodology is developed to assess the exposure of individual modules in a software system. A Bayesian approach is adopted to estimate the likelihood of software failure. Estimates of module exposure and expected number of failures are then combined to develop an overall estimate of software failure risk.

The application of this risk assessment methodology is illustrated with three studies, each with financial implications: a commercial loan system (Chapter 5), a funds-transfer security system (Chapter 6), and a payables processing system (Chapter 7). Each study presents the detailed steps involved in the methodology: assessing external risk, analyzing module exposure, and estimating failure likelihood. In addition, each case study demonstrates the application of the methodology using varying types and amounts of information.

Part III illustrates the implications of the methodology for software development and use. Examples are drawn from the case studies in Part II. Chapter 8 discusses the key decisions and concerns in managing the software development process and describes how failure risk assessment contributes to improved system management by focusing efforts on the high-risk components of the system. Chapter 9 specifically addresses the software testing process, providing a model to determine the optimum amount of test time to allocate to different modules in a software system. Chapter 10 discusses how risk measurements can be used to guide software maintenance. And Chapter 11 presents the key considerations in the decision to make or buy software and discusses how failure risk assessment can be used to guide these decisions.

In short, this book provides an alternative framework for software quality, one firmly grounded in the economic significance of software failure. It demonstrates how to measure and use more meaningful measures of software quality than traditional software reliability metrics. These measures include software exposure and software failure risk—the magnitude of the potential loss due to software failure and the expected value of this loss, respectively.

REFERENCES

Andrews, N., "Software Bug Cost Millions at Airline," *New York Times*, September 12, 1988, Section D, p. 3, Column 4.

Boehm, B., *Software Engineering Economics*, New Jersey: Prentice-Hall, 1981.
Boehm, B. and P. Papaccio, "Understanding and Controlling Software Costs," *IEEE Trans. Software Engrg.* **SE-14**(10), (October 1988), 1462–1477.
Brooks, F. P., *The Mythical Man-Month*, Reading, MA: Addison-Wesley, 1982.
Burgess, J., "Searching for a Better Computer Shield: Virus Incident Underscores Vulnerability of Companies as Role of Machines Widens," *The Washington Post*, November 13, 1988, p. H1.
Business Insurance, "Software Firms Discover E&O Cover," November 30, 1987, p. 54.
Davis, B., "Costly Bugs: As Complexity Rises, Tiny Flaws in Software Pose a Growing Threat," *The Wall Street Journal*, January 28, 1987, p. 1.
Elmer-Dewitt, P., "Ghost in the Machine," *Time*, January 29, 1990, pp. 58–59.
Fass, S., " 'Canned' Software Vendors Fear Liability Lawsuits," *Journal of Commerce*, March 30, 1984, p. 22B.
Haack, M. T., "Insuring the Data Processing Risk," *Best's Review*, January 1984, pp. 44–50.
Jacky, J., "Programmed for Disaster: Software Errors that Imperil Lives," *The Sciences* **29**(5), (1989), 22–27.
Juris, R., "EDP Auditing Lessens Risk Exposure," *Computer Decisions*, July 15, 1986, pp. 36–42.
Los Angeles Times, "Reservation System Breaks Down," May 13, 1989, Financial Desk, Part 4, p. 2.
——"Program Error Halts Hospitals' Computer Work," September 20, 1989, p. 23.
Mabry, M., and E. Bradburn, "The Tarnishing of AT&T's Reliable Image," *Newsweek*, January 29, 1990, pp. 70–71.
Neumann, P. G., "A Comment on SEN's Anthologized Tales of Woe," *Software Engineering Notes* **10**(1), (January 1985), ACM SIGSOFT, p. 9.
——"Risks to the Public in Computer and Related Systems," *Software Engineering Notes* **14**(1), (January 1989), ACM SIGSOFT, 6–21.
Parnas, D., "Software Aspects of Strategic Defense Systems," *Comm. ACM* **28**(12), (December 1985), 1326–1335.
San Jose Mercury News, "Travel Agents in a Holding Pattern after Airline Ticket Computer Stalls," May 13, 1989, p. 4D.
Schmitt, E., "Computer Failure Let Scud Through," *The Morning Call*, Allentown, PA, May 21, 1991, p. A1.
Selby, R. W., V. R. Basili, and F. T. Baker, "Cleanroom Software Development: An Empirical Evaluation," *IEEE Trans. Software Engrg.* **SE-13**(9), (September 1987), 1027–1037.
Software Engineering Notes **10**(3), "Risks to the Public in Computer and Related Systems," (P.G. Neumann, ed.), (July 1985), ACM SIGSOFT, p. 13.
——**13**(4), "Risks to the Public in Computer and Related Systems," (P. G. Neumann, ed.), (October 1988), ACM SIGSOFT, 3–20.
——**16**(1), "Risks to the Public in Computer and Related Systems," (P. G. Neumann, ed.), (January 1991), ACM SIGSOFT, 11–19.
Williamson, M., "Getting a Handle on CASE," *CIO*, (April 1990), pp. 42–51.
Woolnough, R., "Britain Scrutinizes Software Quality," *Electron. Engrg. Times*, June 13, 1988, p. 19.
Zonana, V. F., "$23-Million Computer Snafu Adds to B of A's Troubles," *Los Angeles Times*, July 24, 1987, Part 4, p. 1.

Chapter 2

Risk Analysis and Management

Tools and Techniques

Modern society is replete with risk. Information systems risk, and software failure risk in particular, are but two of the many risks organizations face. To understand how to deal with such risk, we begin by reviewing techniques and tools to deal with all risks in the environment, especially those in the information systems environment.

As new and increasingly complex software is created, traditional risk measurement methods based on historical failure information are of limited use in software failure risk analysis. However, new probabilistic risk assessment tools developed for newly engineered and complex technological systems provide a foundation for risk assessment that can be extended to software failure. This chapter introduces these tools as well as some of their limitations.

2.1. WHAT IS RISK?

Risk is usually defined as the chance of injury, damage, or loss. In most contexts, risk incorporates not only the chance of loss, but the value of that loss as well. In the insurance industry, risk is the average of the long-run value of loss (Doherty, 1985). The term is also used to describe the subject of a policy or the peril that is insured against. Reliability engineers measure risk as consequence or loss per time period (Henley and Kumamoto, 1981). A statistical interpretation is given in an actuarial context: What average value of total loss payment is expected, and what is the level of variability around this average level? Financial risk management is also concerned with the degree of variability, known as *portfolio riskiness* (Doherty, 1985).

These definitions share several concepts. First, risk involves the occurrence of future events. Second, risk exposes someone or something to physical or financial loss. Third, the occurrence of the loss can be described as a random event with some likelihood of occurring. Both probability that the event will occur and its potential consequence may vary with the type of risk and the environment. Therefore, it is appropriate to include both likelihood and consequence in any risk estimate.

People have long recognized exposure to personal risk as a normal aspect of life. In fact, people often voluntarily take risks solely for personal satisfaction. They may be willing to accept high risk levels for high benefits: witness the mountain climber who justifies the high risk of this sport by the personal benefit of thrill and self-satisfaction.

Organizations have similarly accepted and dealt with risks justified by the benefits accruing from being in business. Marketing risks are associated with variations in potential product demand. Financial risks result from capital market fluctuations. Resource management risks have long plagued corporations. These include changes in availability and cost of resources, the potential for physical destruction of resources, and technological changes. Interactions with the public and government have introduced environmental risks (Doherty, 1985).

Organizations and individuals evaluate risks and develop appropriate mechanisms to cope with them. In some cases, the level of risk is sufficient to support the acquisition of safety features, such as car seat belts, smoke detectors, and labor contracts. These risk mechanisms can be regulated by common law, governmental intervention, or private sector self-regulation (Covello and Mumpower, 1985). Risk recovery procedures, such as fire extinguishers or backup production equipment, are sometimes warranted. Insurance is one of the oldest strategies for dealing with risks, its origins traced to attempts at setting interest rates on agricultural loans in ancient Babylon (Covello and Mumpower, 1985). Finally, some risks are simply accepted because they are necessary or have a high cost of avoidance or reduction.

Risk management involves developing strategies to handle risk, controlling the application of these strategies, and monitoring their results. While risks may be speculative, offering a chance of gain or loss, risk management is concerned with pure risks, those that offer the prospect of loss (Doherty, 1985). Strategies are developed to avert and/or minimize the impact of risk. Once these plans are implemented, they are monitored, comparing consequences with expectations to identify opportunities for altering risk management plans.

Implicit in the decision to accept risk and to incorporate various risk management techniques is an evaluation of the level of risk and an implicit definition of an acceptable level of risk. *Risk analysis* involves identifying what the risks are, measuring them, and prioritizing them. Techniques to manage risk cannot be developed unless the components of risk are identified. Every system or environment has different types of risks; some may have greater consequences or greater chances of occurring than others. Therefore, it is necessary to *measure* the amount of risk. If we include in this measurement both the likelihood and the potential loss, the measurement can be used to *evaluate* the risks, allowing them to be *prioritized*.

2.2. RISK ANALYSIS

Risk analysis involves three processes (Charette, 1989):

Risk Identification:	What can go wrong?
Risk Measurement:	What is the magnitude of the risk—the expected consequence?
Risk Evaluation:	How can risks be prioritized, and how are the risk measurements related to acceptable levels of risk?

2.2.1. Risk Identification

Risk identification involves speculation about the future to determine what can possibly go wrong. The risk identification phase is meant to reduce uncertainty and to increase understanding (Charette, 1989), although the availability of information strongly influences the risks considered. Some traditional sources of evidence to identify risk are traditional or folk knowledge, analogies to well-known cases, common-sense assessments, results of experiments or testing, and surveys (Charette, 1989).

In information systems applications, many of these information sources, such as analogies and traditional knowledge, can identify such hardware risks as physical destruction due to fire, water, sabotage, or component breakdown. However, identification of risks associated with the software can be more difficult, especially when one encounters new environments, technologies, and applications and the increasingly complex interrelationships among software components. Software risk identification requires focused analysis of interrelationships in the environment in which the software will operate.

Implicit risk measurements provide the boundaries for risk identification. Attention is directed toward those risks having sufficient probability and consequence to cause managerial concern. Some losses are so remote that they are of minor concern within the context of the environment and are, therefore, not considered in the risk analysis. For example, the crash of an airplane into a distillation column at a petroleum refining facility is generally not included in a risk study. However, airplane crashes, seismic risk, and other low-probability hazards do enter into calculations of nuclear power plant risks because one can protect against them and because theoretically, a nuclear power plant can kill more people than a distillation column (Henley and Kumamoto, 1981). On the other hand, some losses may have insignificant consequences but a very high probability of occurrence. Few large firms are concerned with routine broken windows other than to budget a general provision for such minor contingencies.

2.2.2. Risk Measurement

Estimation of the magnitude of loss and the likelihood of occurrence generally requires subjective judgement in conjunction with any data on past losses. But as new technology becomes available and systems become more complex, the amount of historical input becomes less significant compared to the degree of subjective estimation. This increases the bias associated with estimates. "There literally are no complete models, paradigms, or algorithms by which one can identify the consequences of a given technology" (Coates, 1974). Identifying impacts requires a combination of experience, skills, imagination, and creativity.

Traditionally, risk measurement relied primarily upon historical information. Acceptable risk levels were based upon an individual's or corporation's risk profile. Disaster sequences were fairly straightforward. For example, the risk of fire in a home or corporation could be assessed using historical information on the cause and extent of fires in similar structures. Evaluation of the impact of a labor strike on a corporation's output and profit could be based on historical information, adjusted by forecasts of a company's future position.

Major societal technical systems, such as transportation and energy systems, have created the need for new methods to analyze risk. There is often little historical information on the reliability of these systems or the consequence of accidents. The number of interrelationships involving new technology and applications requires system-level approaches to risk assessment. In fact, the complexity and coupling of these systems means that it is impossible to demonstrate that their design is correct and that failure-prone components have been completely eliminated (Lauber, 1980).

Since 1970, problems associated with product liability, environmental constraints, and governmental intrusions into plant design, construction, and operating procedures have created a new technology for assigning risk in these large, complex systems. The extensive risk assessment of nuclear power plants sponsored and completed by the U.S. Atomic Energy Commission in 1974—"WASH 1400, The Reactor Safety Study"—introduced a wide variety of techniques that have since been adopted by the chemical and other industries (U.S. Nuclear Regulatory Commission, 1975). These techniques provide a uniform, consistent approach to understanding and working with the components of risk in a large system so that they can be identified and measured. These techniques also provide a foundation for analyzing risk in software systems which similarly involve complex interrelationships where historical failure information is often minimal or nonexistent.

Since many complex interrelationships are involved, it is necessary to elaborate the various events and consequences that may result from such accidents, the probabilities of all direct and higher-order effects, and some measures of their costs (Slovic *et al.*, 1984). Two of the most useful tools applied to risk assessment are the logic models known as event and fault trees. *Event trees* describe initiating events along with subsequent successes or failures of the systems designed to cope with them. They contain accident sequences that result from various initiating events. An event tree is made up of a sequence of random events and is constructed using deductive (or forward) logic. In short, starting with the initiating event, all possible sequences of subsequent events and their outcomes are described.

Fault trees, on the other hand, describe the ways in which the systems involved in the accident sequence could fail. A fault tree displays relationships among events leading to an event identified in an event tree. A fault tree is developed using inductive (or backward) logic. First, an event shown in an event tree, failure of all or part of the system, is assumed to have occurred. Then a set of possible causes is determined. Necessary preconditions are described at the next level of the fault tree with either an AND or an OR relationship. Events are thereafter expanded at each sublevel until they can no longer be subdivided.

The advantage of these descriptive models is that they describe cause–effect relationships of failures in very complex systems. This can be useful for analyzing software failure risk. However, it is necessary to recognize that, although these tools have been adopted as the most important policymaking tool available to the Nuclear Regulatory Commission (MacKenzie, 1984), they have limitations. These limitations must be understood before these assessment tools are used to evaluate and manage risk, whether that risk involves damage to a nuclear reactor component or a software failure in an airline reservation system. Differences in results can arise when different groups perform the analysis and from any of the following uncertainties: determination of the dominant risk paths, accident phenomonology, the data base characterizing system failure, the treatment of common-mode and human factor failures, and various underlying assumptions (Vesely and Rasmuson, 1984).

2.2.2.1. Uncertainties in Probabilistic Risk Assessment

Two major types of uncertainty have been differentiated in probabilistic risk assessment (PRA): uncertainty due to physical variability and uncertainty due to lack of knowledge. Physical variability gives rise to the underlying uncertainty associated with risk. The incorporation of physical variability is the basic purpose of probabilistic risk assessment.

Knowledge uncertainties, however, are much more critical. These include parameter uncertainties, modeling uncertainties, and completeness uncertainties.

Parameter uncertainties refer to imprecisions and inaccuracies in the parameters used in a probabilistic risk assessment. These uncertainties include not only imprecisions due to lack of data but also uncertainties in judgments by experts of parameter values.

Modeling uncertainties refer to uncertainties in the applicability and precision of the models used in a probabilistic risk assessment. They include indefiniteness in the models' comprehensiveness, uncertainty as to whether the model accounts for all the variables that can significantly affect the results, indefiniteness in the models' characterization, and uncertainties in the relations and descriptions used in the model. These uncertainties are also affected by the perceptions of experts.

Completeness uncertainties are uncertainties about whether all significant phenomena and relationships have been considered in the risk assessment. Contributor uncertainties refer to the uncertainty as to whether all the pertinent risks and important possible accidents have been included. Relationship uncertainties refer to the uncertainty about whether all significant relationships among the contributors and variables have been identified.

"Completeness uncertainty acts as a constraint and limitation on a PRA" (Vesely and Rasmuson, 1984). Its limitations in software failure risk assessment will be further discussed when the use of probabilistic risk assessment to assess software failure risk is introduced in Chapter 4.

2.2.2.2. Bias in Probabilistic Risk Assessment

Many of the uncertainties in a probabilistic risk assessment are due to problems that arise from bias in risk perception (Tversky and Kahneman, 1974). Characteristics that affect people's attitude toward hazards are voluntariness, controllability, familiarity, immediacy of consequences, threat to future generations, the ease of reducing the risk, and the degree to which benefits are distributed equitably to those who bear the risk (Slovic *et al.*, 1980). These characteristics can bias perceptions of risk in an information system.

Risk assessors make judgments using heuristics that have been found to bias their perceptions (Tversky and Kahneman, 1974). One such heuristic is the *representativeness* heuristic, in which probabilities are evaluated by the degree to which an event is representative of a class of events. Thus, the assessment of risks arising from the use of software may be biased by the degree to which the software is representative of a class of software applications. Prior probabilities about this software's development may be ignored.

Risk assessors may also rely on the *availability* heuristic, assessing the frequency of a class or the probabilities of an event by the ease with which instances or occurrences can be brought to mind. A recent disaster, such as the bug planted in the Internet network in 1988, which snarled processing in many academic institutions, could seriously distort risk judgments. Experience plays a vital role in risk assessment. Widespread or alarmist discussion of a low-probability hazard may increase its memorability and imaginability and therefore its perceived riskiness (Slovic *et al.*, 1980).

Third, risk assessors may use *adjustment* and *anchoring* heuristics, making estimates by starting from an initial value that is adjusted to yield the final answer.

People generally have great confidence in their own judgment, often lacking awareness that their knowledge is based on assumptions. Moreover, experts, once they are forced to go beyond their data and rely on judgment, may be as prone to overconfidence as are laypeople (Slovic *et al.*, 1980). Slovic *et al.* (1980) identified several ways in which experts may overlook or misjudge pathways to disaster:

- Failure to consider how human error can affect technological systems
- Overconfidence in current scientific knowledge
- Failure to appreciate how technological systems function as a whole
- Slowness in detecting chronic, cumulative effects
- Failure to anticipate human response to safety measures
- Failure to anticipate common-mode failures, which simultaneously affect systems designed to be independent

Software failure risk assessment, which is based upon probabilistic risk assessment, suffers similar limitations and biases. However, if the risk assessor is consciously aware of the types of biases and factors often overlooked in these analyses, probabilistic risk assessment can provide a foundation that will make software failure risk assessment as useful a tool in managing software risk as probabilistic risk assessment is in managing risk in complex engineered systems.

2.2.3. Risk Evaluation

Once risks have been identified and measured, they can be evaluated and then prioritized. Strategies to manage risks depend upon the priorities they have been assigned.

Risks can be prioritized by their expected value. Utility functions can also be used if the decision maker is not risk neutral. When multiple risk factors exist, scoring methods can combine these factors. Risk management plans can then be developed using these measures.

The expected value of a risk is the product of the expected consequence and its likelihood of occurrence. Some risks have high consequence but little chance of occurring, while others have high probability of occurrence but little consequence. The overall contribution of *both* likelihood and consequence should be considered when determining the type of risk management plan needed. The risk manager would first consider the risks with the highest expected losses. Risk management strategies would be based on the relative degree of risk.

Utility functions may also be used to evaluate risk. Utility functions incorporate attitudes toward risk. They are obtained by asking people to express their preferences in terms of various risk situations. For example, one might prefer a guaranteed payoff of $60,000 to an option with a 50% chance of a payoff of $150,000 and a 50% chance of a loss of $30,000. While both have the same expected value, the first option has a higher utility.

Scoring methods obtain priority rankings for risks by multiplying risk scores by preference weights for different risk factors. Preference weights are assigned to the different risks according to the significance of the risk factors. For example, in an information systems environment, software failure risk may be more significant than hardware failure because of the existence of backup hardware systems. Thus, when evaluating the failure risk of operational systems, both hardware and software failure risk is measured and an overall score is obtained for each system by incorporating relative weights for the general risk of hardware and software failure. Risk management procedures can then be based on the relative scores of the systems.

There are three types of scoring models: additive, multiplicative, and nonlinear (von Mayrhauser, 1990). The form of the scoring function simulates the trade-offs one is willing to make when prioritizing risks. Additive scoring models allow complete trade offs among all factors, especially when weights are approximately equal. In these models, preference weights are multiplied by corresponding scores, then summed up and normalized by the sum of all preference weights. Multiplicative models are useful when there are factor dependencies—for example, when the overall risk increases unless a set of factors is below a certain value.

In the multiplicative model, the scores incorporate preference weights as exponents and the weighted scores are multiplied with one another. The resulting product is normalized by an exponent which is the inverse sum of the preference weights. Multilinear models can be used when some factors can be traded off against one another but others cannot. These models include both additive and multiplicative components.

If it is not possible to measure the likelihood of different risks, priorities are established based upon the degree of optimism of the risk manager or by assuming that all risks are equally likely. The evaluation can sometimes proceed by obtaining a ranking that is insensitive to a wide range of assumptions. A preferred alternative or strategy may become clear without numerical estimates. For example, when Merrill Lynch had to decide whether to allow its subsidiary, Bloomberg Financial, to market its analytics software package to Merrill's largest competitors, quantification of all the risk factors, potential payoffs, and negative impacts proved extremely difficult and some of the data were impossible to obtain. It was found that restructuring the alternatives transformed the problem into one that could be solved without this data. The lack of quantitative data often arises when the operating environment can be radically altered such as by the introduction of strategic information systems (Clemons, 1991).

It is necessary when evaluating risks to be aware of the biases and uncertainties in risk identification and measurement. The analyst must recognize that assessments are laden with value judgments and make an effort to avoid these judgments or at least make them explicit. "No general method of dealing with differences between perception and technical assessment exists in the societal decision-making process" (Starr *et al.*, 1976). Thus, while the role of the technologist is to provide an assessment of risk, the risk manager must evaluate that assessment, its biases, and its uncertainties.

In most cases, risk is judged against some implicit level of acceptable risk. In the Space Shuttle program, the risk that was the ultimate determining factor—the system-wide risk referent—was the risk to the lives of the crew (Charette, 1989). All risks were prioritized relative to this risk referent. In a business application, the risk referent might be a certain magnitude of financial loss or type of loss, such as a nonrecoverable loss.

2.3. RISK MANAGEMENT

Risk management involves planning strategies to deal with risk. Once planned, these strategies are then implemented, and feedback is continuously monitored to alter and update risk management plans.

2.3.1. Risk Planning

Risk planning occurs within the framework of the environment, which includes economic, political, social, and technological components. Planning establishes objectives that define the role of risk in the organization. It helps managers coordinate their actions, gives them a sense of direction, provides decision making guidelines, and serves as standards against which actual performance may be checked. Subsequent to the establishment of organizational objectives, a strategic plan should be developed for the types of risk tools to be employed. This provides a basis for operating plans to address each risk.

Individuals and organizations have historically employed a number of techniques to manage risk (Covello and Mumpower, 1985; Doherty, 1985):

- Avoidance or elimination
- Regulation or modification of the activity to reduce the magnitude and/or frequency
- Reduction of vulnerability of exposed persons and property
- Development and implementation of postevent mitigation and recovery procedures
- Institution of loss-reimbursement and loss-distribution systems
- Transference to another party, e.g., a subcontractor

Each of these types of risk management procedure exists in information systems environments. Some systems are not developed because they simply generate excessive risk. Some systems are engineered to reduce different components of risk. For example, project management scheduling methods can help minimize the risk of not completing development on time. Various software development methodologies address ways to minimize the risk that the system will fail to meet user requirements. The various risks that can be managed in software development are discussed in Chapter 3. The measurement of software failure risk can be used to modify software development so as to minimize the likelihood of failure, particularly in the high-exposure portions of the system.

Vulnerability can be reduced by developing physical safeguards, fault-tolerant software, or manual and automated audit controls. American Airlines reduced the vulnerability to earthquakes, floods, and high winds of its system by burying its computers in a bunker topped with seven and a half feet of dirt and steel-reinforced concrete (Burgess, 1988). Fault-tolerant software, often used in safety-critical systems, can keep a system functioning in the event of programming and design errors as well as physical damage, lessening vulnerability due to failure or damage. Audit controls can check the accuracy of software output, lessening risk exposure (Juris, 1986). To determine where controls are needed, auditors should analyze the factors that contribute to failure. Software failure risk assessment can demonstrate where controls are needed.

Postevent recovery procedures and contingency planning have become important components of information system planning (Haack, 1984; Krauss, 1980; Murray, 1980). Organizations keep backup data offsite, use shell sites, or develop hot sites. Shell sites are geographically removed alternative computers minus the hardware. It is assumed that hardware vendors can bring in replacements quickly and that key data will be available. Hot sites are complete with software and compatible hardware, and offer immediate service and recovery. (They are, of course, more expensive.) The choice depends upon the cost of maintaining the site as well as the perceived risk. Since it may take three or four weeks for shell sites to become fully operational, organizations must consider the resulting loss. A fire that destroys an airline's computer center could contribute to a 50% decline in revenue each day that it takes to make the shell site operational (Haack, 1984).

Insurance, one of the oldest strategies for coping with risks, is an important supplement in disaster recovery planning. It is best used to cover large risks not controllable by other techniques and security measures (Haack, 1984). Standard policies insure against external physical threats such as fire and hardware breakdown. As hardware has become more reliable, software emerges as a more significant component of risk. Software errors and omissions policies, while available since the '50s, have recently become more popular. To measure the risk of errors and omissions, underwriters usually analyze the type of data being processed, the kinds of services being performed, the staff's experience, the type of equipment being used, how long the company has been in business, and employee turnover (*Business Insurance*, 1987). The ability to measure the failure risk of a specific application could supplement such information, improving the evaluation of these risks.

2.3.2. Risk Controlling

Once risk management plans are developed, they must be implemented. The actual resources, in both personnel and capital, needed to carry out the plans must be obtained. Project management techniques, such as network scheduling models, can be used to control the implementation of the risk management plans. Resource conflicts between competing organizations must be resolved in accordance with risk management plans based upon risk evaluations.

2.3.3. Risk Monitoring

Risk monitoring involves comparing actual performance against planned actions and taking corrective action. It is necessary to determine if the implemented risk management strategies correspond with expectations. Risk monitoring can identify opportunities to alter risk management plans. Continuous feedback is essential for future risk management decisions.

Management audits, reviews, and walkthroughs serve to evaluate risk management techniques and their effectiveness. Internal auditors now play a larger role in monitoring risks in information systems (Ward and Harris, 1986). Internal audit programs are designed to test compliance with accounting-related computer controls, to identify overcontrolled situations, and to pinpoint weaknesses and procedures in need of change. The auditing function provides another level of assurance that controls are functioning as they should.

REFERENCES

Burgess, J., "Searching for a Better Computer Shield; Virus Incident Underscores Vulnerability of Companies as Role of Machines Widens," *The Washington Post*, November 13, 1988, p. H1.

Business Insurance, "Software Firms Discover E&0 Cover," November 30, 1987, p. 54.

Charette, R. N., *Software Engineering Risk Analysis and Management*, New York: Multiscience, 1989.

Clemons, E. K., "Evaluation of Strategic Investments in Information Technology," *Comm. ACM* **34**(1) (January 1991), 22–36.

Coates, J. F., "Some Methods and Techniques for Comprehensive Impact Assessment," *Technological Forecasting and Social Change* **6**. (1974), 341–357.

Covello, V. T., and J. Mumpower, "Risk Analysis and Risk Management: An Historical Perspective," *Risk Analysis* **5**(2), (1985), 103–120.

Doherty, N. A., *Corporate Risk Management: A Financial Exposition*, New York: McGraw-Hill, 1985.

Haack, M. T., "Insuring the Data Processing Risk," *Best's Review*, January, 1984, pp. 44–50.

Henley, E. J., and H. Kumamoto, *Reliability Engineering and Risk Assessment*, Englewood Cliffs, NJ: Prentice-Hall, 1981.

Juris, R., "EDP Auditing Lessens Risk Exposure," *Computer Decisions*, July 15, 1986, pp. 36–42.

Krauss, L., "EDP Contingency Planning: How to Survive a Disaster," *Management Rev.*, June, 1980, pp. 20–26.

Lauber, R., "Strategies for the Design and Validation of Safety-Related Computer-controlled Systems," in *Real-Time Data Handling and Process Control*, (G. Meyer, ed.), Amsterdam: North-Holland, 1980, pp. 305–310.

MacKenzie, J. J., "Rx for Nuclear Power," *Tech. Rev.* **87**, (February–March 1984), 33–39.

Murray, J., "Developing a Contingency Plan," *Data Management*, January, 1980, pp. 10–48.

Pate-Cornell, M. E., "Fault Trees vs. Event Trees in Reliability Analysis," *Risk Anal.* **4**(3), (1984), 177–186.

Slovic, P., B. Fischoff, and S. Lichtenstein, "Facts versus Fears: Understanding Perceived Risk," in *Societal Risk Assessment: How Safe is Safe Enough?* (Schwing, R., Albers, W. A., eds.) New York: Plenum, 1980.

Slovic, P., S. Lichtenstein, and S. Fischhoff, "Modeling the Societal Impact of Fatal Accidents," *Management Sci.* **30**(4), (April 1984), 464–474.

Starr, C., R. Rudman, and C. Whipple, "Philosophical Basis for Risk Analysis," *Annual Rev. Energy* **1**, (1976), 629–662.

Tversky, A. and A. Kahneman, "Judgment under Uncertainty: Heuristics and Biases," *Science* **185**, (September 1974), 1124–1131.

U.S. Nuclear Regulatory Commission, *Reactor Safety Study: An Assessment of Accident Risks in U.S. Commercial Nuclear Power Plants*, WASH-1400, October, 1975.

Vesely, W. E. and D. M. Rasmuson, "Uncertainties in Nuclear Probabilistic Risk Analyses," *Risk Anal.* **4**(4), (1984), 313–322.

von Mayrhauser, A., *Software Engineering: Methods and Management*, San Diego, CA: Academic Press, 1990.

Ward, G. M. and J. D. Harris, *Managing Computer Risk: A Guide for the Policymaker*, New York: Wiley, 1986.

Chapter 3

Software Failure Risk

What It Is and What It Is Not

While organizations face many different types of risks, the increasing reliance on computer systems introduces new elements of risk. Some risks, such as physical destruction of hardware, are managed with the same techniques as other risks in our society. Risks associated with the development and use of software, however, pose some special problems. Software is often unique; little historical information is available to analyze its risk. The complex interrelationships found in software complicate risk measurement. Moreover, the introduction of software can change an organization's environment, making it difficult to both analyze and manage risk. While there is always the risk that the software will not be developed effectively, there is also the risk that, once developed, the software may not meet the needs of the organization.

Software failure risk incorporates some but not all components of risk in software development and use. This chapter will provide, first, a definition of what software failure risk is; then, a review of the major components of software risk to clarify what software failure risk measures; and finally, a discussion of what it does not measure.

3.1. SOFTWARE FAILURE RISK: WHAT IT IS

> *Software failure risk* is the expected loss due to failure of software to operate correctly.

Let's consider this definition. First, what is software? *Software* is the set of instructions that tell a computer what to do. It is made up of modules, or components, which are related subsets of instructions. Software failure risk is concerned with computer failures that are either caused or exacerbated by these instructions. For example, an error in the software's logic can cause the computer to generate invalid results. Inaccuracies in First Boston's inventories of its mortgage-backed securities resulted in losses of between $10 and $50 million (*Information Week*, 1988). Or the software may be missing the logic necessary to recover properly from hardware failure. When a hardware problem activated normal recovery routines in AT&T's New York switching system, it was a software error that triggered the collapse of the long distance network (Elmer-Dewitt, 1990; AT&T, 1990).

Software design errors in the man–machine interface may also contribute to failure. When software controlling the beam intensity switch on the Therac-25 radiation machine failed, operators ignored the cryptic error message displaying a number rather than describing the problem in words. Moreover, this message was one of forty messages per day indicating minor problems that were typically ignored. As a result, a patient was provided with one hundred times the prescribed amount of radiation (Jacky, 1989).

If software fails, what is the impact on the organization? Software failure risk measures *loss* as the economic consequence to the organization. This includes actual loss, future lost business, business interruption, and extra clerical work. When Bank of New York's government securities clearance system failed, the bank borrowed over $20 billion from the Federal Reserve Bank of New York to pay sellers for the securities it had been receiving. Its loss amounted to the $5 million in interest on these loans (Juris, 1986). AT&T lost a substantial amount of money when it offered its day of discounts to recoup its public image after the network disaster of January, 1990. When the American Airlines computerized reservation system went down for 12 hrs, the firm had to pay for employee time to write reservations manually and then later confirm them. Not only did this involve extra labor, but American Airlines probably lost business since travel agents could not confirm reservations (*Los Angeles Times*, 1989).

Is there a loss every time software fails? No, sometimes users recognize that information is wrong before any loss occurs. If there are controls in the system environment, the loss estimate can be reduced by the expected efficacy of such controls.

Let's look closely at what we mean by two terms: failure and fault. A *failure* is a departure of the program's output from what the user needs. Information is either invalid or missing. It is important to note that a failure is not a departure from formal requirements, but rather a departure from what the user needs. This is a significant distinction, since formal requirements may themselves be invalid. In fact, over 60% of errors discovered during software development arise during the requirements or design phase (Lipow, 1979).

A *fault* is an error in the computer instructions. A failure may occur when a fault in the software is encountered. Faults that exist in obsolete portions of the code do not produce failure. Software failure risk is concerned only with faults that can produce failure.

Software can fail because of incomplete or incorrect requirements analysis, poor design, and inadequate testing or quality assurance. Faults can be introduced at any time prior to the use of the software. Faults are often introduced when software is changed during maintenance or testing. The software fault that brought down the AT&T network was introduced when the network software was updated to improve its reliability. A fault can be introduced when the software is written or when the design is developed. The programmer may misunderstand the design specifications, or the designer may not correctly translate the specifications into a design. A programming error in a hospital bookkeeping system caused one hundred hospitals to revert to manual records. Finally, and most importantly, a fault can be introduced in the requirements definition or prototype development. The developer may not correctly understand what the user needs. The excess radiation administered by the Therac-25 machine was caused, in part, by a poor interface. Developers did not adequately consider the environment in which the machines would operate.

3.2. SOFTWARE RISKS

Now let us look at all the components of software risk to determine what software failure risk measures and what it does not measure. First, we review the components of software risk and the various risk management techniques used in the development of software. We suggest how software failure risk assessment can be used to help manage some of these risk components.

The components of risk in software development have been defined as (Clemons *et al.*, 1990; Clemons, 1991):

Project Risk:
1. The system cannot be developed on time or within budget, or
2. The system does not perform adequately.

Functionality Risk:	The system fails to meet current or future needs of users because 1. it is not what the user wants, or 2. the environment changes so that it is no longer functionally appropriate.
Political/Internal Risk:	Interorganizational factors hinder progress as a result of perceived system threats.
Financial Risk:	The system will not generate the forecasted returns on investment because benefits are too low or costs are too high.
Technical Risk:	Development attempts to go beyond what is technologically feasible.
Systemic Risk:	The system is so successful that it creates a large-scale discontinuity in an industry due to competitive, customer, user, or regulatory responses.

Software failure risk measures one component of *project risk*, namely, the risk that the system fails due to faults in the software. This differs from software reliability, software safety, and software security, all of which are components of project risk. Software failure risk also measures the *functionality risk* arising from development of a system that is not what the user wants. Finally, software failure risk measures the *financial risk* associated with loss. However, software failure risk does not measure schedule, environmental, technical, or systemic components of risk. Nevertheless, the process of measuring software failure risk, introduced in Part II of this book, can indicate the existence of these components of risk as well.

3.2.1. Project Risk

Project risk is the risk that the system cannot be completed on schedule, within budget, with adequate performance, or in accordance with some measure of project success. The firm may not be able to complete the project because of its scale, its technical complexity, or its poor fit with the organization's expertise. Project risk includes six of the top ten software risk items identified by experienced project managers: personnel shortfalls, unrealistic schedules and budgets, real-time performance shortfalls, a continuing stream of requirements changes, and shortfalls in externally furnished components or tasks* (Boehm, 1989).

To identify project risk, it is necessary to understand not only the project tasks but the degree to which the completion of each task involves uncertainty.

*The other four risk items are functional or technical components of risk.

Increased uncertainty in any of the following areas generally increases project risk:

Task:	What has to be done?
Process:	How will it be done?
Technology:	What resources are available?
Management:	How will the project be controlled?

A clearly defined *task* generally reduces project risk. Larger projects are riskier because they are more difficult to schedule and control. Tasks that differ markedly from previous ones are harder to schedule, thereby increasing project risk.

If the *process* is well understood, if the designers have developed a similar system, or if an experienced project team is assembled, then project risk is often reduced. Conversely, a new project team or the use of new techniques to build a system generally increases project risk. The level of *process maturity* affects project risk (Humphrey, 1989; Pfleeger, 1991). As the software development process matures, the degree to which a project can be monitored increases and the risk of project failure decreases.

The five possible maturity levels for a process are shown in Table 3.1. At the *initial* level, the absence of structure and control implies high project risk. The organization typically has no formalized procedures, cost estimates, and project plans. The *repeatable* process provides control over how the organization establishes plans and commitments based upon prior experiences. However, changes in applications, technology, or organizational structure provide major project risks at this level of maturity. At the *defined* process level of maturity, the organization has the foundation for examining the software development process and deciding how to improve it. Organizations operating at this level have established a process group, a development process architecture, and a family of software engineering methods and technologies. However, the defined process lacks quantitative measures of effectiveness. These are introduced in the *managed* process and then used to identify and fix the weakest elements of the process at the *optimizing* level of process maturity. Studies by the Software

Table 3.1. Process Maturity Levels

Maturity level	Description
Initial	*Ad hoc*, chaotic
Repeatable	Stable process, repeatable levels of statistical control
Defined	Defined process, qualitative information
Managed	Comprehensive process measurement and analysis
Optimizing	Continuous improvement and process optimization

Engineering Institute found that 85% of 113 software development projects were at the initial level, 14% were at the repeatable level, and 1% were at the defined level. None of the projects were developed at either the managed or the optimizing level of process maturity (Pfleeger and McCowan, 1990). Thus, it is expected that project risk resulting from low process maturity is substantial.

New *technology* can increase project risk since there is more uncertainty regarding the impact of technology on project performance. The learning curve is often underestimated, leading to cost and schedule overruns.

"The techniques of communication and organization demand from the manager much thought and as much experienced competence as the software technology itself" (Brooks, 1982). Project risk generally increases with *management* difficulty and uncertainty. In fact, the Defense Science Board's task force on military software is convinced that today's major problems with military software are not technical but management problems (*Electronics*, 1987). Many system interfaces provide opportunities for increased risk.

"More software projects have gone awry for lack of calendar time than for all other causes combined" (Brooks, 1982). A mid-80s Peat Marwick Mitchell and Co. survey of 600 of the accounting firm's largest clients revealed that 35% had major overruns. In fact, the problem was so significant that a group at Peat Marwick, set up to control overruns, generated $30 million in revenues in less than 2 years from nearly 20 clients (Rothfeder, 1988).

In many cases, schedule and cost overruns result in systems with inadequate performance. Companies, anxious to cut costs further, take short cuts in testing and quality assurance. A government investigator claimed that the IRS was concerned more with completing its new $103 million computer network in time for the 1985 tax processing season than with testing the system. The untested program produced many errors that took weeks, even months to locate (Howe, 1985). Any tradeoff between software quality and cost can have disastrous results when systems are released that either do not perform adequately or fail to perform at all. The measurement of software failure risk provides information regarding the cost of failure so that the impact of schedule changes on operational failure can be measured.

A number of different techniques are available for analyzing and managing various elements of project risk. First, meeting cost/schedule deadlines can be managed with more accurate schedules, better tools to monitor and control schedule progress, and process improvements such as a modular approach to development and the use of process measurements to continually improve the software development process. Second, developing a system with adequate quality can be managed with development techniques that may differ depending upon the measure of project success. Finally, project risk can be managed by outsourcing the project to organizations better equipped to deal with this risk component.

3.2.1.1. Managing Cost and Schedule

Several techniques are available to manage the risk that the system is not developed on schedule or within budget. First, software cost estimation models have been developed to improve schedule and cost estimates. Second, project management tools help not only to plan but to monitor and control schedule progress. Finally, modular development reduces the risk of overruns by reducing the size of the project.

a. Cost Estimation Models. One of the factors that contribute to cost and schedule overruns is the difficulty in developing schedule estimates. Several models have been developed to estimate schedules and costs (Putnam, 1987; Boehm, 1981). But while these can aid in producing schedules, they contribute little to the information needed to allocate resources to effectively meet schedule deadlines while producing quality software.

The Putnam SLIM model uses historical data to generate likely costs and schedules (Putnam, 1987). It assumes that all software development projects follow a Raleigh distribution so that peak personnel usage occurs when 40% of the budget is utilized. It is a macroestimation model: while estimating total effort for each phase of development, it does not focus on individual components of the system. Hence, it is of limited use for developing individual components. If resources are limited; it cannot aid the manager in allocating resources to minimize failure risk. Moreover, this model has not been found to be accurate in predicting actual costs and schedules, particularly on smaller projects (Charette, 1989).

Boehm's COCOMO model has three levels of cost estimation. Basic COCOMO estimates software development and cost as a function only of the size of the software product. Additional predictor variables are incorporated in the intermediate model. These include product attributes, such as required software reliability, data base size, and product complexity; computer attributes; personnel attributes; and project attributes. The intermediate model claims to estimate costs within 20% of actual costs 68% of the time for the class of projects to which it is calibrated—mostly scientific, human–machine interface, and control software (Boehm, 1981)—but is not as accurate in other environments such as business data processing, where recalibration is required (Kemerer, 1987).

In the intermediate COCOMO model, reliability cost multipliers are based upon the effect of a failure or the level of its exposure, as shown in Table 3.2. Higher-exposure applications are assumed to require more effort. In the detailed level of COCOMO, the multipliers are broken down by the following four phases: requirements and product design, detailed design, code and unit test, and integration and test. The effort multipliers for high-exposure applications

Table 3.2. Required Software Reliability in COCOMO Software Cost Estimation Model[a]

Rating scale	Effect of software failure	Overall effort multiplier
Very low	Inconvenience to developer to fix	0.75
Low	Easily recoverable loss	0.88
Nominal	Moderate loss to users	1.00
High	Major financial loss or massive human inconvenience	1.15
Very high	Loss of human life	1.40

[a]From Boehm (81)

are significantly greater during the final two phases of development. While the degree of reliability may vary among subsystems in detailed COCOMO, the degree of required reliability generally does not vary from module to module within a subsystem. However, the required reliability would differ if financial exposure differs. This information can be obtained from software failure risk assessment.

b. Project Management Tools. Software development managers can use project management tools to plan and monitor schedule progress. Network models, such as PERT, can be helpful in managing the project. The task breakdown required in PERT models can aid in showing what the key schedule elements may be. Moreover, milestones can be developed and the schedule monitored so that slippages or slack activities and times are identified early. Opportunities to catch up when behind schedule can be investigated before it is too late. Software failure risk can measure the impact of schedule changes on the failure risk of the software.

c. Process Improvement. Modular development and steps toward continual process improvement can also help manage project risk. The software development process is the set of tools, methods, and practices used to produce a software product (Humphrey, 1989).

Project risk associated with size can be reduced by working on smaller modules or phases. The "spiral" software process model is an evolutionary software development paradigm that specifically focuses on risk (Boehm, 1988). The development process is broken down into a series of phases or cycles of a spiral, providing an opportunity to re-evaluate risks before proceeding further. Objectives, alternative implementation plans, and constraints are identified and evaluated before proceeding with each cycle of the spiral. If the risks from proceeding with the next cycle of the spiral exceed the benefits, then the spiral is terminated. One result of the use of this technique is that specifications are not necessarily uniform, exhaustive, or formal. Instead, the level of detail is driven by risk. Prototyping is used at any stage of development, and the developer returns to earlier stages as new risk issues need resolution. Risk driven documents are important features of the development process. This approach manages development risk not only by focusing on risk elements, but by dividing the project up into smaller, more manageable phases.

Checklists of risk components can be reviewed at each process stage. The U.S. Air Force guidebook, "Software Risk Abatement," provides a set of risk drivers in the areas of performance, support, cost, and schedule (U.S. Air Force Systems Command, 1988). The U.S. Department of Commerce Guide for EDP Audit describes risk considerations in five dimensions: criticality/mission, impact, size/scale/complexity, environment/stability/reliability/integrity, and integration (Ruthberg and Fisher, 1986). In addition, software failure risk can be reevaluated before proceeding with the next cycle.

As the software development process improves, risk is reduced. To improve process capabilities, an organization must (Humphrey, 1989):

1. Understand the current status of its development process or processes.
2. Develop a vision of the desired process.
3. List required process improvement actions in order of priority.
4. Produce a plan to accomplish actions.
5. Commit necessary resources.
6. Start over at step 1.

The organization must assess its maturity status as shown in Table 3.1 and then develop a system to implement priority improvement actions.

The improvement in maturity from the *initial* process level to the *repeatable* level requires implementation of a project management system, management oversight, a quality assurance group, and change control. To further mature to the *defined* process level, the organization would establish a process group, software development process architecture, and a family of software engineering methods and technology. The establishment of process measurements, data bases, and the resources to gather data and assess the relative quality of each project help move a process to the *managed* level. Finally, the *optimizing* process requires the gathering and use of process data to analyze and modify the process. As the organization gains these tools and learns how to effectively use them, the process will mature, and risk will be reduced.

3.2.1.2. Managing Performance/Quality Risk

Different applications require the analyst to address or emphasize different components of software quality and performance, including efficiency, usability, flexibility, maintainability, reusability, testability, security, safety, and reliability (Arthur, 1984). The latter three are related to software errors or failures and their consequences. It is important to distinguish these quality components from risk. Software *security* problems can occur from intentional modification of data or physical destruction of the computer center. They need not result from faults in the software. Software *safety* issues arise when computers are used to control real-time, safety-critical problems where the consequences of failure go beyond economic loss. Software *reliability* incorporates only one aspect of software failure risk, the likelihood of failure. Each of these three components will be reviewed in more detail below, not only to understand how software failure risk differs, but to draw upon applicable research results and describe how software failure risk assessment can complement them.

a. Software Security. Information systems security is the protection of information from unauthorized disclosure, modification, or destruction, whether accidental or intentional (Fisher, 1984). Security includes physical security threats such as fire, water, and intrusion; controls and procedures, including organizational, personnel, operational, interface, and application development; and contingency planning (for emergency backup and recovery). Software failure risk is concerned with exposure due to faults in the software, but software is only one aspect of the control plan. Security problems can also result from organizational weaknesses and deficiencies in management skills including personnel, availability, and access problems (Tate, 1988).

The security of information systems is critical because information can mean power—power to manipulate and power to control (Fisher, 1984). While most security experts believe that most security breaches are unintentional, it is deliberate access to and modification and removal of data that are often brought to mind when security issues are considered. A lot of attention has focused on outside hackers who access computers and add bugs or viruses. The 1988 capture of three members of a major spy ring who stole U.S. military information for Soviet intelligence agents from Internet, coupled with the worm planted by a Cornell University graduate student, which snarled processing on 6000 computers at a number of academic centers, caught the attention of the computer community (Burgess, 1988; Fitzgerald, 1989). The availability of this information and the spectacular nature of these cases probably biased perceptions regarding the source of computer security problems.

Most experts believe that dishonest and incompetent employees are a far greater security risk than outside saboteurs. According to surveys by the computer security consulting firm RCI of Port Ewen, N.Y., only 3% of the loss of money because of compromised data is caused by people outside the company; 32% is due to dishonest or disgruntled employees, while the remaining 65% is attributable to employee mistakes (Fitzgerald, 1989). Nevertheless, it is difficult to estimate the impact of intentional software sabotage since most computer crime is not reported. In fact, it is estimated that less than 2% of computer crime is reported; computer crime may be costing at least $10 billion per year (Hull and Serio, 1987).

Software failure risk does not specifically address intentional breaches of security, those that generally receive the most publicity. Intentional disclosure, modification, or destruction results from software failure only if software controls are missing or inadequately installed. Software failure risk does, however, measure breaches of security resulting from software design flaws. This is accomplished by analyzing the external environment to see how the software will be used and what can go wrong. Such analysis is similar to that suggested by software security experts, with the focus of software failure risk assessment being on software flaws rather than on external controls.

Most security problems arise from simple errors and omissions in the data life cycle (Fisher, 1984). Many systems can be penetrated because they lack basic data security controls for such functions as control of manual interfaces, disaster/recovery planning, adequate segregation of functions, provision of training programs, and formalization of input/output controls. The methodology for assessing software failure risk analyzes these functions as they relate to the use of the software in the external environment.

The approach to security risk measurement endorsed by the federal government focuses on data exposure control points in the data control life cycle (National Bureau of Standards, 1979). The eleven basic data exposure control points are data gathering, input movement, conversion, communication, receipt, processing, preparation, output movement, communication, usage, and disposition. The security risk for each defined exposure at a control point is subjectively estimated as the product of the probability of an exposure occurring and the cost or loss attributed to such an exposure. Exposure includes software faults as well as many other sources of security problems, including inadequate physical controls. Since software failure risk assessment actually analyzes the code to measure the likelihood of software failure, it can improve estimates of one source of security risk, software errors.

The objective of security risk analysis is to determine where controls are needed and what types of controls are needed (Fisher, 1984). Preventive controls such as training programs, personnel background checks, shatterproof glass, or segregation of duties offer the first line of defense. Detective controls, such as alarms, printouts, and system termination are generally paired with corrective controls, such as automatic error corrections, backup procedures, and investigation of audit reports. All these controls can minimize exposure. When software can contribute to loss, the software failure risk assessment measures the impact of external controls on software failure exposure. These assessment measures can therefore also be used by software security analysts to illustrate what external controls related to software faults may be missing.

b. Software Safety. While software failure risk addresses all economic loss due to software errors, software safety is concerned only with software whose failure can result in death, injury, damage to or loss of equipment, or environmental harm (Leveson, 1986). Modern systems—energy, transportation, defense and medical systems, for example—increasingly rely on software technology for control functions previously performed only by humans or hardware. The greater amounts of logic that current technology makes it practical to incorporate in the software is easier to change than if it were implemented in the hardware. Moreover, the flexibility of software enables operators to be provided with more information in a more useful form (Parnas *et al.*, 1990). These advantages make it difficult to resist incorporating control software.

Despite the advantages to be gained from the use of software technology, the problem remains that it is impossible to guarantee that software is free of errors. While there has been a great deal of progress in the development of hardware fault- tolerant architectures (Hecht, 1976), achieving the same degree of confidence in software has not been possible. Several problems, not easily resolvable, contribute to lack of confidence in software: its complexity, error sensitivity, testing difficulty, correlation of failures, and lack of professional standards (Parnas *et al.*, 1990).

Failures in "completely tested, reliable" systems have demonstrated that safety should be a major concern when systems are used in life threatening situations. Examples of software problems affecting the safety of individuals abound. In the medical equipment industry, software related recalls tripled since 1984 to 34 recalls in 1990 (Richards, 1990). Software errors resulted in a blood analyzer displaying incorrect values; a system for monitoring heart rate, blood pressure, and other vital signs mixing up data and relaying information on the wrong patients; and a ventilator allowing concentrations of oxygen and other vital gases to drop without warning (Jacky, 1989).

The medical industry is not the only one plagued with safety problems involving software. In 1979, a software flaw in the computer aided system that designed nuclear reactors and their cooling systems left the plants vulnerable to seismic damage in earthquakes (Leveson, 1986). The tragedy of Iran Air Flight 655, shot down by the U.S.S. Vincennes on July 3, 1988, was related to a software design error: altitude data was not shown on the target display (U.S. House of Representatives, 1989).

Software safety involves ensuring that software will execute its task within a system context without unacceptable mishap. *Mishap* denotes unplanned events or series of events that result in death, injury, occupational illness, damage to or loss of equipment or property, or environmental harm (Leveson, 1986). Mishap, however, does not include economic loss resulting from invalid or missing information or inability to provide service. It does not include, for example, AT&T's costs to regain customer acceptance after software error cut off telephone service to tens of millions of customers in January, 1990, or the lost business and costs of delays when the American Airlines Sabre system failed for nearly twelve hours.

Safety is the probability that conditions that can lead to a mishap do NOT occur, whether or not the function of the software is performed. In fact, software can perform as intended but still be unsafe because a mishap can occur. System safety modeling involves demonstrating that a system is safe if it operates as intended and in the presence of faults. It is necessary to show that no single fault implies a mishap or that mishaps resulting from sequences of failures are sufficiently remote. Similarly, software failure risk is concerned with determining the probability that failure will occur, whether or not software faults exist. The software may operate as intended but still fail because the environment was incorrectly evaluated or misunderstood or because the environment changed.

Software safety, however, is concerned with verifying not that software is *failure free* but that it is *mishap free*. Trustworthiness is the key concern in software safety. Trustworthiness is the probability that no serious design error leading to mishap remains after the software passes a set of randomly chosen tests (Parnas *et al.*, 1990). This is not the same as failure risk, which deals with the probability and consequences if an input causes a failure. Safety is concerned only with a subset of software errors that result in actual mishaps.

Safety-critical applications justify stringent design, development, and testing criteria. Software design tries to ensure that faults and failures cannot cause mishaps because the software design is intrinsically safe and the number of mishaps is minimized. Problems can be either prevented or detected and treated.

Fault avoidance techniques are those design principles and practices whose objectives are to prevent errors from ever existing in the software (Myers, 1976). However, mishaps can still occur even without software errors. Furthermore, it is impossible to guarantee error-free software. Modularization and data access limitation have been suggested techniques in which noncritical functions are separated or decoupled from critical functions to ensure that failures of noncritical modules do not put the entire system into a hazardous state (Leveson, 1986).

Fault detection techniques detect failures as soon as possible after they arise. Authority limitation with regard to inadvertent activation can be implemented by retaining a person in the loop (Leveson, 1986). In some systems, like the Boeing 737-300 and Airbus A510 avionics systems, nondigital backup systems, either analog or including human attendants, are immediately given control in the event a software error is detected (Leveson *et al.*, 1990).

Fault correction techniques go further: after an error is detected, either the error itself or the effects of the error are corrected by the software. Given the seriousness of mishaps and the real-time nature of control, simply detecting an error or even correcting it after the fact can have disastrous consequences.

Design fault–tolerant strategies have been proposed as the only acceptable alternatives to simply accepting that software can not be guaranteed to be entirely fault free (Randell *et al.*, 1978). These strategies keep the software system functioning in the presence of errors.

Software fault–tolerant strategies have been borrowed from concepts in hardware fault tolerance. But whereas identical backup modules can provide hardware redundancy, identical copies of a software program are of little use in recovering from a fault. Redundancy requires programs that are deliberately *different* from one another. Common strategies for software fault tolerance, such as recovery blocks and *n*-version programming, all require the development of independent versions of a program (Scott *et al.*, 1987). But most important, the *results* must be independent if any of these methods is to be effective. Researchers have demonstrated that programs produced independently do not necessarily result in independent software versions (Knight and Leveson, 1986), thereby minimizing the effectiveness of these methods.

Inadequate design foresight and specification errors are the greatest source of safety problems (Leveson, 1986). Moreover, since fault-tolerant designs are not 100% effective, software safety requirements analysis and design verification should be performed. While it is not possible to insure the safety of a system by analysis and verification alone (Leveson, 1986), software safety analysis investigates the ways in which the software and the system can fail safely and determines to what extent failure is tolerable. It focuses on what the system should *not* do, including ways to eliminate and control system hazards and limit damage in case of a mishap (Leveson, 1986).

Several techniques have been proposed and used in limited contexts for safety requirements analysis (Leveson, 1986). One such technique, fault tree analysis (Cha *et al.*, 1988; Fryer, 1985; Leveson and Harvey, 1983), has been used to determine safety requirements, detect software logic errors, identify multiple failure sequences involving different parts of the system, and guide the selection of run-time checks and testing. Fault tree analysis attempts to verify that the program will never allow an unsafe state to be reached. However, in its application to software safety, fault trees say nothing about incorrect but safe states.

The methodology for software failure risk assessment extends fault tree analysis to all failures that result in loss, not just unsafe states. It is similar to software safety analysis, because the concern is with software that produces loss, not just incorrect software. Both software failure risk assessment and software safety requirements analysis focus on what the system must not do. They do not focus on what the system should do, the traditional role of functional requirements analysis. Moreover, fault tree analysis in both cases considers interaction of the software with hardware, human error, and other environmental factors. However, the definition of loss in software failure risk assessment is different from that in software safety requirements. Whereas software safety analysis is used to determine how software faults and failures could adversely affect system safety, software failure risk assessment considers how software faults and failures could adversely affect the intended use of the system.

The question of how to assess safety is still very much unresolved (Leveson, 1986). Mishaps are almost always caused by multiple factors often in supposedly redundant components, and failure probabilities tend to be very small. Trustworthiness can not be practically evaluated by testing. It must be obtained by formal, rigorous inspections (Parnas *et al.*, 1990). Moreover, the consequence of a mishap is difficult to measure. How does one quantify the cost of the loss of a life? Is the loss of one hundred lives one hundred times the cost of the loss of one life? How does this compare with the destruction of property?

c. Software Reliability. Software failure risk was previously defined as the cost of failure multiplied by the probability of failure—a definition that differs significantly from that of software reliability. The major difference is the inclusion of the cost of failure in the measure of software risk. Software reliability models do not consider the cost of failure. They have been adapted from hardware reliability assessment, which generally models failure resulting in a single known consequence, generally total system failure. However, the consequences of software failure are more varied. Furthermore, the causes of failure differ: hardware may fail after use as components fatigue or wear out; software may fail as a new use encounters old errors. We may therefore expect different statistical properties for hardware and software failures. Since software failure risk assessment differs from hardware reliability assessment, it is not surprising that traditional software methods, grounded in the hardware tradition, should prove less than wholly satisfactory for measuring software failure.

Several definitions have been advanced for *software reliability*. Early software reliability models defined reliability in terms of the number of residual errors in a program (Jelinski and Moranda, 1972; Moranda, 1981; Ohba, 1984; Shooman, 1972, 1973; Schneidewind, 1975; Shooman and Trivedi, 1976). Other models adopted the traditional hardware definition of reliability, mean time to failure. Software reliability is thus defined as the probability of failure-free operation of a program for a specified time period in a specified environment (Goel and Okumoto, 1979; Musa, 1975; Musa and Okumoto, 1984). Littlewood uses a more subjective interpretation, defining reliability in terms of the strength of belief in the operation of the software without failure for a given period (Littlewood and Verrall, 1973; Littlewood, 1975, 1979, 1980).

The major problem with each of these definitions lies in the assumption that all errors or failures are equal. Whereas hardware reliability theory typically assumes that failures have the same consequence (i.e., the system is not operational), a software error can have a variety of consequences, primarily because different types of software failure exist. A software failure can be a system crash or a misread number. If the latter, the consequence of the misread number can vary. In an air traffic control system, if the hardware fails, we typically lose sight of all aircraft. However, if the software fails, we might lose sight of all aircraft, or we might unknowingly lose sight of a single aircraft, or we could transpose a digit on the aircraft identification. The consequence of these different failure modes can be quite different. The point is that, because software errors and resulting failures have varying consequences, while hardware failures have been modeled with a single consequence, hardware models of software failure are of limited usefulness.

Other differences exist between software and hardware that distinguish software failure risk assessment from hardware reliability measurement. Hardware failures can be due to degradation of components as well as design errors. The former source of failure produces statistically measurable failure patterns. Software components, however, do not degrade as a result of environmental stress or fatigue. In fact, an older program is usually more reliable. Reliability increases with use although it may decrease as maintenance takes place. Software failures are often due to design and implementation errors that occur as a result of unanticipated or untested inputs. Correction of software errors usually alters the software; it does not just replace it as in a hardware correction. Finally, software can be copied, thereby retaining its reliability, whereas hardware can not.

Another problem with the definition of software reliability is that a reliable program needs to be correct only for inputs or specific environments for which it is designed (Ramamoorthy, 1982). What if an error in design occurs? What if the environment changes? Reliability is not solely a property of a program; it is also dependent on the user environment:

> A reliable program correctly performs the functions desired by the users of that program for all conditions under which the program will be used. . . . A computer program may terminate its execution as expected and produce numerical results of considerable accuracy, but if it has answered a question different from what the user asked, it cannot be considered reliable. (Rubey, 1977)

Software failure risk assessment evaluates the environment to assess the probability that the software will fail to provide what the user needs in the relevant environment, even if the designer did not initially recognize this need.

A number of different software reliability models have been proposed. Most describe failure as a random process that varies with time. The randomness occurs with the introduction of faults and the variation in the conditions of execution of a program (Musa *et al.*, 1987). In addition, most models assume that failures are independent of one another.

A few time-independent models have been developed. The general approaches include fault seeding and input domain analysis (Goel, 1985). In *fault seeding*, a known number of faults is planted in the program. After testing, reliability is estimated from the proportion of seeded faults found. Fault seeding has proven difficult to implement because it is hard to introduce seeded faults that present the same difficulty of discovery as inherent faults do. In the *input domain*–based approach, reliability is estimated from the number of failures observed during execution of a set of test cases from the input distribution (Brown and Lipow, 1975; Ramamoorthy and Bastani, 1982). This approach is limited because it is difficult to estimate the input distribution.

Most software reliability models are time-dependent. More than fifteen early models were classified by Musa and Okumoto (1983) according to the following dimensions:

Time domain:	calendar time or execution time
Category:	the number of failures that can be experienced in infinite time is finite or infinite
Type:	the failure quantity distribution, e.g., Poisson, binomial, negative binomial
Class:	the functional form of the failure intensity in terms of time, e.g., exponential, Weibull (finite failure category only)
Family:	the functional form of the failure intensity in terms of the expected value of failures experienced, e.g., geometric (infinite failure category only)

Software reliability parameters are generally estimated once test data become available. Prior to testing, some of the models have parameters that can be predicted from characteristics of the code. Researchers have studied the psychological and social aspects of the tasks involved in programming (Brooks, 1982; Weinberg, 1971). Many empirical studies have looked at the factors affecting software quality in terms of error content (Akiyama, 1971; Basili and Hutchens, 1983; Basili and Perricone, 1984; Basili and Phillips, 1982; Card *et al.*, 1986; Endres, 1975; Feuer and Fowlkes, 1979; Gremillon, 1984; Glass, 1981; Schneidewind and Hoffman, 1979; Shen *et al.*, 1985; Takahashi and Kamayachi, 1989; Youngs, 1981). However, much additional work must be done to understand the software development process: how is better software developed and who develops it. This information can be used in conjunction with information about the differential impact of failure of system functions when making critical decisions about the design of the system as well as the allocation of effort in development.

Once test data are obtained, parameters are usually estimated with maximum likelihood estimation techniques (Musa *et al.*, 1987), although several Bayesian approaches have also been developed (Jewell, 1985; Langberg and Singpurwalla, 1985; Littlewood and Verrall, 1973). This book adopts one of the most widely tested software reliability models to estimate failure likelihood, a finite failures execution time model of Poisson type and exponential class. The model's parameters are updated with Bayesian estimation techniques as test data become available.

The proposed applications of software reliability measurement have included system engineering, project management during development and particularly during testing, operational software management, and evaluation of software engineering technology (Musa *et al.*, 1987). It has been proposed that specified reliability objectives be used to evaluate design trade-offs, monitor progress and scheduling (particularly during systems testing), and control preventative maintenance. However, each of these uses requires trade-offs between the operational cost of failure and the cost of development, testing, maintenance, and schedule delays. Reliability estimates alone do not provide information about the cost of failure. Their use either assumes that all failures have the same consequence or requires additional information regarding the significance of different failures. Since different faults can lead to different failures with varying consequences in distinct environments, reliability measures alone are insufficient. Moreover, since the environment can change, it is important to continually evaluate the impact of these changes on software failure. Software failure risk that incorporates the economic significance of failure together with the reliability of the software provides information that is necessary to make the trade-offs needed to manage the development and use of software.

d. Using Software Failure Risk to Manage Project Risk. The software failure risk assessment methodology includes procedures to determine external software risks. In addition, it includes procedures to assess the potential magnitude of loss due to faults in different portions of a software system. This analysis can then be used to guide the development process. Any additional information about the software development process that becomes available improves the organization's ability to allocate development effort to the portions of the system where the greatest potential magnitudes of loss reside.

Managing project risk also improves the chance of developing quality systems on time. One important component of the quality assurance process is testing. Often there is an implicit trade-off between quality and schedule. Complete testing of a software system, conclusively demonstrating the absence of any errors, is usually impossible. Therefore, the key issue in software testing has been the selection of the subset of all possible test cases that has the highest probability of detecting the most errors (Myers, 1979). While more testing generally results in fewer faults, it also implies longer schedules.

Since errors can have very different chances of causing a failure with different consequences, management often makes decisions concerning the allocation of limited resources by considering the differential probability and impact of software failure. A testing strategy has been suggested whereby the manager queries designers and programmers about which sections of the system are most difficult, giving those sections very thorough testing (Jones, 1986). Although management may have some opinions regarding the differential risk of software failure, no theoretical basis has been developed to actually measure the consequence of failure due to faults in different parts of a system. Hence, no theory to guide management choices of test cases considers the fact that errors vary in their consequence. Software failure risk assessment addresses the issue of assessing risk in various portions of a system.

3.2.1.3. Outsourcing and Purchase

Outsourcing can reduce the risk of producing a system that cannot be developed by inhouse personnel. The purchase of generic software can decrease the risk of not installing a system on time, provided that not too many revisions are required. However, outsourcing and purchase introduce new risks: functionality may be sacrificed, internal business secrets may need to be divulged, and dependence on outsiders for support is created (Clemons *et al.*, 1990). Software failure risk can guide the acquisition and implementation of purchased software by providing information on the differential risk of failure.

3.2.2. Functionality Risk

Functionality risk, the risk that the software may fail to meet user needs, is most critical in rapidly changing environments. Functionality risk arises from two sources. First, a system may fail to provide needed functionality because the developer did not understand what the user wanted. Second, the environment may change so that a system is no longer functionally appropriate. Software failure risk measures that first source of functionality risk.

Traditional approaches to software development have tried to reduce uncertainty in systems development by focusing on what the system should do, not what it should not do. Software failure risk assessment analyzes the environment to determine not only what the software should do, but what can go wrong. It considers how to identify operational risks of software, generating information that can be used to guide development efforts. Such an approach can help reduce functionality risk.

The earliest approaches to managing functionality risk centered on improving and verifying requirements definitions and design (DeMarco, 1979; Gane and Sarson, 1979; Hamilton and Zeldin, 1976; Jackson, 1975; Myers, 1975; Orr, 1977; Ross, 1977; Teicherow and Hershey, 1977; Yourdon and Constantine, 1979). The variety of tools and techniques provided by these methods was intended to enable the software developer to define more clearly how a system was supposed to operate. Validation of software requirements is a starting point for identifying and resolving functionality problems early in the life cycle of a system, but such validation assumes that requirements will not change as the system is used. Moreover, none of these methodologies tests the assumptions underlying the designers' concepts which are often the source of error.

Requirements specifications are often too difficult for users to understand. Traditional requirements documents, such as textual lists of requirements that the system must fulfill or an interpretative model of the proposed system, may not adequately explain how a system will operate (Carey and Mason, 1983). This has led to the use of prototypes (Boar, 1984; Carey and Mason, 1983; Nauman and Jenkins, 1982) that allow users to view a working model of the system. These may be more readily understood by users and can improve communication.

Because uncertainty in the environment often cannot be reduced, new and more flexible approaches to development are needed. In a changing environment, software failure risk assessment and the use of prototypes do not guarantee functionality. What is needed is the ability to revise the software to keep up with environmental changes. Fourth-generation languages and CASE technology offer some opportunities not only to stay close to the user but to respond to changes. The use of new technology, while increasing technical risk, can reduce functionality risk if the technology allows rapid changes. First Boston, a securities trading company, chose to decrease functionality risk (while increasing technical risk) when replacing all its systems in order to keep up with changing global markets, financial instruments, strategies, and regulatory climates in the 1980s. To minimize functional risk, it developed new CASE tools that were previously unavailable even from commercial software vendors in order to provide the capability of responding to functional changes (Clemons, 1991).

3.2.3. Political/Internal Risk

Political/internal problems contribute to functionality as well as project risk. A group within an organization may perceive a new or increased disadvantage with the information system. This can result in producing a system that is not used or is used improperly (either intentionally or unintentionally). The support and commitment of management must be gained, and all users who have a stake in the problem must be involved to assure user acceptance (Lucas *et al.*, 1990).

Theory W is a new theory of software project management geared toward making each of the parties in the software process a winner. This is accomplished by establishing a set of win–win preconditions and structuring a win–win process and product. The project manager plays a key negotiation role in creating win–win situations by focusing attention on portions of the project most likely to cause trouble and to compromise participants' win conditions in a project (Boehm and Ross, 1989).

3.2.4. Financial Risk

Financial risk results when a systems project does not generate expected financial returns because of one or more of the following events: environmental factors such as competition or new technology; development project cost overruns, perhaps due to poor project planning and control; or losses resulting from operational failure of the system. Only the latter event is measured by software failure risk assessment.

Financial risks must often be accepted in uncertain environments. McKesson Drug took a significant financial risk when it implemented its Economost order-entry system (Clemons and Row, 1988). Had Economost not generated sufficient volume as a result of price cuts incorporated into the system, the cost of the system would not have been recouped. Manufacturers Hanover, on the other hand, anticipated a volume that was never achieved when installing its worldwide communications network for GeoNet (Clemons *et al.*, 1990).

Financial risk can be managed by forming alliances to develop shared resources, thereby spreading costs and risk. Participants in the MAC system, a shared automatic teller machine network, lowered their individual costs by sharing switching and processing facilities. This reduced the benefits needed by each participant to justify the investment, a highly desirable change, since ATMs were a competitive necessity rather than a competitive advantage (Clemons, 1990). Consortiums can also prove valuable when the potential damage from not having the system greatly exceeds the potential benefit (Clemons and Knez, 1988).

Financial risk arising from cost overruns can be managed by improved planning and monitoring of costs. Since uncertain environments create financial risk, the risk can be managed by phased modular development, thereby deferring an upfront total commitment. Using the spiral model of development, a project is terminated if the software can no longer improve the mission, as for example if the product misses its market window or a superior product becomes available (Boehm, 1988). Sensitivity analysis should be performed that considers adoption rates, system utilization, and anticipated staff reductions (Clemons *et al.*, 1990).

Financial loss associated with operational failure can have a large impact on financial returns. The system that Electronic Data Systems developed in 1983 for Blue Cross and Blue Shield United of Wisconsin produced $60 million in overpayments and duplicate checks. The loss of 35,000 policyholders was attributed to problems with this system (Rothfeder, 1988). To minimize financial loss associated with operational failure, these risks must be identified and measured, the subject of Part II of this book.

3.2.5. Technical Risk

Technical risk can occur if development attempts to go beyond what is currently technologically feasible with software, hardware, telecommunications, or algorithms (Clemons *et al.*, 1990). It may not be possible, for example, to achieve required levels of overhead in a multiprocessor operating system, desired levels of computer security protection, necessary speed and accuracy of new algorithms, or desired man–machine performance (Boehm, 1984).

The New Jersey Department of Motor Vehicles faced a technical risk when it employed a fourth-generation language never used to build a comparable system. The completed system crashed, and the resulting backlogs left thousands of the state's motorists driving with invalid registrations or licenses. Hundreds of thousands of others encountered errors and delays while overtime pay totalled hundreds of thousand of dollars (Kull, 1986).

Technical risk can be managed by staying abreast of technological innovation, using inhouse Research and Development or links with organizations skilled in more advanced technology, using alternative approaches with existing technology, or outsourcing development to organizations with greater technical expertise.

Operational failure risk does not specifically address technical risk. However, by evaluating the relationships between the use of the software and its environment, the application of the methodology may raise some concerns if the technology appears inadequate.

3.2.6. Systemic Risk

Systemic risk is the risk that a successful system changes the industry. Competitors may imitate the product, develop alternative and possibly more successful systems, or attempt to prevent advantage by other means. Competitors of Girard Bank, who formed MAC, a shared ATM network, were far more successful than Girard and ultimately acquired Girard's ATM operations (Clemons, 1990).

Users or customers may also threaten the success of an information systems project. Rosenbluth Travel developed a system for determining the best airfares from a number of airline reservation systems, reducing the advantages gained by the larger airline reservation systems (Clemons and Row, 1990).

Regulatory changes can also threaten success. The American Airlines SABRE system was required to eliminate bias from its displays of available flights.

Since many of these responses are not controllable, risk is managed by trying to anticipate reactions and by being prepared to change. Again, the spiral model of development would be useful since it continually reevaluates risk throughout the cycle (Boehm, 1988).

Since operational failure risk assessment does not measure systemic risk, nor is it very helpful in forecasting or managing uncontrollable responses, external risks need to be continually reviewed. As the environment changes, software failure risk can be re-evaluated to determine whether system changes are necessary.

3.3. SOFTWARE FAILURE RISK: WHAT IT IS NOT

This review of the various components of risk in software development and use illustrate what software failure risk does and does not measure. First, it measures risk resulting from software errors only. It is *not* concerned with physical threats to the computer center and hardware, such as fire or equipment theft. It is concerned with hardware failures only if they are caused or exacerbated by software problems.

Software failure risk does *not* measure all aspects of software security. It does *not* measure the risk resulting from malicious destruction of data introduced, for example, by viruses or worms. However, software failure risk does incorporate risk resulting from destruction or modification of data due to software deficiencies. Moreover, it incorporates the impact of external controls.

Software failure risk measures risk resulting from poor quality and poor functionality introduced during development, but does *not* measure technical risk. It does *not* measure the system's capability to meet future unanticipated environmental changes, although software failure risk can be re-evaluated to incorporate the effect of a new environment on failure risk.

Software failure risk is concerned with expected economic loss. Thus, it measures more than just reliability or probability of loss. The measurement, also includes the magnitude of economic loss.

Software failure risk is concerned with loss due to software failure, but is *not* concerned with loss due to either poor planning and control or reduced benefits accruing from the use of software.

While software failure risk does *not* measure all components of risk in software development, it does measure a very significant factor, the economic loss that may occur if the software fails to operate correctly. This may be due to errors in developing the requirements, design, or code. The ability to measure the differential risk of failure in the components of a software system can be used to manage the development process. The process of assessing this risk can decrease functionality risk due to the misunderstanding of requirements in the operational environment. It decreases the project risk associated with inadequate quality assurance. Moreover, information on differential risk can be used to manage the project schedule by focusing efforts on high-risk components. This will decrease financial risk due to failure as well as schedule overruns. While software failure risk does *not* forecast environmental changes, risk can be continually reevaluated as the environment changes.

REFERENCES

Akiyama, F., "An Example of Software System Debugging," *Proc. IFIP Congress* (August, 1971), Ljubljana, Yugoslavia, Amsterdam: North Holland, pp. 353–359.

Arthur, J., "Software Quality Measurement," *Datamation* **30**, (December 15, 1984), 115–120.

AT&T Bell Laboratories, "Technical Report on AT&T's Network Slowdown," January 15, 1990, Summit, NJ.

Basili, V. R. and D. H. Hutchens, "An Empirical Study of a Syntactic Complexity Family," *IEEE Trans. Software Engrg.* **SE-9**(5), (November 1983), 664–672.

Basili, V. R. and B. T. Perricone, "Software Errors and Complexity: An Empirical Investigation," *Comm. ACM* **27**(1), (January 1984), 42–52.

Basili, V. R. and T. Y. Phillips, "Evaluating and Comparing Software Metrics in the Software Engineering Laboratory," *NASA Collected Software Engineering Papers: Volume 1* (July, 1982), Section 4, pp. 18–36.

Boar, B., *Application Prototyping*, New York: Wiley, 1984.

Boehm, B., *Software Engineering Economics*, Englewood Cliffs, NJ: Prentice-Hall, 1981.

——"Verifying and Validating Software Requirements and Design Specifications," *IEEE Software*, (January 1984), pp. 75–88.

——"A Spiral Model of Software Development and Enhancement," *Computer* (May, 1988), pp. 61–72.

——*Software Risk Management*, Washington: IEEE Computer Society Press, 1989.

Boehm, B. and R. Ross, "Theory-W Software Project Management: Principles and Examples," *IEEE Trans. on Software Engrg.* **SE-15**(7), (July 1989), 902–916.

Brooks, F. P., *The Mythical Man-Month*, Reading, MA: Addison-Wesley, 1982.

Brown, J. R. and M. Lipow, "Testing for Software Reliability,"*Proc. Internat. Conf. Reliable Software* (April, 1975), Los Angeles, CA, New York: IEEE, 1975, pp. 518–527.

Burgess, J., "Searching for a Better Shield; Virus Incident Underscores Vulnerability of Companies as Role of Machine Widens," *Washington Post*, November 13, 1988, p. H1.

Card, D. N., V. B. Church, and W. W. Agresti, "An Empirical Study of Software Design Practice," *IEEE Trans. Software Engrg.* **SE-12**(2), (February 1986), 264–271.

Carey, T. T and R. E. A. Mason, "Information Systems Prototyping: Techniques, Tools, and Methodologies," *INFOR—The Canadian Journal of Operational Research and Information Processing* **21**(3), (February 1983), 177–191.

Cha, S. S., N. G. Leveson, and T. J. Shimeall, "Safety Verification in MURPHY using Fault Tree Analysis," *Proc. 10th Internat. Conf. Software Engrg.*, (April 11-15, 1988), Singapore, Washington: IEEE, 1988, p. 377–386.

Charette, R. N., *Software Engineering Risk Analysis and Management*, New York: McGraw-Hill, 1989.

Clemons, E. K., "Evaluation of Strategic Investments in Information Technology," *Comm. ACM* **34**(1), (January 1991), 22–36.

——"MAC—Philadelphia National Bank's Strategic Venture in Shared ATM Networks," *J. Management Information Systems*, **7**(1), (Summer 1990), 5–26.

Clemons, E. K. and M. Knez "Competition and Cooperation in Information Systems Innovation," *Information and Management* **15**, (1988), 25–35.

Clemons, E. K. and M. Row, "Rosenbluth Travel: A Case Study in the Strategic Use of Information Technology," Working Paper #90-07-05, Wharton School, University of Pennsylvania, 1990.

——"McKesson Drug Company: A Case Study of Economost—A Strategic Information System," *J. Management Information Systems* **5**(1), (1988), 36–50.

Clemons, E. K., B. W. Weber, and D. Brennen, "Components of Risk in Strategic IT Programs: Implications and Risk Management," Proc. Conf. Strategic Information Architectures, Wharton School, University of Pennsylvania, 1990.

DeMarco, T., *Structured Analysis and System Specifications*, Englewood Cliffs, NJ: Prentice-Hall, 1979.

Electronics, "Task Force Slams DOD for Bungling Military Software Efforts," Military/Aerospace Newsletter, November 12, 1987, p. 121.

Elmer-Dewitt, P., "Ghost in the Machine," *Time*, January 29, 1990, pp. 58–59.

Endres, A., "An Analysis of Errors and Their Causes in System Programs," *IEEE Trans. Software Engrg*. **SE-1**(2), (June 1975), 140–149.

Feuer, A. R. and E. B. Fowlkes, "Some Results from an Empirical Study of Computer Software," *Fourth Internat. Conf. Software Engrg.*, (September 17–19, 1979), Munich, Germany, New York: IEEE, pp. 351–355.

Fisher, R. P., *Information Systems Security*, Englewood Cliffs, NJ: Prentice-Hall, 1984.

Fitzgerald, K., "The Quest for Intruder-proof Computer Systems," *IEEE Spectrum*, August, 1989, pp. 22–26.

Fryer, M. O., "Risk Assessment of Computer Controlled Systems," *IEEE Trans. Software Engrg*. **SE-11**(1), (January 1985), 125–129.

Gane, C. and T. Sarson, *Structured Systems Analysis: Tools and Techniques*, Englewood Cliffs, NJ: Prentice-Hall, 1979.

Glass, R. L., "Persistent Software Errors," *IEEE Trans. Software Engrg*. **SE-7**(2), (March 1981), 162–168.

Goel, A., "Software Reliability Models: Assumptions, Limitations, and Applicability," *IEEE Trans. Software Engrg*. **SE-11**(12), (December 1985), 1411–1423.

Goel, A. and K. Okumoto, "Time Dependent Error Detection Rate Model for Software Reliability and Other Performance Measures," *IEEE Trans. Reliability* **R-28**(3), (August 1979), 206–211.

Gremillon, L. L., "Determinants of Program Repair Maintenance Requirements," *Comm. ACM* **27**(8) (August 1984), 826–832.

Hamilton, M. and S. Zeldin, "Higher Order Software—A Methodology for Defining Software," *IEEE Trans. Software Engrg*. **SE-2**(1), (March 1976), 9–32.

Hecht, H., "Fault-Tolerant Software for Real-Time Applications," *Computing Surveys* **8**(4), (December 1976), 391–407.

Howe, A., "How the IRS Acquired Its Troubled Computers," *The Philadelphia Inquirer*, August 5, 1985, p. A1.

Hull, R. P. and L. E. Serio, Jr., "What Managers Should Know about Computer Security," *Business*, October–December 1987, pp. 3–8.

Humphrey, W. S., *Managing the Software Process*, Reading, MA: Addison-Wesley, 1989.

Information Week, "Executive Summary," March 7, 1988, p. 8.

Jackson, J. A., *Principles of Program Design*, London: Academic Press, 1975.

Jacky, J., "Programmed for Disaster: Software Errors that Imperil Lives," *The Sciences* **29**(5), (September–October 1989), 22–27.

Jelinski, Z. and P. Moranda, "Software Reliability Research," *Statistical Computer Performance Evaluation* (W. Frieberger, ed.), New York: Academic Press, 1972, pp. 465–484.

Jewell, W. S., "Bayesian Extensions to a Basic Model of Software Reliability," *IEEE Trans. Software Engrg.* **SE-11**(12), (December 1985), 1465–1471.

Jones, C., *Programming Productivity*, New York: McGraw-Hill, 1986.

Juris, R., "EDP Auditing Lessens Risk Exposure," *Computer Decisions*, July 15, 1986, pp. 36–42.

Kemerer, C., "An Empirical Validation of Software Cost Estimation Models," *Comm. ACM* **30**(5), (May 1987), 416–429.

Knight, J. C. and N. G. Leveson, "An Empirical Evaluation of the Assumption of Independence in Multi-Version Programming," *IEEE Trans. Software Engrg.* **SE-12**(1), (January 1986), 96–109.

Kull, D., "Anatomy of a 4GL Disaster," *Computer Decisions*, February 11, 1986, pp. 58–65.

Langberg, N. and N. Singpurwalla, "A Unification of Some Software Reliability Models," *SIAM J. Sci. Statist. Computing* **6**(3), (July 1985), 781–790.

Leveson, N. G., "Software Safety: Why, What, and How," *Computing Surveys* **18**(2), (June 1986), 125–163.

Leveson, N. G. and P. R. Harvey, "Analyzing Software Safety", *IEEE Trans. Software Engrg.* **SE-9**(5), (September 1983), 569–579.

Leveson, N. G., S. S. Cha, J. C. Knight, and T. J. Shimeall, "The Use of Self Checks and Voting in Software Error Detection: An Empirical Study," *IEEE Trans. Software Engrg.* **SE-16**(4), (April 1990), 432–443.

Lipow, M., "On Software Reliability," *IEEE Trans. Reliability* **R-28**(3), (August 1979), 178–180.

Littlewood, B., "MTBF is Meaningless in Software Reliability," *IEEE Trans. Reliability* **R-24**(1), (April 1975), 82.

——"Theories of Software Reliability: How Good are They and How Can They Be Improved?" *IEEE Trans. Software Engrg.* **SE-6**(5), (September 1980), 489–500.

——"How to Measure Software Reliability and How Not To", *IEEE Trans. Reliability* **R-28**(2), (June 1979), 103–110.

Littlewood, B. and J. L. Verrall, "A Bayesian Reliability Growth Model for Computer Software," *IEEE 1973 Computer Software Reliability Conf.*, New York, (1973), New York: IEEE, pp. 70–77.

Los Angeles Times, "Reservation System Breaks Down," May 13, 1988, Financial Desk, Part 4, Column 1.

Lucas, H.C., M. J. Ginzberg, and R. L. Schultz, *Information Systems Implementation: Testing a Structural Model*, Norwood, NJ: Ablex Publishing, 1990.

Moranda, P. B., "An Error Detection Model for Application during Software Test Development," *IEEE Trans. Reliability* **R-30**(4), (October 1981), 309–312.

Musa, J. D., "Theory of Software Reliability and its Application," *IEEE Trans. Software Engrg.* **SE-1**(3), (September 1975), 312–327.

Musa, J. D. and K. Okumoto, "Software Reliability Models: Concepts, Classification, Comparisons, and Practice," *Electronic Systems Effectiveness and Life Cycle Costing* (J. K. Skwirzynski, ed.), NATO ASI Series F3, Heidelberg: Springer-Verlag, 1983, pp. 395–424.

——"A Logarithmic Poisson Execution Time Model for Software Reliability Measurement," *Proc. 7th Internat. Conf. Software Engrg.* (March 26–29, 1984), Orlando, FL, Washington: IEEE, pp. 230–238.

Musa, J. D., A. Iannino, and K. Okumoto, *Software Reliability: Measurement, Prediction, Application*, New York: McGraw-Hill, 1987.

Myers, G. J., *Reliable Software Through Composite Design*, New York: Van Nostrand Reinhold, 1975.

——*Software Reliability*, New York: Wiley, 1976.

——*The Art of Software Testing*, New York: Wiley, 1979.

National Bureau of Standards, "Guidelines for Automatic Data Processing Risk Analysis," Federal Information Processing Standards Publication 65, August 1, 1979.

Neumann, J. and M. Jenkins, "Prototyping: The New Paradigm for Systems Development," *MIS Quarterly*, September, 1982, pp. 29–44.

Ohba, M., "Software Reliability Analysis Models," *IBM J. Res. Develop.* **28**(4), (July 1984), 428–443.

Orr, K., *Structured Systems Development*, New York: Yourdon Press, 1977.

Parnas, D. A., J. van Schouwen, and S. P. Kwan, "Evaluation of Safety-Critical Software," *Comm. ACM* **33**(6), (June 1990), 636–648.

Pfleeger, S. L., *Software Engineering: The Production of Quality Software*, New York: Macmillan, 1991.

Pfleeger, S. L. and C. L. McCowan, "Software Metrics in a Process Maturity Framework," *J. Systems and Software*, **12**, (July 1990), 255–261.

Putnam, L., "Key Issues in Managing Software Cost and Quality," Quantitative Software Management, Inc., McLean, VA., 1987.

Ramamoorthy, C. V. and F. B. Bastani, "Software Reliability—Status and Perspectives," *IEEE Trans. Software Engrg.* **SE-8**(4), (July 1982), 354–371.

Randell, B., P. A. Lee, and P. C. Treleaven, "Reliability Issues in Computing System Design," *Computing Surveys* **10**(2), (June 1978), 123–165.

Richards, E., "Software's Dangerous Aspect; Problem During Medical Treatment Tied to Deaths, Injuries," *Washington Post*, December 9, 1990, p. A25.

Ross, D. T., "Structured Analysis for Requirements Definition," *IEEE Trans. Software Engrg.* **SE-3**(1), (January 1977), 6–16.

Rothfeder, J., "It's Late, Costly, Incompetent—But Try Firing a Computer System," *Business Week*, November 7, 1988, pp. 164–165.

Rubey, R., "Planning for Software Reliability," *Proc. Reliability and Maintainability Symposium*, (1977), Philadelphia, New York: IEEE, 1977, pp. 495–499.

Ruthberg, Z. G. and B. T. Fisher, "Work Priority Scheme for EDP Audit and Computer Security Review," U.S. Department of Commerce, National Bureau of Standards Technical Report NBSIR 86-3386, March, 1986, p. iii-B-14.

Scott, R. K., J. W. Gault, and D. F. McAllister, "Fault-Tolerant Software Reliability Modeling," *IEEE Trans. Software Engrg.* **SE-13**(5), (May 1987), 382–392.

Schneidewind, N. F., "Analysis of Error Processes in Computer Software," *Proc. Internat. Conf. Reliable Software* (April, 1975), Los Angeles, New York: IEEE, 337–346.

Schneidewind, N. F. and H. Hoffman, "An Experiment in Software Error Data Collection and Analysis," *IEEE Trans. Software Engrg.* **SE-5**(3), (May 1979), 276–286.

Shen, V. Y., T. Yu, S. Thiebaut, and L. Paulsen, "Identifying Error-Prone Software—An Empirical Study," *IEEE Trans. Software Engrg.* **SE-11**(4), (April 1985), 317–323.

Shooman, M. L., "Probabilistic Models for Software Reliability Prediction," in *Statistical Computer Performance Evaluation* (W. Frieberger ed.), New York: Academic Press, 1972, pp. 485–502.

——"Operational Testing and Software Reliability Estimation during Program Development," *Proceedings IEEE Computer Software Reliability Conference*, New York, New York: IEEE, 1973, pp. 51–57.

Shooman, M. L. and A. Trivedi, "A Many State Markov Model for Computer Software Performance Parameters," *IEEE Trans. Reliability* **R-25**(2), (June 1976), 66–68.

Takahashi, M. and Y. Kamayachi, "An Empirical Study of a Model for Program Error Prediction," *IEEE Trans. Software Engrg.* **SE-15**(1), (January 1989), 82–86.

Tate, P., "Risk: The Third Factor," *Datamation*, April 15, 1988.

Teicherow, D. and E. Hershey, "PLA/PSA: A Computer-Aided Technique for Structured Documentation and Analysis of Information Processing Systems," *IEEE Trans. Software Engrg.* **SE-3**(1), (January 1977), 41–48.

U.S. Air Force Systems Command, "Software Risk Abatement," Air Force Logistics Command Pamphlet 800-45, September 30, 1988.

U.S. House of Representatives, "Bugs in the Program: Problems in Federal Government Computer Software Development and Regulation," Staff Study by the Subcommittee on Investigations and Oversight, transmitted to the Committee on Science, Space, and Technology, U.S. Government Printing Office, Washington, D.C., September, 1989.

Weinberg, G. M., *The Psychology of Computer Programming*, New York: Van Nostrand Reinhold, 1971.

Youngs, E., "Human Errors in Programming," in *Tutorial: Human Factors in Software Development* (W. Curtis, ed.), New York: IEEE, 1981, pp. 383–392.

Yourdon, E. and L. Constantine, *Structured Design: Fundamentals of a Discipline of Computer Program and Systems Design*, Englewood Cliffs, NJ: Prentice-Hall, 1979.

Part II

Software Failure Risk Measurement

Chapter 4

A Methodology for Software Failure Risk Measurement

This chapter deals with the economic significance of software malfunction by presenting a framework for measuring software failure risk followed by a detailed examination of components of that methodology to assess software failure risk.

4.1. FRAMEWORK FOR SOFTWARE FAILURE RISK MEASUREMENT

Software failure risk is the expected loss due to failure during a given period; it is measured by the frequency or *likelihood of loss* (events resulting in loss per unit time) multiplied by the magnitude of loss or the *level of exposure* due to loss (consequences of events).*

Several functions must be performed to measure software failure risk:

1. *External Exposure Identification*
   What actions by the organization can result in losses, and what are the consequences of those actions?

*This is analogous to the work of Henley and Kumamoto (1981).

2. *Structural Exposure Analysis*
   What system failures can result in these actions?
   What is the potential magnitude of loss due to failures caused by faults in each module?
3. *Prior Predictions of Failure Likelihood and Risk*
   What is the *a priori* estimate of the likelihood of failure due to faults in each untested module?
   What is the resulting estimate of risk?
4. *Using Test Results to Update Prior Predictions*
   How can test results be used to update failure assessments?

Figure 4.1 depicts the framework for risk assessment methodology. The components are briefly described here, followed by specific procedures to perform each step.

4.1.1. External Exposure Identification

The first step in the measurement of software failure risk is the identification of external exposure. This involves an assessment of factors that can contribute to loss operating in the environment external to the software. First, potential actions that can result in loss must be identified. Then, the magnitude of possible loss due to these actions must be assessed.

For several reasons, the software failure risk assessment methodology begins outside the software itself. First, failure risk is not always an inherent feature of the software, but is frequently affected by the operator or user of a system. On the one hand, users may commit errors which affect the overall chances of an accident; on the other, they can intervene to halt accident sequences and limit the damage. Second, a software error often results from a misunderstanding or an omission of external user requirements. Study of the software alone might not help uncover such analysis and design errors. Assessment of the external environment involves identification of sources of catastrophe—typically operator actions (or inactions) that can cause disaster by violating norms of behavior. For example, in an air traffic control system, the collision of two airplanes may be caused by a controller failing to direct the pilots to change headings when their two planes are on a collision course.

Analysis of behavior linked to catastrophic events may reveal items that were inadvertently left out of the system requirements (errors of omission). By focusing on actions in the environment that can cause loss, design requirements not previously evident from the requirements definition may be recognized. In short, such analysis provides another technique for validating the system design.

The magnitude of loss that may result from inappropriate actions is a function of the environment and the context in which the system operates. The

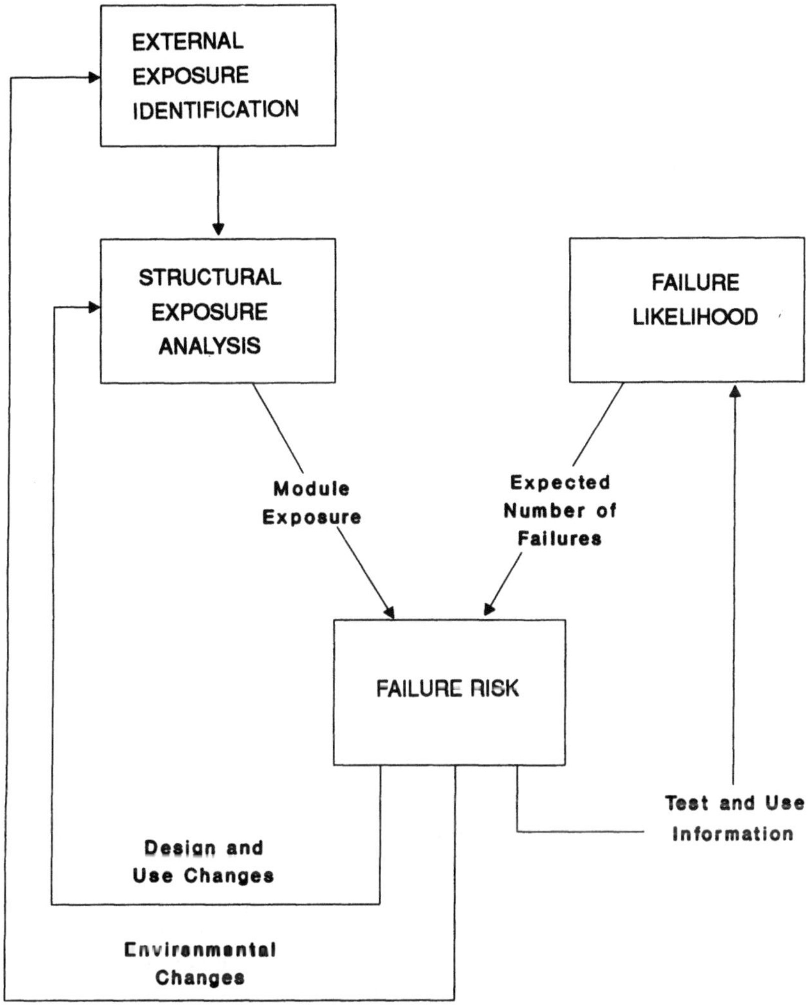

Figure 4.1. Framework for software failure risk measurement.

potential loss from an air traffic controller operating inappropriately in situations where planes are on a potential collision course is much larger if the controller is working during rush hour in a large airport than if he or she were working an off-hour shift in a small airport that does not handle wide-bodied aircraft. Generally, many environmental factors must be considered. We begin by assuming a linear utility function for the user organization, using expected values for the magnitude of loss.

The methodology for assessing external exposure draws upon probabilistic risk assessment techniques, such as event and fault trees. These techniques have been used to describe the set of interrelated conditions that can lead to failure in complex, potentially hazardous engineered systems such as nuclear power and chemical plants (Henley and Kumamoto, 1981; Levine, 1984; MacKenzie, 1984; McCormick, 1981; Pate-Cornell, 1984; Sheridan, 1980; U.S. Nuclear Regulatory Commission, 1975; Veseley and Rasmuson, 1984) as well as to determine software safety requirements (Cha *et al.*, 1988; Leveson and Harvey, 1983). Procedures for using some of these techniques to assess external exposure of complex software systems are presented later in this chapter. Application of these procedures to several selected software systems follows in subsequent chapters.

4.1.2. Structural Exposure Analysis

In structural exposure analysis, inappropriate operator actions identified during the external exposure identification stage are mapped back to system causes. These system causes are associated with potential faults in various modules to identify the magnitude of loss due to faults in different portions of the system.

The magnitude of loss due to actions that can result from system failure is defined as their *exposure level*. *Failures* are due to *faults*, or defects, in the system. The objective is to assign an exposure level due to faults in the basic interconnected components or individual modules of the system.

Operator, or environmental, malfunction can cause or result from invalid system output. Note that the absence of *anticipated* output may itself be considered invalid output. This invalid output is a result of a failure caused by one or more faults in the system. Hence, inappropriate actions must first be related to system failures. For example, failure of an operator to respond to aircraft on a collision course may be due to the system failing to display more than one aircraft with collision-course headings.

After identifying potential system failures, it is necessary to determine which modules or paths in the system may have faults that can result in these failures. In the above example, modules that process data related to the display of aircraft heading must be identified. This requires determining how the output resulting from the system malfunction is produced. Invalid output that triggers actions which result in losses is produced by invalid processing of data by the system. The specifications may be used to show how data flows through the system.

In order to assign exposure levels to modules, the relationship between the data the module processes and the invalid outputs must be determined. It is also necessary to determine how the function of each module relates to the data it processes. It is assumed that the fault potential of a module is a function of the type of processing that occurs in that module. Thus, functions related to data with the potential for loss are identified. Design documents may help in understanding how the specifications were packaged into modules, in turn facilitating the mapping of the relationship between the invalid output and the data processed in each module.

A module's function at any time, as well as its associated exposure level, may vary with the way the system uses it; this use, in turn, is related to the way the system itself is being used. For example, response to an air traffic control display produced by a module can result in different actions, based upon the purpose of the display at the time of failure. Hence, the complex relationship between module functions and system functions must be clearly understood.

To summarize, the exposure level of a module is based on actions that can result from failures due to faults in the module. It depends on what data are processed by the module and how that data relate to invalid output. Exposure level also depends on how the module processes data, which itself is a function of the module's use. The methodology for estimating the exposure level of a module includes procedures for assessing software failure modes, determining module fault potential, and estimating module use.

Exposure assessment, combined with an estimate of failure likelihood, can guide the testing of a software system. In addition, estimates of the exposure of various portions of a proposed software system can guide design decisions. Design trade-offs can be made that will minimize the likelihood of failure in portions of the system where exposure is estimated to be high. Alternative designs can be compared. The use of the structural exposure analysis in software development is discussed in Chapter 8.

4.1.3. Prior Prediction of Failure Likelihood and Risk

The likelihood of a software failure depends on

1. the number of faults or errors in a program, and
2. the probability that a fault or program defect will be encountered in operation

The number of faults is a function of the product as well as the development process. Most research has concentrated on studying the relationship between characteristics of the final product, such as size and complexity, and the number of faults found. Many researchers have found that the size of a program, measured in terms of the number of executable source statements, has the most impact on the number of faults it contains (Feuer and Fowlkes, 1979; Gremillon, 1984; Musa *et al.*, 1987). For modules, research has suggested that a linear model be used to predict the number of faults as a function of size (Basili and

Perricone, 1984; Shen *et al.*, 1985), because of interface errors, extra care taken in coding larger modules, and the possibility of undetected errors in larger modules (Basili and Perricone, 1984). The existence of a constant inherent fault component unrelated to size is, however, still in dispute (Card *et al.*, 1986).

Research that relates measures of program complexity to the number of faults has been inconclusive (Akiyama, 1971; Basili and Hutchens, 1983; Basili and Perricone, 1984; Basili and Phillips, 1982; Card *et al.*, 1986; Feuer and Fowlkes, 1979; Gaffney, 1984; Gremillon, 1984; Lipow, 1982; Lipow and Thayer, 1977; Schneidewind and Hoffmann, 1979; Shen *et al.*, 1985).

Characteristics of the development process can affect the number of faults (Basili and Hutchens, 1983; Card *et al.*, 1986; Selby *et al.*, 1987; Selby and Porter, 1988; Takahashi and Kamayachi, 1989; Youngs, 1981). Such factors as the skill level of the development team, communication among team members, the quality of reviews, deadline pressure, and familiarity with application and techniques are expected to affect the error density of a program. However, it is difficult to develop and relate objective measures of many of these characteristics to the error density of a program. Therefore, most researchers have used the size of a program as the key factor in predicting the number of faults in that program. Although the methodology presented here uses program size to predict the number of faults prior to test, it is believed that better methods of predicting errors based on characteristics of the development process would improve operational performance of the methodology. In particular, appropriate collection and recording of the historical performance of individual programmers might improve the ability to predict errors. (Appendix A provides some background in fault prediction methods and suggests some future work in this area.)

The probability that a fault will produce a failure depends on the number of ways a module can be used and the frequency with which it is used. The risk assessment methodology assumes that each fault in a module is independent and has the same per fault hazard rate, since it appears excessively difficult to determine what specific portions of a module have the greatest potential for producing failures. If the location of all faults were known, those faults could be fixed, and the problem of predicting failure would no longer exist.

The probability that a fault will cause a failure when a module is used may depend on the number of paths (or distinct sequences of control) and the number of input classes (or sets of similar input variables). If a module has a large number of paths and input classes, the probability of a specific fault causing a failure on any given run is expected to be less than if a module has only a single path and a single input class. However, research establishing this relationship has not been conclusive, and researchers have used similar programs to estimate a fault exposure ratio—the fraction of the number of times that a program is used that a fault results in failure (Musa *et al.*, 1987).

Typically, certain modules are used more often than others, resulting in unequal *per fault hazard rates* for faults in different modules. The operational profile, or set of all possible input states with their associated probabilities of occurrence, determines which modules are used most frequently. If a fault is located on a main branch of the code or in a portion of code that is well traversed, it should have a higher probability of causing a failure than if it were located in a section of the code that is rarely traversed. Previous studies of software reliability assign the same per fault hazard rate to all portions of a system (Musa *et al.*, 1987). The operational profile can help to assign different hazard rates based upon expected frequency of use.

The estimate of *risk* for each module is the product of the *expected exposure level* and the *expected number of failures* within a given period resulting from faults in that module. The expected exposure level depends on the expected use of the system during operation, whereas the expected number of failures depends on the number of faults and the probability that faults will produce failures.

4.1.4. Using Test Results to Update Prior Predictions

Prior to testing, exposure level assessment is based on identification of the types of failures that could occur and their consequences. The number of faults is estimated along with the likelihood of failure using *a priori* perceptions of the development process and characteristics of the code. Information about software failure risk obtained as testing proceeds may change initial perceptions or prior assessments of the magnitude and location of that risk. Examining the failure and debugging information can provide new knowledge about the system. If types of failure that were not previously considered are encountered during testing, the external and structural exposure analyses may need to be repeated. As additional information on failure rates and location of faults is gathered, the perception of the number of faults and, thus, the likelihood of failure due to faults in each module may be altered. Prior estimates can be updated based on this new information.

One means of using failure data to update prior estimates is based on the observation that in many systems errors tend to cluster. In one of IBM's S/370 operating systems, 47% of total errors were associated with only 4% of the modules in the system (Myers, 1979). In a recent AT&T electronic switching project, 80% of the changes were concentrated in 20% of the modules (Levendel, 1991). This phenomenon prompted one of the testing principles stated by Myers: "The probability of the existence of more errors in a section of a program is proportional to the number of errors already found in that section" (Myers, 1979, p. 15). Thus, the location of many faults in a single module may change the prior estimate of the number of faults still to be found in that module.

A second means of using failure information involves assuming a statistical distribution for software reliability growth. As failure data become available, statistical inference procedures are used to update the parameters of the distribution (Goel and Okumoto, 1979; Kubat and Koch, 1980; Littlewood and Verrall, 1973; Musa, 1975). In most cases, these parameters are the number of faults and the probability that a fault will cause a failure. This approach has been adopted in developing the methodology presented here. Since module failures have low probabilities of occurrence, predictions are based primarily on prior estimates. When a failure occurs, however, those prior estimates are adjusted to account for the occurrence of a low-probability event. Such a framework suggests a Bayesian model.

4.2. EXTERNAL EXPOSURE ASSESSMENT

Assessment of external software exposure begins with an analysis of the environment in which the software will operate. The objectives of external exposure assessment are

1. to determine what actions in the environment *external* to the software can contribute to loss, and
2. to assess the significance of the loss.

To accomplish these objectives, a procedure involving the following steps is presented:

1. risk identification,
2. definition of environmental hazards,
3. identification of accident sequences,
4. failure modes analysis, and
5. consequence analysis.

First will come a discussion of the risk identification process and implications of assumptions made when identifying risk in the external environment. That will be followed by details of the steps required to identify and assess potential loss.

4.2.1. Risk Identification

The ability to measure software failure risk is predicated upon the assumption that risk can be adequately identified. This identification requires an understanding of the nature and impact of software failure on current and potential future activities of the user organization.

> Risk identification is equivalent to risk diagnosis. During this stage, we seek to reduce the uncertainty, in descriptive terms, about the identity and potential impact of the key variables that characterize risk in the problem situation under consideration. (Hertz and Thomas, 1983)

Identification of these variables, in turn, requires a clear understanding of the environment in which the software will operate: how users will interact with the software and what the organization will do with the output of the software. Risk identification is based on a risk assessor's definition of the environment and assumptions about hazards within that environment. Software failure may be due to errors of omission or commission that arise when user requirements are translated into specifications, design, and code. Analysis of developers' understanding of a problem may not uncover their errors of omission. Risk identification must, therefore, focus on the environment and use of software beyond the software developers' descriptions of the problem. Moreover, risk is strongly affected by the operator or user of a system. Hence, actions external to the software that can contribute to loss must be considered.

As potential hazards and parts of the system or environment that give rise to the hazards are defined, it is found that "It is necessary to put some boundary on the technical system and the environment under study" (Henley and Kumamoto, 1981). The boundaries can be set within the context of reasonable risk. The "probability-threshold" position* assumes that hazards whose probabilities are very low are considered insignificant or unimportant by the risk assessor. This position regarding risk has been supported by the National Academy of Sciences, regulatory agencies such as the Environmental Protection Agency and the Nuclear Regulatory Commission, scientists, engineers, policymakers, and environmental risk assessors (Shrader-Frechette, 1985). This book will assume that this is a reasonable viewpoint to consider in the analysis of the risk of software failure.

Identifying risks in the software environment expands the understanding of future impacts and thus generates a thought process that may bring about the design of better software. However, it is important to recognize that this procedure can lead to "tunnel vision" because risk assessors can anchor perceptions of the future around current concerns (Tversky and Kahneman, 1974).

> The trustworthiness of the analysis hinges on the experts' ability to enumerate all major pathways to disaster and on the assumptions that underlie the modeling effort. Unfortunately, a modicum of systematic data and many anecdotal reports suggest that experts may be prone to certain kinds of errors and omissions. (Fischhoff *et al.*, 1981)

*Defined by Shrader-Frechette (1985).

The Nuclear Energy Agency Committee on the Safety of Nuclear Installations concluded that the Three Mile Island accident consisted of a sequence of plant failures and errors that led to physical situations evolving over several hours. These sequences had not been studied in sufficient depth because safety assessments had been focused on design-based accidents that happen very quickly (Nuclear Energy Agency, 1980).

Hence, it is important to recognize that software failure risk assessment is based on a procedure for identifying risk that cannot be proven complete or unbiased. It has been stressed that the conscientious application of probability analysis cannot be sufficient proof of safety when considering very improbable events in nuclear power systems (Roberts, 1984). Likewise, scrupulous application of the software failure risk assessment methodology cannot be sufficient proof that all risks of failure have been identified. Due to the problem of obtaining a clear and explicit formulation of the boundaries of the analysis, one researcher concluded that

> The main benefit to draw from an analytical risk assessment will probably not be the quantitative risk figure derived, but the possibility of using the structure and assumptions of the analysis as tools for *risk management* to secure the proper level of risk during the entire plant life. (Rasmussen, 1982)

Similarly, the main benefit from software failure risk assessment is the information on differential software exposure and risk used to guide the software development process in order to minimize overall operational risk. This use of software failure risk assessment will be discussed in Part III.

4.2.2. Definition of Hazards

External exposure assessment begins by investigating the environment(s) in which the software will operate. A thorough understanding of the environmental context is necessary to identify the major consequences resulting in loss. It is also essential to the satisfactory design of a software system. This understanding is obtained through discussion with users rather than software developers. Software developers tend to emphasize what the software is supposed to do. The external picture is desired: how the software will be used and what can go wrong. Although each software application is unique, some general questions can focus user discussions. Some suggested questions are listed in Table 4.1. These questions force the risk assessor to go beyond the system and its intended operation to focus on the environment in which the software will operate.

When defining hazards, it is important to consider how the organization plans to use the system. Hazards are identified for this purpose. It is often helpful to consider system output. What actions or decisions are made using that output? What hazards can occur if that output is invalid or missing?

Table 4.1. External Risk Identification Focus Questions

How will this system be used?
How can the use of this system contribute to the organization's financial hazards?
Who are the users who will directly access the system?
Who are the users who will use the outputs from this system?
What decisions will be made based upon outputs from this system?
What is the impact on financial resources of errors in decisions based upon system outputs?
What are the general plans for processing data?
Will there be any manual checks on the system?
How might the environment change in the future?
Are there attributes of the system whose use might increase or change in the future?
What types of enhancements to the system can be foreseen, and what are the impacts of their use?
What operator actions can cause disaster by violating norms of behavior?
What are the opportunities for deliberate misuse of the system?
What hardware failures can result in loss?
What environmental circumstances can cause situations that may lead to the hazards?
What functions can alter the effect of these operator actions, hardware failure, and environmental conditions?

It is also important to consider how the environment can change in order to determine what hazards may subsequently occur. This is critical because many failures are due to changes in system use. Failure in The Bank of New York's securities trading system occurred when trading volume exceeded 32,000 issues, much greater than original expectations. This failure might have been avoided if designers had considered the need to process a higher-than-anticipated volume of data (Juris, 1986).

4.2.3. Identification of Accident Sequences

After identifying the environment and its hazards, the investigation considers how these hazards can occur. Consideration is given to all events that can precipitate these hazards, called *hazard initiators*, as well as to events that can alter the course of an accident, called *hazard mitigators*. Event trees are useful in displaying the accident scenarios.

The most important questions in the identification of events that can lead to hazards are

- What operator actions can cause disaster by violating norms of behavior?
- What hardware failures can result in loss?

- What environmental circumstances can cause situations that may lead to these hazards?
- What functions can alter the effect of these occurrences?

The suggested procedure differs somewhat from traditional probabilistic risk assessment. It does not begin by focusing on failures of system components, as is traditional in probabilistic risk assessment (Henley and Kumamoto, 1981). The analysis at this point focuses on operator actions or failures of systems *external* to the software that can result in loss, not on portions of the software. If this procedure is used before the system is developed, it may help determine what the design criteria of the software system should be. This technique can also be used to discover errors of omission in any existing design. By focusing on actions in the environment that can cause loss, design requirements not previously evident from the requirements definition may be discovered.

Typically, the sequences of events are linked by conditional probabilities. This lends itself to the use of event trees that display relationships among juxtaposed events on the basis of conditional probabilities (Pate-Cornell, 1984). Event tree construction begins by listing the critical external factors or personnel as preliminary headings. Starting with the initiating event, all possible sequences of events are considered by investigating independent success and failure states for each factor. Figure 4.2 shows a generic event tree for scenario analysis. First to be determined are headings that include all external personnel involved in processing data related to the hazard. The events are specific actions

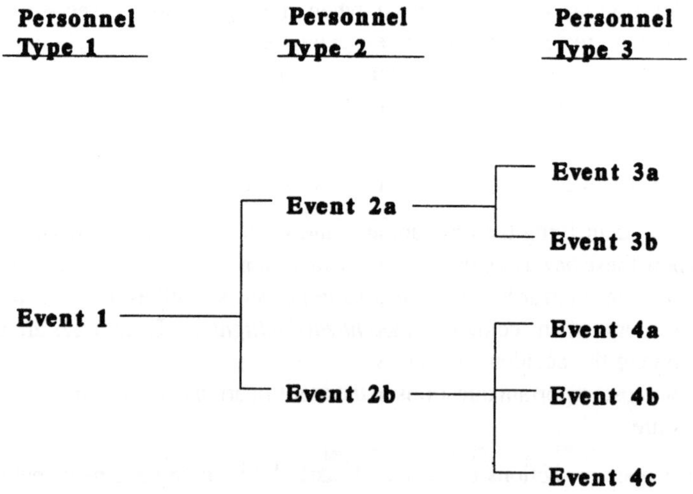

Figure 4.2. Generic event tree for scenario analysis.

that can initiate a hazard or mitigate the effect of a hazard. For example, in the air traffic control example, personnel may include the primary controller (personnel type 1) who may fail to see two planes on a collision course (event 1). A second controller (personnel type 2) could mitigate this hazard by correcting the course (event 2a) or may also fail to see the two planes about to collide (event 2b). The pilot (personnel type 3) could also take action to mitigate this hazard.

4.2.4. Failure Modes Analysis

The analysis next identifies the failure modes of the events identified in the accident sequences. These become top events in the fault tree. Consideration is given to contributing events and conditions that can result in these top events and the relationships among these contributing events. The ultimate objective is to determine where software failure can affect the accident scenario.

Failure modes of top events are revealed by working backward, considering relationships among all events leading to the top event. Fault trees have proven useful in complex, hazardous engineered systems—providing graphical aids, directing the analysis, and pointing out important aspects of the failure of interest (Henley and Kumamoto, 1981). An undesired top event can be linked to more basic fault events using logic gates, symbols that define relationships among events. An OR gate signifies that a top event would occur if any one of the input events occurs, whereas an AND gate means that all the input events would have to occur simultaneously to cause the top event. Developing fault trees forces the analyst to consider all events and relationships.

Events in the software failure risk analysis can typically be categorized as either environmental events, human interactions, failures of hardware components, or erroneous information and control procedures. Environmental events are occurrences that take place due to conditions in the environment. Human interactions include all operator interfaces; actions or inactions are also typically dependent upon a variety of environmental conditions. Hardware failures are sometimes a function of similar environmental conditions. If the system is under stress, there may be a greater chance of hardware failure. Erroneous information and control procedures are often the result of software failure; they are also often dependent upon environmental conditions.

Fault trees are used to investigate the causes of events and relationships in the event trees. Figure 4.3 is a fault tree depicting conditions that, together with lack of information or erroneous information, may cause events leading to hazards. In most fault trees, a diamond denotes an event that is not further analyzed because of a lack of information, money, or time to perform a detailed analysis (Henley and Kumamoto, 1981). This symbol is used here to represent events such as the existence of erroneous information or lack of information because their causes have not yet been analyzed. They will be analyzed in the

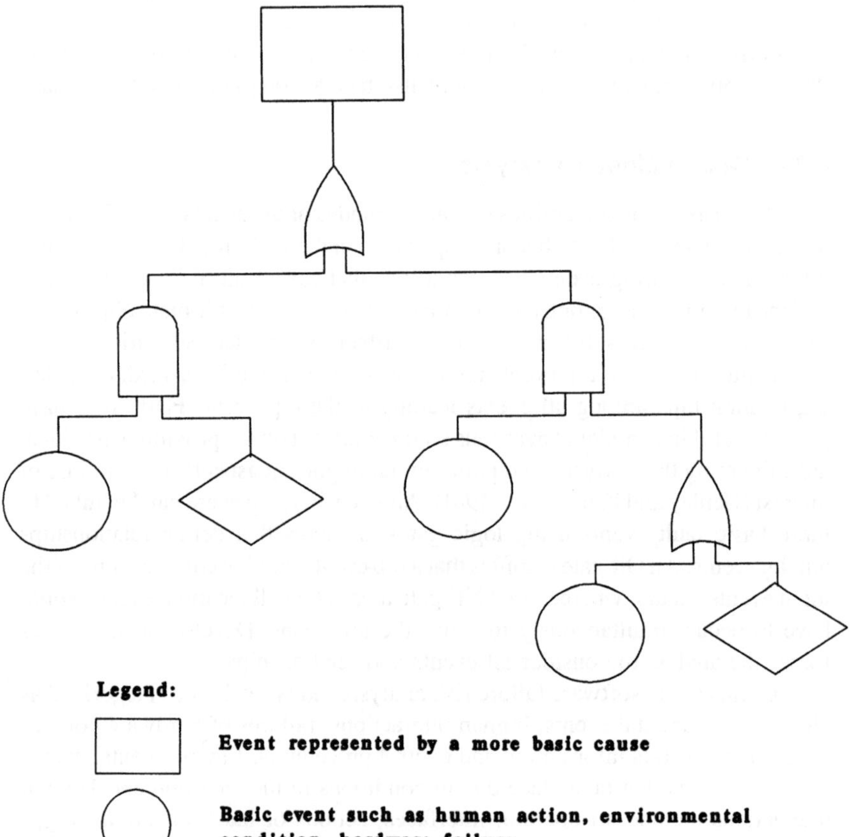

Figure 4.3. Fault tree showing conditions that may lead to hazards.

next phase. The objective at this point is solely to find out how information deficiencies can affect the course of an accident.

4.2.5. Consequence Analysis

To assess the consequence of the hazards, the conditions that affect the loss associated with each consequence are identified. Since an almost unlimited number of environmental factors can affect loss, the information is consolidated utilizing expected values for each condition. This procedure is similar to the *collective scenario* concept (Lind, 1986). A scenario is a model of the environment qualified by the likelihood of occurrence. Since a scenario has a large number of possible outcomes, they are consolidated by assigning typical or expected values.

The potential exposure is computed by weighing the loss estimated for each accident scenario by the likelihood of the accident scenario, given software failure. The probability of occurrence of each accident scenario in an event tree is determined by computing the conditional probabilities of each of the events. These, in turn, are based upon the probability assessment of events in the fault trees conditional upon software failure.

If the software for an organization will be located in different, readily distinguishable environments, it may be appropriate to consider a separate analysis for each. In addition, in some cases, it may be useful to categorize certain environmental conditions into several groups, especially when the value of a variable varies widely depending upon the value assigned to a preceding event. The degree of classification is a function of the ability to estimate losses. In either case, the decision is application dependent.

4.3. MODULE EXPOSURE ASSESSMENT

External exposure assessment procedures determine where invalid information resulting from software failure can contribute to loss. Then, structural analysis or module exposure assessment, is performed to discover how and where software faults could contribute to loss. The objective is to assign an exposure estimate to each module of a system based upon its relationship to the external exposure assessment.

The analysis begins by identifying software failure modes, located in the external exposure analysis, which contribute to erroneous information. A procedure is outlined to determine which modules may have potential faults related to each failure mode. Since the impact of erroneous information due to software failure may depend on the environment in which the software operates, a methodology for analysis of the functional use of the software is described. Finally, a model is developed for module exposure assessment.

4.3.1. Software Failure Modes

Once external exposure assessment indicates where erroneous information can contribute to loss, the software is investigated to determine how it may fail, resulting in the provision of that erroneous information. The following question is considered: What software functions can produce the erroneous information shown in the diamond symbols in the fault trees? This yields a set of software failure modes that can be assigned to each accident scenario.

These software failure modes are determined by analyzing the expected use of the software in the external environment. As is the case in any probabilistic risk assessment, a good deal of subjective judgment is used to produce these scenarios. The probabilistic risk assessment evaluates the risk from only those accident scenarios and relationships identified in the assessment. Therefore, the analysis suffers from both subcategories of completeness uncertainty, contributor and relationship uncertainty, uncertainty as to whether all the significant phenomena and all the significant relationships have been considered (Vesely and Rasmuson, 1984).

As in any probabilistic risk assessment, completeness uncertainty acts as a constraint and limitation since exposure estimates may be low if all risks and relationships are not anticipated. However, the advantages resulting from clearly defining identifiable risks have still made probabilistic risk assessment a useful tool in assessing risk in large complex systems such as nuclear power plants. MacKenzie, in his report on the limitations of probabilistic risk assessment (PRA), concludes that despite its limitations, "PRA's dual role as both a technical design tool and an instrument in setting public policy will surely continue" (MacKenzie, 1984). Levine concludes this is because these assessments have provided fundamental insight into which factors are truly significant in the safety of nuclear reactors. The thought processes and logic structures effectively force attention onto issues genuinely important to risk (Levine, 1984).

> The real question is whether the results of PRA are useful, even with their associated uncertainties. The answer is a resounding yes—because the principal engineering and safety insights gained by PRA are usually not significantly affected by uncertainty, and because in any case these insights cannot be derived in any other way. (Levine, 1984)

It is felt that, with detailed knowledge of design and engineering principles, reasonable risk assessments can be produced that reduce the risks of incompleteness (Levine, 1984). Similarly, it is argued that if one has detailed knowledge of the design, structure, and use of the software, the analysis of software exposure using this technique is a reasonable approach to the analysis of exposure due to failure in complex software systems, and is definitely preferable to current procedures that do not attempt to assess exposure at all.

4.3.2. Module Fault Potential

After assessing how the software can fail, the structure of the software system is reviewed to determine the location of potential faults related to each software failure mode. "Gray-box" analysis of the system is proposed. This is defined as analysis of the structure and use of the software system: the modules, their interactions, and how they are used. Gray-box analysis requires examination of the software specifications. Consideration of the function of the module as it relates to the potential for loss makes it possible to determine the potential (not actual) location of faults related to each failure mode.

The size and interrelationships of most software systems make it impractical to consider the analysis of all software branches and conditions (white-box analysis). On the other hand, the analysis of all software functions (black-box analysis) does not give us sufficient information about the potential location of faults. However, if the code is reviewed at the module level, it is feasible to consider module function and relate it to potential loss.

It is necessary to determine whether each module performs any functions related to each software failure mode. Software system failure is manifested by invalid system output or lack of anticipated output. Any modules involved in producing that output could be the source of failure. Thus, the procedure begins by identifying all modules involved in the production of output related to each failure mode.

How can all modules related to the particular failure mode be identified? First, critical data are determined. Then, when determining the potential location of a fault leading to failure, a process is used similar to procedures involved in debugging software. It is necessary to determine where the critical data are maintained. The specifications are used to identify all critical program modules that use or update these data. Reverse engineering is used, working backward to determine what input provides these data. Key input transactions are identified as well and used to initiate a forward review of the system to find out how and where this information is updated. Significant reports are identified and all programs involved in the production of these reports are determined.

Some modules may not be directly involved in the flow of the critical data, but their failures may nevertheless affect the critical data. Therefore, in addition to reverse engineering in order to identify modules processing specific data, each module is individually reviewed, asking the following questions:

- What is the module's function?
- Is it reasonable for the module to be connected with each identified hazard?
- Should it be associated with any other identified hazards?
- Can additional hazards be identified that might be associated with this module?

Again, this procedure is limited by completeness uncertainty. Although some of the modules involved in the processing of the critical data might be missed, if designers structure their programs to minimize module coupling and maximize module strength* (Myers, 1976), it will be more difficult to omit significant modules related to the critical data.

By mapping modules to hazards, the *module fault potential set* is defined. This is the set of all modules that could be related to a hazard.

4.3.3. Use Distribution

Modules processing data related to each software failure mode are now determined. However, invalid data processing may not always result in loss; it depends upon the way in which the module is used, itself a function of system use. Thus, it is necessary to assess and relate use to external risk assessment. A procedure will be described to partition the system's input space functionally, estimating the probability that a system will be used in various ways. The external risk assessment is mapped onto the system input space. An approach to estimating the module use distribution, the probability distribution of expected use of the modules, is presented.

4.3.3.1. System Use Distribution and External Exposure

Various uses of the same software system result in events with different consequences. Therefore, in order to analyze the impact of loss, it is necessary to consider different ways in which a system can be used. This use must be related to the external exposure assessment.

It is assumed that the system's operational use can be described. This is a reasonable assumption; a system should not be designed without an understanding of its intended use. The questions to be considered are

- What are the uses of the system?
- What is the probability that the system will be used in each way?

From this analysis, the system's input space is partitioned by use or function.

Once system use is analyzed, external exposure assessment is mapped onto this use. The external exposure assessment is analyzed by asking what function the system is performing when failure occurs, examining conditions that exist in conjunction with software failure, and reviewing the environmental characteristics upon which the fault trees are based. This demonstrates how the system will be used when loss could occur. Use is mapped onto the functional

*Module coupling is a measure of the data relationship among modules, whereas module strength is a measure of the relationships within a module.

partitions of the system use space. If there is no direct correspondence, the use space can be further partitioned. A *failure use set*, or set of all system uses related to each hazard, is defined.

Once each event due to software failure is related to the software system use space, the loss is adjusted for anticipated system use. The software exposure then reflects expected environmental conditions just as the external assessment reflected expected environmental conditions.

4.3.3.2. Module Use Distribution

Not all modules are invoked for each system use. Therefore, to estimate module exposure, it is necessary to estimate the module use distribution and relate this to the system use distribution and external exposure. To estimate the probability distribution describing how modules are expected to be used, the software system is partitioned into sets of modules invoked for each system use.

If a module is invoked for a particular use of the system, it is assigned a use probability for that function from the system use distribution. The total probability of use of each module is equal to the sum of its expected use for each function for which the module might be invoked.

4.3.4. Hazard Probability Distribution

Although the types of faults that exist in the modules are unknown, some estimates can be made of the relative proportion of errors contributing to hazards of different severity. This is necessary to determine the expected consequence for each module use—the probability of occurrence of each hazard (conditional upon software failure), weighted by the potential consequence of the hazard. It is believed that, even in the absence of a formal methodology for assessing risk, software developers pay more attention to more critical functions, reducing the probability of major losses relative to minor losses. Thus, the relative proportion of each type of error is based on the assumption that high-consequence errors will be encountered less frequently than low-consequence errors.* A hazard probability distribution can then be computed. This is the relative probability of occurrence of each of the hazards resulting from each use of a module.

Little research exists that classifies errors according to their impact. One study of failures in the Space Shuttle Ground System reported the proportion of critical, major, and minor errors to be 2%, 34%, and 64% of all errors, respectively (Misra, 1983). It is expected that this proportion will vary with the classification and application. For example, it is anticipated that the proportion

*Otherwise, a uniform distribution could be assumed for each failure mode.

of critical errors in the Space Shuttle System would be less than in a financial application due to the former's stringent safety requirements. Furthermore, the definition of critical errors would differ for each system. Future research is required to investigate factors that might improve predictions of the relative proportion of failures of different levels of severity. The applications that follow employ reasonable assumptions based upon this data.

4.3.5. Module Exposure

Module exposure may be estimated by summing the expected use of the module, weighted by the expected consequence of all hazards that may result for each module use. A hazard may result if

1. the module is involved in the processing of any invalid data produced by the system in the course of the accident scenario resulting in the hazard (i.e., if the module is in the module fault potential set defined for the hazard), and
2. the module use is related to the accident scenario resulting in the hazard (i.e., if the module use is in the failure use set defined for the hazard).

The expected consequence of all hazards for each use of the module is determined by weighing each potential consequence by the hazard probability distribution. Figure 4.4 shows a decision tree that can be constructed to illustrate the exposure assessment.

The exposure of module M can be expressed as

$$X^M(T) = \sum_i p(U_i^M) \sum_j p(H_j/U_i^M) C_j(T) \tag{4.1}$$

where

$X^M(T)$ = exposure of module M during time T
$p(U_i^M)$ = probability of use i for module M
$p(H_j/U_i^M)$ = probability that hazard j occurs when module M has use i
$C_j(T)$ = consequence of hazard j during operational time T

4.4. SOFTWARE FAILURE LIKELIHOOD

A model describing the software failure process estimates the expected number of failures resulting from faults in a module. It is suggested that prior information about the code and its development be used to estimate the parameters of this model, the mean number of faults in a module and the per fault hazard rate. As testing proceeds, new information becomes available regarding failure likelihood. A Bayesian approach updates the basic parameters of the model with this information.

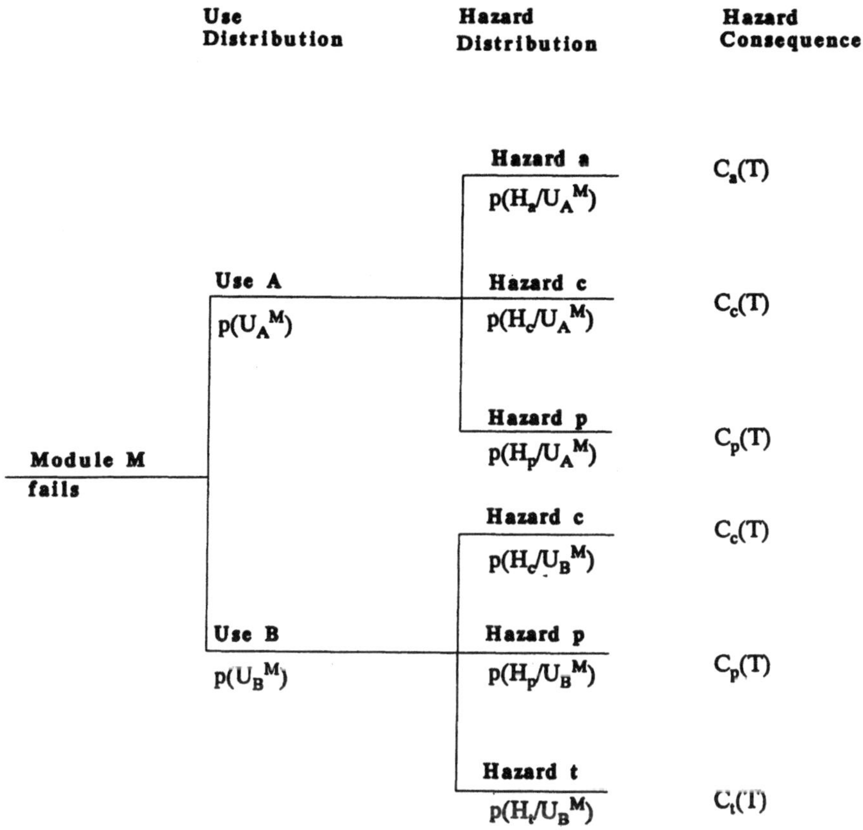

$$X^M(T) = p(U_A^M)[p(H_a/U_A^M)C_a(T) + p(H_c/U_A^M)C_c(T) + p(H_p/U_A^M)C_p(T)]$$
$$+ p(U_B^M)[p(H_c/U_B^M)C_c(T) + p(H_p/U_B^M)C_p(T) + p(H_t/U_B^M)C_t(T)]$$

Figure 4.4. Decision tree for evaluation of module exposure.

4.4.1. Software Reliability Model

Many software reliability models have been developed to describe the software failure process. (A summary of these models can be found in Musa *et al.* [1987].) These models describe software failure as a stochastic process. The models can be classified by category (finite or infinite number of failures experienced in infinite time), by type (distribution of number of failures in time), and by class or family (functional form of the failure intensity) (Musa and Okumoto, 1983).

Although almost any one of the software reliability models could be used to assess software failure risk in our analysis, we use a model in the finite-failures category, of the Poisson type, and of the exponential class. This model has been shown generally to predict satisfactorily, to be simple and easy for practitioners to understand, and to be the one most thoroughly developed and widely applied to actual projects (Musa *et al.*, 1987). In addition, its parameters have a clear physical interpretation and can be related to information that exists prior to program execution. The assumptions underlying this model are summarized in Scheme 4.1. Expressions have been derived for the expected number of software failures within a given period, remaining failures, and the likelihood of software failure (Musa *et al.*, 1987):

$$E[M(t)] = \mu[1 - \exp(-\theta t)] \tag{4.2}$$

$$E[R(t)] = \mu \exp(-\theta t) \tag{4.3}$$

$$P[T_i \leqslant t^*/N(t_e) = n] = 1 - \exp\text{-}[\mu(e^{-\theta t_e} - e^{-\theta t^*})], \qquad t^* \geqslant t_e \tag{4.4}$$

where

$E[M(t)]$ = expected number of failures by time t
$E[R(t)]$ = expected number of remaining failures at time t
μ = mean number of inherent faults
θ = per fault hazard rate
t = execution time of module
$P[T_i \leqslant t^*/N(t_e) = n]$ = the probability of software failing by time t^* conditional upon the number of failures up until the current execution time
t_e = current execution time

4.4.2. Rationale for Bayesian Estimation

Maximum likelihood estimation is typically used to estimate the parameters of software reliability models. However, it has been shown that, under certain conditions, maximum likelihood estimates may be misleading or may not even exist (Forman and Singpurwalla, 1987; Littlewood, 1975). Although several software reliability researchers have developed Bayesian approaches to software reliability analysis (Jewell, 1985; Langberg and Singpurwalla, 1985; Littlewood and Verall, 1973), Bayesian analysis has not been widely accepted. It has been felt that the Bayesian approach is "markedly inferior to maximum likelihood from a practical viewpoint" (Musa *et al.*, 1987). However, several arguments support the contention that Bayesian methods are appropriate because of the nature of the problem and because, from a practical viewpoint, they

1. The software failure process can be described by a nonhomogeneous Poisson process:
   a. There are no failures experienced at time $t = 0$.
   b. The process has independent increments. This assumption implies the Markov property that the future of the process depends only upon its present state and is independent of its past.
   c. The probability that a failure will occur during $(t, t + \Delta t)$ is $\lambda(t)\Delta t + o(\Delta t)$, where $\lambda(t)$ is the failure intensity of the process $[\lim_{t \mapsto 0} o(\Delta t)/t = 0]$.
   d. The probability that more than one failure will occur during $(t, t + \Delta t)$ is $o(\Delta t)$.
   e. The failure intensity is a function of time.
2. The total number of faults in a module at time $t = 0$ is a Poisson random variable with parameter μ.*
3. Each failure, caused by a fault, occurs independently and randomly in time, according to its hazard rate, θ, defined as the probability density (per unit time) of failure given that failure has not occurred up to the present.**
4. Each fault in a module has the same hazard rate.***
5. The fault causing a failure is corrected before testing resumes or its rediscovery is not counted again.

*This distinguishes this model from models of binomial class that assume that the number of faults at time 0 is fixed and known with certainty (Jelinski and Moranda, 1972).

**Although each fault has a constant hazard rate, the module hazard rate can be shown to be $\mu\theta \exp(-\theta t)$ (Musa *et al.*, 1987). Since the module hazard rate varies with time, the process can be described as a nonhomogeneous process.

***This model has been used previously to describe software failure in a system. The assumption of a uniform operational profile for systems is not valid. However, at a module level, it is more reasonable, especially as more cohesive modules are developed. In addition, it would be extremely difficult to attempt to determine what portions of a module have the greatest potential for producing failures and in all likelihood this would yield at best only marginally superior results.

Scheme 4.1. Assumptions of the Poisson-type Exponential-Class Software Reliability Model. (Adapted from Musa *et al.*, 1987).

make it possible to use software reliability models to estimate module failure likelihood early in the test cycle.

Traditional sampling theory techniques such as maximum likelihood estimation are based on the frequency notion of probability. Supporters of this notion assume that many observations are made under similar conditions in order to measure the relative frequency of an event. Since each software module is a unique creation of an individual or group of programmers, not enough information is available upon which to establish a long-run relative frequency of errors, or resulting failures, for this program. However, a degree of belief in the relative error-proneness of a piece of software can be subjectively estimated. The problem is more adequately described by a subjective, or Bayesian, viewpoint.

Developers of software reliability models use information about the code to predict parameters of the software models. However, once test data are obtained, these predictions are usually no longer considered. Only test data are used to estimate parameters. It has been suggested that for the initial estimates, whose accuracy can be low due to small failure samples, a weighted average of previous parameter predictions and maximum likelihood estimates of parameters be used (Musa *et al.*, 1987). Bayesian inference would provide a satisfactory means of explicitly introducing and keeping track of assumptions about the likelihood of failure in different modules based on the code and the development process. Since some designs are evolutionary rather than revolutionary, known facts about modules could be utilized in prior estimates.

Sampling theory methods have been shown to have several disadvantages in traditional hardware reliability theory. In particular, they require much more sample data than Bayesian analysis does and are especially inappropriate for reliability analysis on scarce data. For hardware that is intrinsically reliable, e.g., nuclear equipment, sufficient failure data is often unavailable for traditional sampling theory. Bayesian analysis is often used in these cases (Martz and Waller, 1982). Similarly, well-developed individual software modules would be expected to yield scarce failure data. Thus, Bayesian analysis would be more appropriate for parameter estimation. In addition, it is hoped that the failure likelihood estimate and subsequent risk assessment can be used early in the test cycle to help guide further testing and development. At this stage of the analysis, prior expectations of software failure likelihood must be relied on. Data requirements of traditional sampling theory are such that estimates would not be useful until much of the testing is complete.

4.4.3. Bayesian Methodology

An overview of the Bayesian approach and resulting posterior estimates of the parameters of the finite-failures, Poisson, exponential software reliability model are provided here. (The mathematics of the approach are described in

Appendix B.1.) These updated model parameters re-estimate the likelihood of failure and the expected number of failures conditional upon the test data.

Bayes' Theorem derives the posterior joint distribution of the parameters, the mean number of inherent faults in the module, and the per fault hazard rate from the product of the likelihood function and the joint prior distribution (Box and Tiao, 1973). Marginal distributions for each of the parameters are derived from this joint distribution. Mean estimators of these distributions are then used to estimate the expected number of failures.

4.4.3.1. Prior Estimates

First, let us look at some reasonable prior distributions; then we shall discuss estimators of the parameters of these distributions.

a. Distributions. First, some assumptions concerning prior distributions:

1. The prior distribution of the mean number of faults μ is $\Gamma(a,b)$
2. The prior distribution of the per fault hazard rate θ is $\Gamma(c,d)$
3. These prior distributions are independent.

The Γ prior distributions were chosen because they are reasonable distributions to describe the mean number of faults and the per fault hazard rate. In addition, some empirical evidence derived from the case study discussed in Chapter 5 supports the reasonableness of the assumption concerning the prior distribution of μ.

Although these prior distributions are believed to be appropriate, other distributions could also be used. Musa *et al.* (1987) have suggested using a locally uniform prior distribution, assuming complete lack of knowledge of the parameters of the model, even though parameters can be predicted prior to test from characteristics of the code.

b. Estimators. Module size is used to estimate the parameters of the distribution of the mean number of inherent faults. While "it has long been assumed that the size of a program has the most effect on the number of inherent faults" (Musa *et al.*, 1987), it is recognized that other factors characterizing both the code and the development process may also affect the number of errors. (These are discussed in Appendix A.) It is difficult, and extremely time consuming, to objectively measure many development factors such as communication, review quality, and deadline pressures. The number of faults found in similar modules, developed in the same environment by the same or similar personnel, can give a first approximation of the number of faults in modules of similar size.* It is

*Size is measured in terms of number of deliverable, executable source instructions.

assumed that use of data gathered in the same environment can capture, although imperfectly, some of the development factors affecting the number of faults. This approach is illustrated in some of the case studies that follow.

In some situations, historical failure data from the same environment may be unavailable. Some organizations do not record this information. Average values gathered from published results on many systems can be used initially (Musa *et al.*, 1987). While it is recognized that generic fault information may be imperfect, it does provide an initial basis for estimation. The information can be updated as data become available in the actual environment.

The per fault hazard rate, the probability that a fault will produce a failure per unit execution time, can be estimated initially as the product of the linear execution frequency and the fault exposure ratio (Musa *et al.*, 1987).* The linear execution frequency is the average instruction execution rate divided by the number of object instructions. It expresses the number of times a program would be executed per unit time if it had no branches or loops. The number of object instructions can be estimated by multiplying the number of source instructions by the average expansion ratio for different programming languages, which is given by Jones (1986). The fault exposure ratio is the fraction of time that a passage results in failure. It accounts for the fact that programs have many loops and branches and that machine states vary. While it may be possible in the future to somehow relate this factor to program structure, fault exposure ratios are currently determined from similar programs (Musa *et al.*, 1987).

4.4.3.2. Likelihood Function

The likelihood function describes the probability distribution of test results conditional upon prior distributions. The likelihood function for the software reliability model of Poisson type and exponential class (derived in Appendix B.1.2) is as follows:

$$p(S/\mu,\theta) = \frac{(\mu\theta)^n}{n!}\exp(-\theta\Sigma t_i)\exp\{-\mu[1 - \exp(-\theta t_e)]\} \tag{4.5}$$

where

S = test data = $\{t_1, t_2, \ldots t_n, t_e\}$
$t_1, t_2, \ldots t_n$ = times of failure
t_e = elapsed CPU time
n = number of failures
μ = mean number of faults
θ = per fault hazard rate

*It is assumed that each failure results in the correction of one fault and that no new faults are introduced during fault correction.

4.4.3.3. Posterior Distributions

The posterior distribution is proportional to the product of the likelihood function and the prior estimators. Appendix B.1.3 describes the joint posterior distribution and derives the marginal distributions for each of the parameters.

The mean posterior estimators of the two parameters, derived from the posterior marginal distribution in Appendix B.1.4, is as follows:

$$E(\mu) = \int_0^\infty \frac{\dfrac{b^a d^c \mu^{n+a} e^{-\mu(b+1)}}{n!\Gamma(a)\Gamma(c)} \sum_{j=0}^{\infty} \dfrac{\mu^j}{j!} \dfrac{(n+c-1)!}{[jt_e + \Sigma t_i + d]^{n+c}}}{\displaystyle\int_0^\infty \dfrac{b^a d^c \mu^{n+a-1} e^{-\mu(b+1)}}{n!\Gamma(a)\Gamma(c)} \sum_{j=0}^{\infty} \dfrac{\mu^j}{j!} \dfrac{(n+c-1)!}{[jt_e + \Sigma t_i + d]^{n+c}} d\mu} d\mu \qquad (4.6)$$

$$E(\theta) = \int_0^\infty \frac{\dfrac{b^a d^c \theta^{n+c} e^{-\theta(\Sigma t_i + d)}}{n!\Gamma(a)\Gamma(c)} \dfrac{(n+a-1)!}{[(1-e^{-\theta t_e}) + b]^{n+a}}}{\displaystyle\int_0^\infty \dfrac{b^a d^c \theta^{n+c-1} e^{-\theta(\Sigma t_i + d)}}{n!\Gamma(a)\Gamma(c)} \dfrac{(n+a-1)!}{[(1-e^{-\theta t_e}) + b]^{n+a}} d\theta} d\theta \qquad (4.7)$$

where

μ = mean number of faults
θ = per fault hazard rate
a, b = parameters of the prior distribution of μ, $\Gamma\,(a,b)$
c, d = parameters of the prior distribution of θ, $\Gamma\,(c,d)$
t_e = elapsed test time (CPU time)
n = number of failures during time t_e
Σt_i = sum of times of recorded failures

The mean posterior estimators of μ and $e^{-\theta t}$ are used to estimate the expected number of remaining failures at time t and the likelihood of software failure conditional upon the number of failures up until the time of the estimate.

The results are based upon the assumptions regarding the prior distributions of the mean number of faults and the per fault hazard rate. If either the form of the prior distributions or the estimates of the parameters describing these distributions are not valid, then updated estimates will be incorrect. The best information available about the code, its use, and its probability of failure is employed. The subjectivist theory of probability not only allows but demands that our best opinions, including "engineering judgment," be used in evaluations of probability. "The quantification of opinions usually introduces much controversy, which, however, is not a deficiency of the subjectivist theory but an inherent difficulty of the subject matter itself" (Apostolakis, 1978). It is believed that the prior information we use represents our best opinions about the probability of failure and should be used to begin the estimation procedure. As more failure history becomes available, it will override that information.

4.5. MODULE FAILURE RISK

Risk is measured as the product of the magnitude and the likelihood of failure. The methodology for assessing module failure risk is summarized in Fig. 4.5. The failure risk of a module is estimated as the product of the expected exposure resulting from a fault in the module and the expected number of failures resulting from faults in the module:

Risk (Consequence/Time)	=	Magnitude (Consequence/Event)	×	Likelihood (Event/Time)	(4.8)
Estimated Risk of Module m during time t	=	Expected Exposure of fault in module M	×	Expected Number of failures from faults in module M by time t	(4.9)

$$R(T) = X(T)\mu[1 - \exp(-\theta t_o(T))] \quad (4.10)$$

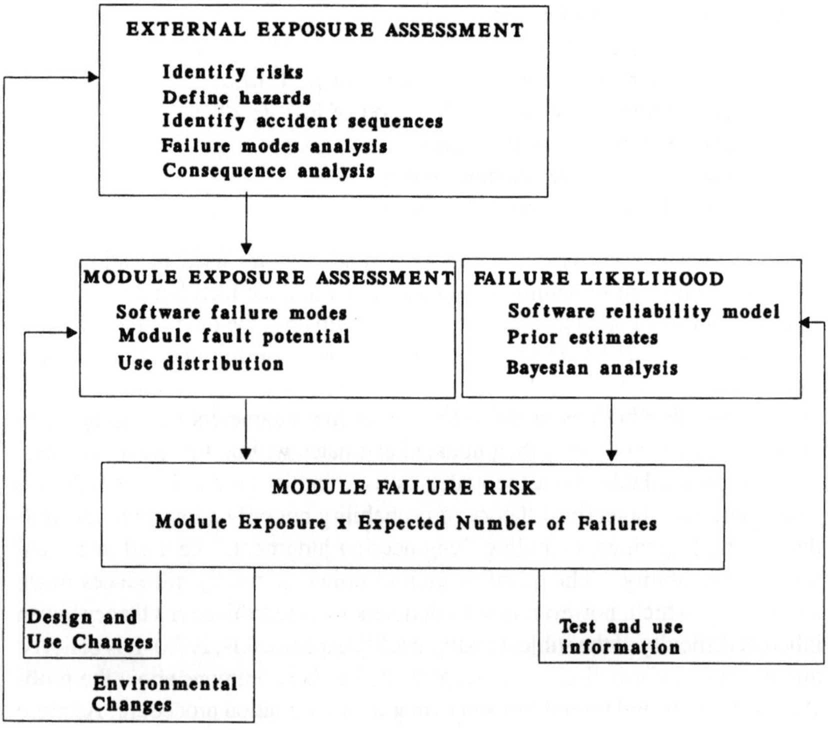

Figure 4.5. Module risk assessment: An overview.

where

$X(T)$ = expected exposure due to failure resulting from fault in the module during operational time T
μ = mean number of faults in the module
θ = per fault hazard rate
$t_o(T)$ = execution time of a module during operational time T

Note that t_o is measured in execution or CPU time while T is measured in calendar time.

The methodology for estimation of software failure risk makes it possible to combine information about the software and its use into an assessment of the criticality of a module as it is being developed and used. Software reliability estimates alone did not make it possible to include information about the exposure of a module, a very significant contributor to the criticality of a module. The following three chapters apply this methodology to several case studies.

REFERENCES

Akiyama, F., "An Example of Software System Debugging," *Proc. IFIP Congress* (August, 1971), Ljubljana, Yugoslavia, Amsterdam: North Holland, pp. 353–359.

Apostolakis, G., "Probability and Risk Assessment: The Subjectivistic Viewpoint and Some Suggestions," *Nuclear Safety* **19**(3), (May–June 1978), 305–315.

Basili, V. R. and D. H. Hutchens, "An Empirical Study of a Syntactic Complexity Family," *IEEE Trans. Software Engrg.* **SE-9**(5), (November 1983), 664–672.

Basili, V. R. and B. T. Perricone, "Software Errors and Complexity: An Empirical Investigation," *Comm. ACM* **27**(1), (January 1984), 42–52.

Basili, V. R. and T. Y. Phillips, "Evaluating and Comparing Software Metrics in the Software Engineering Laboratory," *NASA Collected Software Engineering Papers: Volume 1*, July, 1982, Section 1, pp. 18–36.

Box, G. and G. C. Tiao, *Bayesian Inference in Statistical Analysis*, Reading, MA: Addison-Wesley, 1973.

Card, D. N., V. B. Church, and W. W. Agresti, "An Empirical Study of Software Design Practice," *IEEE Trans. Software Engrg.* **SE-12**(2), (February 1986), 264–271.

Cha, S. S., N. G. Leveson, and T. J. Shimeall, "Safety Verification in MURPHY using Fault Tree Analysis," *Proc. 10th Internat. Conf. Software Engrg.*, (April 11–15, 1988), Singapore, Washington: IEEE, pp. 377–386.

Feuer, A. R. and E. B. Fowlkes, "Some Results from an Empirical Study of Computer Software," *Proc. Fourth Internat. Conf. Software Engrg.*, (September 17–19, 1979), Munich, Germany, New York: IEEE, pp. 351–355.

Fischhoff, B., S. Lichtenstein, P. Slovic, S. Derby, and R. Keeney, *Acceptable Risk*, Cambridge: Cambridge, 1981.

Forman, E.H. and N. D. Singpurwalla, "An Empirical Stopping Rule for Debugging and Testing Computer Software," *J. Amer. Statist. Assoc.* **72**(360), (December 1987), 750–757.

Gaffney, J., "Estimating the Number of Faults in Code," *IEEE Trans. Software Engrg.* **SE-10**(4), (July 1984), 459–464.

Goel, A. and K. Okumoto, "Time Dependent Error Detection Rate Model for Software Reliability and Other Performance Measures," *IEEE Trans. Reliability* **R-28**(3), (August 1979), 206–211.

Gremillon, L. L., "Determinants of Program Repair Maintenance Requirements," *Comm. ACM* **27**(8), (August 1984), 826–832.

Henley, E. and H. Kumamoto, *Reliability Engineering and Risk Assessment*, Englewood Cliffs, NJ: Prentice-Hall, 1981.

Hertz, D. and H. Thomas, *Risk Analysis and its Applications*, New York: Wiley, 1983.

Jewell, W. S., "Bayesian Extensions to a Basic Model of Software Reliability," *IEEE Trans. Software Engrg.* **SE-11**(12), (December 1985), 1465–1471.

Jones, C., *Programming Productivity*, New York: McGraw-Hill, 1986.

Juris, R., "EDP Auditing Lessens Risk Exposure," *Computer Decisions*, (July 15, 1986), pp. 36–42.

Kubat, P. and H. S. Koch, "On the Estimation of the Number of Errors and Reliability of Software Systems," Working Paper Series No. 8013, Graduate School of Management, University of Rochester, May, 1980.

Langberg, N. and N. Singpurwalla, "A Unification of Some Software Reliability Models," *SIAM J. Sci. Statist. Comput.* **6**(3), (July 1985), 781–790.

Levendal, Y., "Improving Quality with a Manufacturing Process," *IEEE Software*, March, 1991, pp. 13–25.

Leveson, N. G. and P. R. Harvey, "Analyzing Software Safety," *IEEE Trans. Software Engrg.* **SE-9**(5), (September 1983), 569–579.

Levine, S., "Probabilistic Risk Assessment: Identifying the Real Risks of Nuclear Power," *Tech. Rev.* **87**, (February–March, 1984), 40–44.

Lind, N., "Methods of Risk Analysis," Working Paper, Institute for Risk Research, University of Waterloo, Waterloo, Ontario, Canada, 1986.

Lipow, M., "Number of Faults per Line of Code," *IEEE Trans. Software Engrg.* **SE-8**(4), (July 1982), 437–439.

Lipow, M. and T. A. Thayer, "Prediction of Software Failures," *Proc. Reliability and Maintainability Symposium*, Philadelphia, New York: IEEE, 1977, pp. 489–494.

Littlewood, B., "MTBF is Meaningless in Software Reliability," *IEEE Trans. Reliability* **R-24**, (April 1975), 82.

Littlewood, B. and J. L. Verrall, "A Bayesian Reliability Growth Model for Computer Software," *IEEE 1973 Computer Software Reliability Conf.*, (1973), New York, pp. 70–77.

MacKenzie, J. J., "Finessing the Risks of Nuclear Power," *Tech. Rev.* **87**, (February–March 1984), 34–39.

McCormick, N. J., *Reliability and Risk Analysis*, New York: Academic Press, 1981.

Martz, H. F. and R. A. Waller, *Bayesian Reliability Analysis*, Wiley, 1982.

Misra, P. N., "Software Reliability Analysis," *IBM Systems J.* **22**(3), (1983), 262–270.

Musa, J. D., "Theory of Software Reliability and its Application," *IEEE Trans. Software Engrg.* **SE-1**(3), (September 1975), 312–327.

Musa, J. D., A. Iannino, and K. Okumoto, *Software Reliability: Measurement, Prediction, Application*, New York: McGraw-Hill, 1987.

Musa, J. D. and K. Okumoto, "Software Reliability Models: Concepts, Classification, Comparisons, and Practice," in *Electronic Systems Effectiveness and Life Cycle Costing* (J. K. Skwrizynski, ed.), Heidelberg: Springer-Verlag, 1983, pp. 395–424.

Myers, G. J., *Software Reliability*, New York: Wiley, 1976.

——*The Art of Software Testing*, New York: Wiley, 1979.

Nuclear Energy Agency, *Nuclear Safety Research in the OECD Area: The Response to the Three Mile Island Accident*, Organization for Economic Co-operation and Development, September, 1980.

Pate-Cornell, M. E., "Fault Trees vs. Event Trees in Reliability Analysis," *Risk Anal.* **4**(3), (1984), 177–186.

Rasmussen, J., "Human Reliability in Risk Analysis," in *High Risk Safety Technology* (A. Green, ed.), New York: Wiley, 1982, pp. 143–170.

Roberts, L., *Nuclear Power and Public Responsibility*, Cambridge: Cambridge, 1984.

Schneidewind, N. F. and H. Hoffman, "An Experiment in Software Error Data Collection and Analysis," *IEEE Trans. Software Engrg.* **SE-5**(3), (May 1979), 276–286.

Selby, R. and A. Porter, "Learning from Examples: Generation and Evaluation of Decision Trees for Software Resource Analysis," *IEEE Trans. Software Engrg.* **SE-14**(12), (December 1988), 1743–1756.

Selby, R., V. Basili, and F. Baker, "Cleanroom Software Development: An Empirical Evaluation," *IEEE Trans. Software Engrg.* **SE-13**(9), (September 1987), 1027–1037.

Shen, V. Y., T. Yu, S. Thiebaut, and L. Paulsen, "Identifying Error-Prone Software—An Empirical Study," *IEEE Trans. Software Engrg.* **SE-11**(4), (April 1985), 317–323.

Sheridan, T. B., "Human Errors in Nuclear Power Plants," *Tech. Rev.* **82**, (February 1980), 23–33.

Shrader-Frechette, K., *Risk Analysis and Scientific Method*, Dordrecht: D. Reidel, 1985.

Takahashi, M. and Y. Kamayachi, "An Empirical Study of a Model for Program Error Prediction," *IEEE Trans. Software Engrg.* **SE-15**(1), (January 1989), 82–86.

Tversky, A. and D. Kahneman, "Judgement under Uncertainty: Heuristics and Biases," *Science* **185**, (1974), 1124–1131.

U.S. Nuclear Regulatory Commission, *Reactor Safety Study: An Assessment of Accident Risks in U.S. Commercial Nuclear Power Plants*, Main Report, Appendix 1, WASH-1400, October, 1975.

Vesely, W. E. and D. M. Rasmuson, "Uncertainties in Nuclear Probabilistic Risk Analyses," *Risk Anal.* **4**(4), (1984), 313–322.

Youngs, E., "Human Errors in Programming," in *Tutorial: Human Factors in Software Development* (W. Curtis, ed.), New York: IEEE, 1981, pp. 383–392.

Chapter 5

Applying the Methodology to a Commercial Loan System

This chapter presents the step-by-step application of the software failure risk assessment methodology to a commercial loan system installed at a savings and loan institution, providing a first opportunity to test that methodology.

5.1. INTRODUCTION

A commercial loan system was installed in 1987 by one of the 25 largest savings and loan associations in the United States. Commercial loans accounted for slightly more than 10% of all loans offered by the association at that time, the commercial loan business at this institution having grown significantly just prior to 1987. The number of loan production offices had grown from three offices in 1983, when deregulation allowed savings and loan associations to offer loans of shorter maturity to twenty offices by early 1987.

By 1987, a system was needed to provide more efficient and effective delivery of commercial customer services as well as more comprehensive management reporting and control. The system had to be consistent with the new loan regulations, such as Financial Accounting Standards No. 91, which required a significant change in the method of accounting and reporting for both loan origination fee income and the related origination costs.

The commercial loan system (CLS) was acquired to meet these needs. It creates and maintains all information describing commercial loans. The system's online data entry functions include the establishment of new accounts or obligors, lines, commitments, loans, takedowns, renewals, participations, syndications, repayment schedules, indirect liabilities, and interest and fee schedules. Changes can be made to existing file information, collateral records may be created, and daily transactions are recorded. Online inquiries access six master files: obligor, obligation, collateral, invoice, security, and control. Daily batch processing updates master files, creates billing information, posts to general ledger, and produces various financial and statistical reports.

All loan information originates with the responsible loan officer. Note tellers encode the appropriate forms and manually maintain Loan-In-Process balances. Completed loan information forms are sent to the Loan Control Center. There, after some additional coding, the data are entered into the system. Audit reports are verified against source documents in the Loan Control Center. Inquiry screens are available to both loan control personnel and loan officers.

5.2. EXTERNAL EXPOSURE

To estimate the risk associated with use of the commercial loan system, the environment at the savings and loan was scrutinized to determine actions that could contribute to loss and to assess the significance of this loss. First, environmental hazards or actions by the lender that could result in financial loss were defined. Second, accident sequences and failure modes that could result in these hazards were identified from study of system use. Finally, the magnitude of potential losses was estimated by expected value analysis.

5.2.1. Hazard Identification

To define the hazards surrounding the use of the commercial loan system at the savings and loan, the operational environment was thoroughly studied from the perspective of future users: clerical workers and loan officers who would directly access the system and loan managers who would use system reports for decision making. Major hazards that could result from improper use of this system were identified through focused discussions with users.

The planned use of the system was investigated to determine financial hazards that could occur. For example, the savings and loan planned to use the software to insure that loan commitments were not exceeded. Since commitments are made at various levels of an organization, the software had to properly maintain records linking organizational levels. One hazard identified therefore was *extending loans beyond the level of commitments*.

Table 5.1. Hazards and Consequences

Hazard	Consequence ($/month)
1. Not producing bills	267,000
2. Incorrect interest accruals	29,000
3. Invalid fees	3,000
4. Incorrect tracking of billing payments and disbursements	5,300
5. Invalid access to financial information	700
6. Overadvancing committed dollars	400
7. Insufficient collateral	850
8. Misposting of transactions to the general ledger	1,000
9. Customer service problems	3,000
10. Not managing collateral documentation	600
11. Additional clerical work	800
12. Invalid government reports	1,000

It was also critical to determine how use might change. The savings and loan expected to begin direct posting to its general ledger at some time in the future. Hence, another hazard was *incorrect posting to the general ledger*. Increased use by loan officers as they became more familiar with the system could increase the potential for *invalid access to financial information*. As loan officers became more familiar with the system they might begin to establish more complex loan structures using such features as tiered interest rates and alternate pricing. This could increase the hazard of *incorrect interest accruals* since the loan officers would not be as familiar with the procedure to set up these loans, and these more complex structures might involve previously unused code.

In determining hazards, one considers system outputs. What actions or decisions would be made using these outputs? The commercial loan system produces bills which are then mailed to customers. The hazard identified is *not sending bills*. The savings and loan is also alerted to take action regarding collateral, such as clipping coupons and renewing insurance through collateral tickler reports. If collateral documentation is not maintained properly, the savings and loan may miss important filings—which introduces another financial hazard, *not properly managing collateral documentation*.

A preliminary list of hazards was developed and reviewed with both the savings and loan's users and software experts who agreed that the list shown in Table 5.1 was sufficiently exhaustive.*

The identification of hazards was bounded by consideration of reasonable

*If all hazards are not identified, risk will be underestimated—an example of the completeness uncertainty in probabilistic risk assessment.

risks. It is not reasonable, for example, to consider complete bankruptcy of the savings and loan resulting just from failure of the commercial loan system. The hazards included in the analysis are those that were considered feasible; i.e., their probability was significant enough to consider in the analysis.

5.2.2. Accident Sequences

How could each of these hazards occur? Accident sequences were identified by analyzing system use in the external environment. Event trees were used to describe this use, indicating events that could precipitate hazards as well as events that could alter the course of an accident.

Examples of some of the event trees for two of the hazards identified for the commercial loan system are shown in Figs. 5.1 and 5.2. Figure 5.1 shows one of the event trees that could lead to *failure to produce customer bills*. One event that can precipitate not billing is the failure by the loan officer to enter a billing schedule. When this occurs, loan control is supposed to notify the loan officer to obtain the billing schedule. In the event that loan control fails to do so, bills may not be mailed. However, the customer may alter the effect of these scenarios by notifying the savings and loan that the loan is not being billed.

One event that can precipitate invalid interest accruals is a loan officer's failure to enter correct interest accrual information (Fig. 5.2). The effect of not entering an accrual schedule or of entering invalid information can be mitigated if loan control notifies the loan officer of an error. However, loan control may either not enter the correct prime rate information or input invalid accrual information. In either case, loan output control may recognize errors before bills are mailed. Finally, the obligor may also recognize an error and notify the savings and loan.

In developing the event trees, the focus was on the external use of the system. Loan information sources (loan officers) were identified, and procedures that could be used by the note tellers as they encoded forms and manually maintained Loan-In-Process balances were analyzed. Manual coding procedures that could be used in the Loan Control Center were studied, as were procedures that could be used to enter the data and review the audit reports. Consideration was given to inquiry screen use by both loan control personnel and loan officers.

5.2.3. Failure Modes

The analysis proceeded with an identification of the failure modes of events involved in the accident scenarios. Consideration was given to the types of events, the conditions that could result in these events, and the relationships among them. These included relationships among environmental events, human

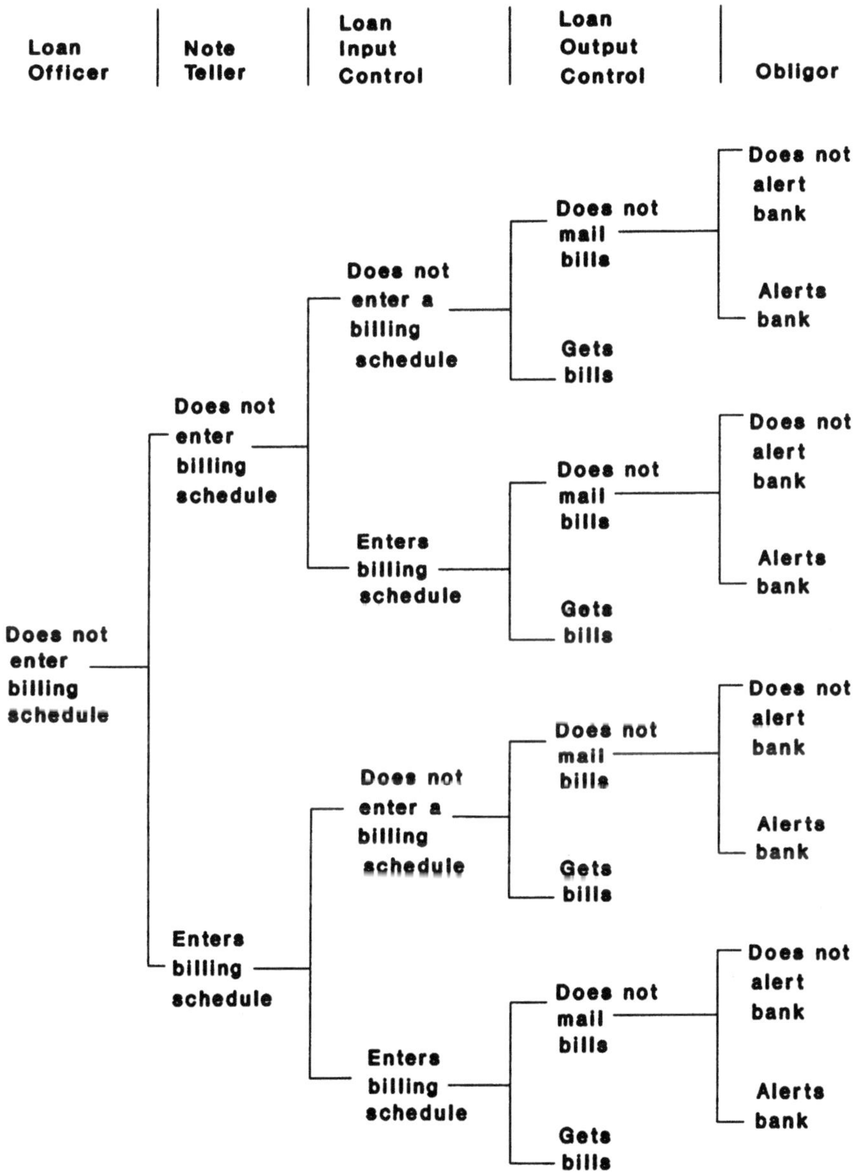

Figure 5.1. Event tree for the hazard of *not producing bills*.

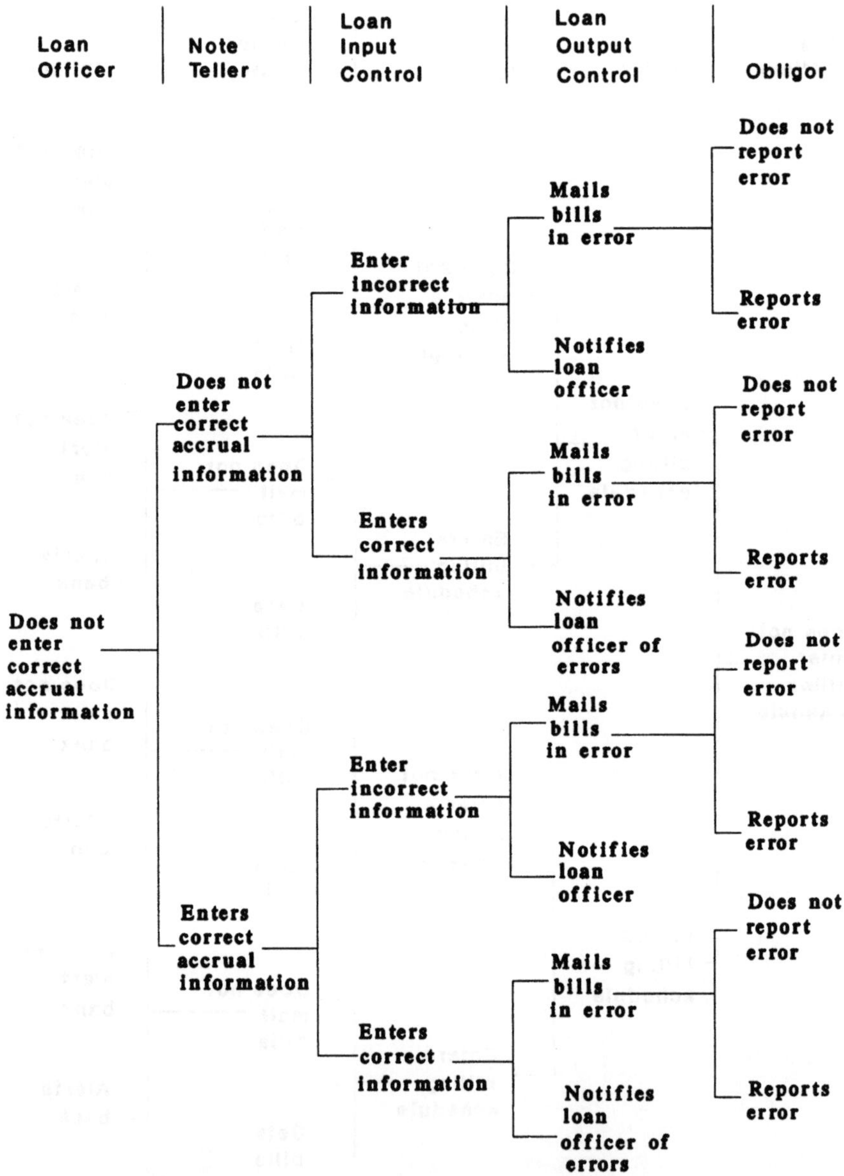

Figure 5.2. Event tree for the hazard of *invalid interest accruals*.

interactions, failures of hardware components, and erroneous information and control procedures that could contribute to the occurrence of the events in the accident scenarios. The ultimate objective was to determine where information deficiencies resulting from software failure could affect the accident scenario. Fault trees were found to be useful to depict the relationships.

Figure 5.3 shows one of the fault trees that can contribute to the events in

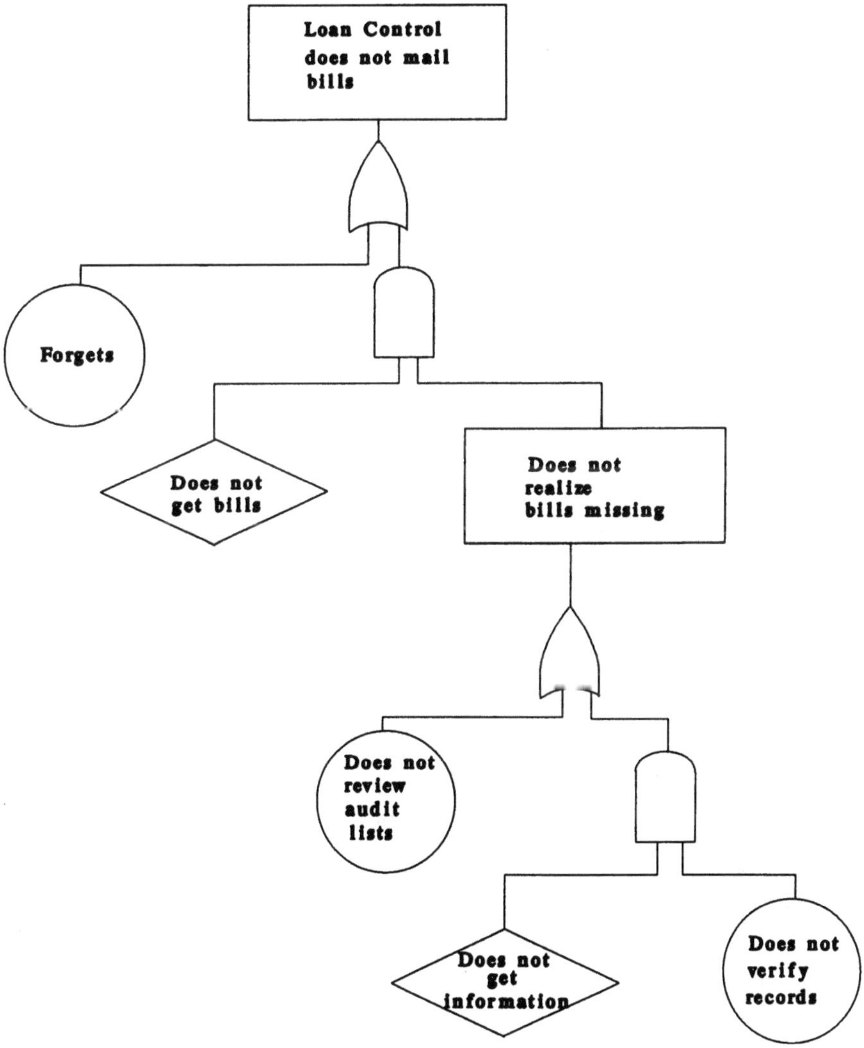

Figure 5.3. Fault tree for the event "loan control does not mail bills."

the accident sequence leading to *not mailing bills*. Loan Control may not mail bills because employees may simply forget to put the bills in the mail, or they may not realize that bills have not been produced. The latter may occur if they do not review the audit lists or if they do not get the correct audit information and do not verify billing information against other records. Several of these events are human errors, such as forgetting to mail bills or review audit lists. Invalid information from the software can arise from two events that can contribute to this hazard. First, bills may not be produced by the system. Second, information regarding missing bills may not be included in the audit information. These events will be further investigated to determine module exposure.

Figure 5.4 shows some of the fault trees involved in the hazard *invalid interest accruals*. Figure 5.4a shows that loan output control can mail bills in error if it does not review the audit information or if it does not get the correct information. The former event is a human error, whereas the latter event represents invalid information that can be produced if the system fails to operate correctly. Figure 5.4b reflects how incorrect information processing can occur when either the accrual schedule or prime rate information is processed. Human error can contribute to invalid interest accruals if incorrect accrual information is entered or the prime rate information is not updated.

5.2.4. Consequence Assessment

Since the actual loss can take on an unlimited number of values based on many environmental factors, information on circumstances affecting the resulting loss was consolidated utilizing expected values for each state. The potential consequence, or external exposure, of each hazard was assessed by weighing the loss estimated for each accident scenario by the likelihood of the accident scenario conditional upon software failure. The probability of occurrence of each accident scenario in an event tree was determined by computing the conditional probabilities of each of the top events, each dependent upon factors in the fault tree.

For example, the total expected value of a loan was estimated to be $170,000, with the expected number of loans equal to 1,700. Assuming an average interest rate of 10% and a 1% administrative fee, the total expected monthly revenue was estimated to be approximately $26.7 million, of which $2.4 million is interest.

If bills were not produced, a 10% chance was estimated to exist that loan control would not realize that bills were missing. The customer would not alert the savings and loan that bills were missing or interest was accrued incorrectly 10% of the time. The expected consequence of not producing bills was estimated to be $267,000, though this would, in fact, remain the borrowers' legal obligation and would be recovered eventually.

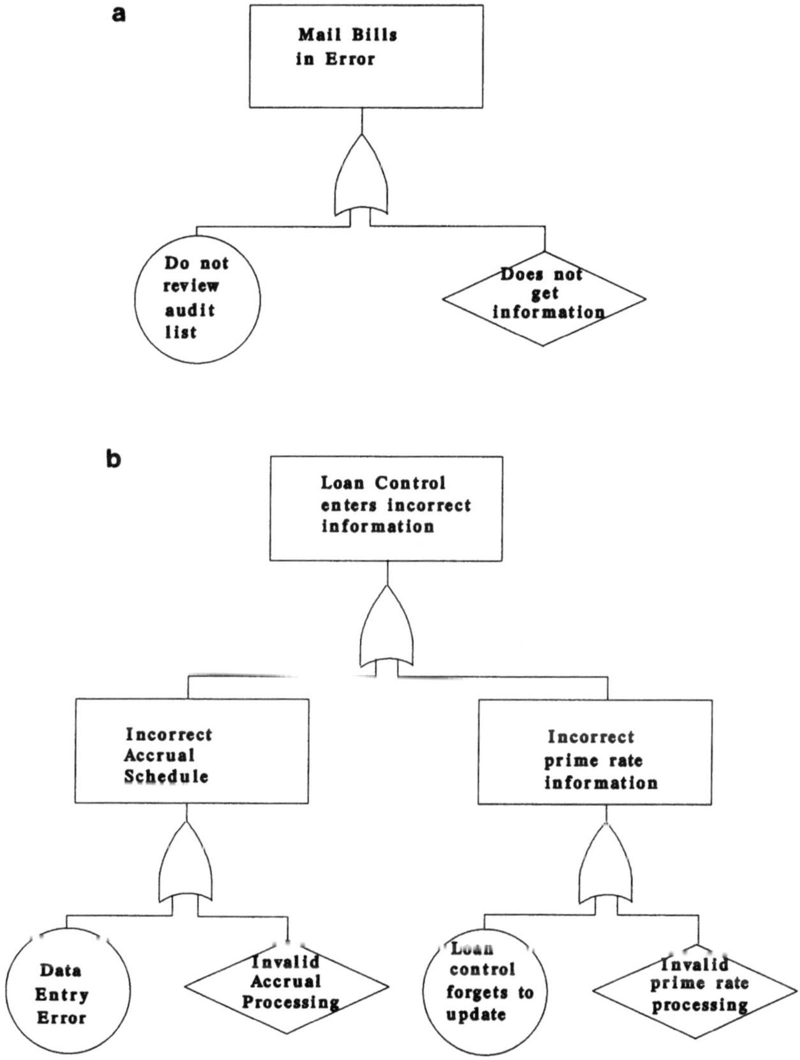

Figure 5.4. Fault trees for events leading to the hazard of *invalid interest accruals*: (a) Loan Output Control mails bills in error. (b) Loan Input Control enters incorrect information.

The potential consequence of invalid interest accruals was estimated to be \$240,000. It was estimated that interest accrual schedules may not initially be set up properly by the loan officer for 10% of all loans. In addition, even if the schedule was entered properly by the loan officer, loan control might not adjust correctly for changes in prime rates. An additional expected loss was possible due to undercharges in interest as well as potential customer service problems due to invalid interest charges, resulting in a total monthly expected consequence of $29,000. (A complete enumeration of the assumptions made when assessing the expected consequence of each of the hazards in the commercial loan system is reflected in Appendix C.1.) A list of the external exposure assessments for each of the hazards is shown in Table 5.1.

The above estimates were based only upon the use of the system at this savings and loan. If the exposure were estimated for several installations, each using different procedures to enter and record information on the commercial loan system, separate analyses or grouping of certain conditions, such as loan size, would be appropriate.

5.3. MODULE EXPOSURE ASSESSMENT

Module exposure is an estimate of the potential loss due to failures that could result from faults in a module. To estimate the exposure of modules in the commercial loan system, each module's function and expected use had to be related to the system's external exposure. Software failure modes that could contribute to the erroneous information and control procedures leading to the hazards were identified. Modules that could have faults leading to these failure modes were identified by analyzing each module's function in the structure of the CLS. Since the consequence of invalid data processing is dependent upon how the module is being used, itself a function of the system use, module use was related to system use and resulting exposure.

5.3.1. Software Description

The CLS software, written in cobol, consisted of 268 program modules. These included 125 online modules operating under CICS, of which 55 were inquiry screens and the remainder were data-entry modules. Sixty-seven batch modules performed file edit and maintenance functions, financial posting, securities repricing, interfacing with the general ledger, producing bills, selecting reports, and performing various statistical, cash flow, and executive analyses. The remaining modules were report modules. The modules ranged in size from 14 to more than 11,000 executable lines of code.

5.3.2. Software Failure Modes

To determine whether a module may have potential faults related to each of the external hazards, the software failure modes that contribute to erroneous information in the external exposure analysis were identified. Fault trees were reviewed, considering all invalid information contributing to the events in the accident scenarios.* These were identified by diamond-shaped symbols in the fault trees.

For example, failure of the software to produce bills may be due to

- failure to produce an audit list of missing bill schedules
- failure to update obligation files with billing information
- failure to print bills
- invalid purging of information
- invalid maintenance of bill-mailing information
- invalid invoice records
- invalid information on control file

Invalid interest accruals may be due to

- failure to produce an audit list of missing accrual schedule
- failure to update obligation file correctly with interest accrual information
- incorrect printing of bills
- invalid processing of prime-rate information

5.3.3. Module Fault Analysis

Software system failure results in invalid system output or lack of anticipated output. Faults in a module could cause a particular software failure if the module is involved in the production of such output.

To relate modules to hazards, the invalid output or lack of anticipated output by which each software failure mode could be manifested was first identified. Then by reverse-engineering the specifications, critical data elements related to this output were revealed, making possible a determination of which modules could be involved in the production of this output. For example, all modules involved in the production of bills were found by considering all transformations of data resulting in bills, working logically backward from the output. Significant reports, such as key audit reports, that could be used to identify missing billing information were also determined, and reverse engineering was again used to ascertain all programs involved in the production of these reports. Key input transactions, such as the billing date transaction, were used to trigger a forward study of the system to determine modules that process information from these transactions.

Failures in modules not directly involved in the flow of critical data may affect the critical data. For example, failure in modules processing control data, such as calendar or divisional reporting information, might affect a loan's billing information. These modules were identified as well.

Thus, for each module, a determination was made as to whether it would

*It is again necessary to recognize the constraints of completeness uncertainty.

Table 5.2. Module Fault Potential Statistics

Hazards	Modules with fault potential
1. Not producing bills	63
2. Incorrect interest accruals	57
3. Invalid fees	47
4. Incorrect tracking of billing payments and disbursements	48
5. Invalid access to financial information	22
6. Overadvancing committed dollars	48
7. Insufficient collateral	66
8. Misposting of transactions to the general ledger	59
9. Customer service problems	112
10. Not managing collateral documentation	49
11. Additional clerical work	143
12. Invalid government reports	75

perform any function related to each of the identified software failure modes. For example, the function of each module was analyzed to determine if it could invalidly maintain bill mailing information or contribute to invalid information on the control file. Again, the analysis was limited by the examiner's ability to completely assess all modules involved in the processing of the data.*

Table 5.2 shows the number of program modules related to each of the identified hazards. Table 5.3 reflects the module fault potential set of all modules that could be related to one of the hazards—not producing bills. The module fault potential set for each of the other identified hazards is available from the author (Sherer, 1988).

5.3.4. Failure Use Analysis

The module's function at any time and its associated exposure level could vary with the way the system uses it; that use, in turn, is related to the way the system itself is being used. For example, the financial posting module may be used to record loan payments or collateral deposits. The module's expected use must be related to the external exposure.

First, the system's input space was partitioned by use. The external risk assessment was then mapped on the system input space so that the hazards that could occur for each system use were determined. Module use distribution was estimated from knowledge of the system's structure and use.

*It is again possible that some of the modules involved in the processing of the critical data may not have been included, i.e., completeness uncertainty. (One can only attempt to be as thorough as possible.)

Table 5.3. Module Fault Potential Set for the Hazard "Not Producing Bills"

Audit list modules
3500 Report extract
3600 Report generator
5200 Print program exceptions

Obligation/obligor file update
2300 Financial update
1155 Sort daily transactions
1150 Off line edit and update
1140 Pre-edit
1122 Create validations
1070 General validation
1065 Sort input transactions
1040 Strip transactions
1005 Sort online transactions
1000 Proof file strip
0021 Payments transactions
0022 Set up billing schedules
0023 New obligor information
0031 Short obligation create
0010 Interface
5200 Program exception report
0998 Data entry—mass change
0092 File error message table
0091 File name table
0071 Obligation segment search
0056 Validation code table
0051 Batch error tables
0050 Processing error tables
0025 Single field transaction
0014 Format parameter list
0011 Storage for IO
0001 Restore master file

Printing bills
2450 Billing print
2445 Sort billing extract file
2400 Billing select
0772 Print selected bills

Information purging
5241 Zero balance report
5354 Chargeoff loan report
3600 Report generator
3595 Sort report work file
3500 Report extract
3495 Sort daily transactions
0024 Delete module

Invoice processing
4410 Delete invoice record
4415 Sort invoice maintenance
4420 Flag delete invoices
2480 Sort invoice file

Control file maintenance
1120 Update
1115 Sort requests
1050 Validate counters
0848 Data base information
0845 Data base information
0842 Calendar information
0825 Data base information
0824 Transaction control
0823 Transaction control
0815 Report control
0812 Program control
0806 Bank control
0803 Control
0802 Control
0800 Date
0054 Error tables

Table 5.4. System Use Distribution

Function	Proportion of total system use
Data entry	
Payments	0.7238
Advances, takedowns	0.0154
New accounts	0.0077
Collateral setup	0.0077
Other	0.0154
Total data entry	0.7700
Data inquiry	
Transaction history	0.2070
Obligor name search	0.0069
Invoice reference	0.0069
Payoff	0.0069
Other	0.0023
Total data inquiry	0.2300

5.3.4.1. System Use Distribution

The use distribution of the CLS was based upon user estimates of the number and types of daily transactions. These transactions could be categorized into ten major classifications, including five data-entry transactions that accounted for 77% of all transactions, as shown in Table 5.4.

External exposure assessment was then reviewed from the perspective of system use. Figure 5.5 reflects the mapping of hazards to functional uses of this system. For example, a software failure when inquiring about payments could allow invalid access to financial information, cause problems with customer service, or generate additional clerical work.

The failure use set or set of all system uses related to each hazard is now defined. The failure use set for the hazard of not producing bills includes advances, takedowns, new accounts and other data entries.

5.3.4.2. Module Use Distribution

The probability distribution describing expected module use was derived from the system use distribution. The financial posting module, for example, would be used for all data entry transactions, but would not be invoked when making system inquiries. The probability that this module would be used for payment is 0.72, derived from the fact that the system is used to process payments 72 percent of the time (Table 5.4). Other examples are shown in Table

Data Entry: 100 transactions/day

PAYMENTS Invalid Access Misposting of General Ledger Invalid Tracking of Payments Customer Service Clerical Work Government Reports	**ADVANCES, TAKEDOWNS** No billing schedule Invalid interest Invalid fees Invalid Tracking Invalid Access Overcommitted $ Insufficient Collateral Customer Service Collateral Documentation Clerical Work Government Reports
COLLATERAL Invalid Access Insufficient Collateral Customer Service Collateral Documentation Clerical Work Government Reports	**NEW ACCOUNTS** No bills Invalid interest Invalid fees Invalid access Overadvance $ Customer Service Collateral Documentation Clerical Work Government Reports
OTHER All hazards	

Data Inquiry: 30 transactions/day

TRANSACTION HISTORY Invalid Access Customer Service Clerical Work	**OBLIGOR NAME SEARCH** Invalid Access Customer Service Clerical Work
PAYOFF Invalid Access Customer Service Clerical Work	**INVOICE REFERENCE** Invalid Access Customer Service Clerical Work
OTHER Invalid Access Customer Service Clerical Work	

Figure 5.5. Mapping hazards to functional use.

5.5. Module 10 (the online interface) and module 1000 (proof file strip) are always used. The probability use distributions of these modules are the same as the system use distribution. Module 18 (obligor number assignment) is used only when setting up a new account, hence the probability 0.0077. Module 111 is used only when inquiring about payoffs, explaining its total use probability of 0.0069.

Table 5.5. Probability of Module Use by Function

		Function									
Module	Total use	Payments	Advances	New accounts	Collateral	Other data entry	Transaction history	Obligor name search	Invoice reference	Payoff	Other inquires
10	1	0.7238	0.0154	0.0077	0.0077	0.0154	0.207	0.0069	0.0069	0.0069	0.0023
18	0.0077			0.0077							
111	0.0069									0.0069	
1000	1	0.7238	0.0154	0.0077	0.0077	0.0154	0.207	0.0069	0.0069	0.0069	0.0023
2300	0.77	0.7238	0.0154	0.0077	0.0077	0.0154					

Table 5.6. Module Exposure

Module	Description	Exposure ($/month)
10	Online interface	1800
18	Obligor number assignment	8
111	Inquiry—Payoff	21
1000	Strip online file	1800
2300	Financial posting	1879

5.3.4.3. Hazard Probability Distribution

For the CLS, the assumption was made that if a module fails, minor hazards with relatively small consequence (hazards 5, 6, 7, 10, and 11 in Table 5.1) are six times more likely to occur than major hazards with large consequences (hazards 1 and 2). Hazards with average consequence of $1000–$10,000 per month were assumed to be three times more likely to occur than major hazards, and half as likely to occur as minor hazards. Although the relative proportion of each type of error was chosen somewhat arbitrarily, it reflects the reality that developers generally pay more attention to the more critical functions.*

5.3.5. Module Exposure

Module exposure is obtained by summing over the probabilities of module use and hazard occurrence for a given use, weighted by the financial consequence of the hazard.

Examples of the exposure assessments for five modules in the system are shown in Table 5.6. For example, faults in inquiry module 111 typically affect customer service. The expected consequence of customer dissatisfaction was estimated to be $3,000.† Since this module is used with probability $p =$ 0.0069, and this use is related to this scenario, the exposure assessment is approximately $21/month.

The decision tree shown in Fig. 5.6 describes a more complex exposure assessment. Here is reflected the assessment for module 2300 (the financial

*The ratio of major, average, and minor hazards, 10%:30%:60%, compares favorably with the data reported by Misra (1983). Misra found a 2%:34%:64% ratio of critical, major, and minor errors in a Space Shuttle system. Since major hazards have only financial consequences in the CLS (not physical loss or injury to people as in the Space Shuttle system), the proportion of these hazards is assumed to be smaller.

†The consequence of customer dissatisfaction was estimated at approximately 0.01% of the anticipated average monthly billings. This is an estimate of potential lost business due to dissatisfaction with handling of current loan account.

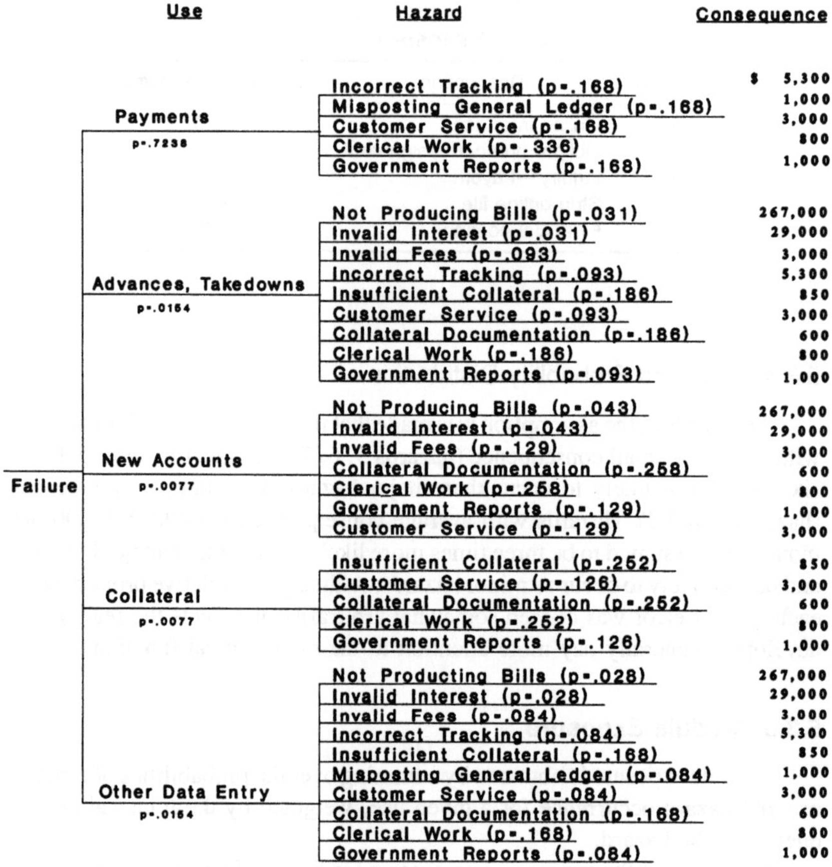

Figure 5.6. Exposure assessment for module 2300.

posting module), which performs many financial computations for the loans. Evaluation of the decision tree yields the exposure when this particular module is used.

Exposure assessment assumes that the module will fail; the likelihood of this failure will be determined later in the analysis. The module use distribution, or probability distribution describing how the module is expected to be used, is then shown. This module is used for payments, advances and takedowns, new accounts, collateral, and other data entries. The probability of each use is shown on the decision tree. Conditional upon a given use, all hazards that may occur are delineated. A hazard could occur if (1) the module performs a function that may lead to the hazard (module fault analysis) or (2) the use of the module can lead to the hazard (failure use analysis). The probability distribution of each of the hazards (hazard probability distribution), conditional upon a given module use, is based upon the assumptions concerning the relative probability of the various types of hazards. Thus, a hazard such as *not producing bills* (a major hazard with an expected external consequence of $267,000/month) is only 1/6 as likely as a minor hazard, such as *extra clerical work*, with an expected external consequence of $800, and only 1/3 as likely as *invalid fees* (expected consequence of $3000). The consequence of each hazard is derived from the external exposure analysis presented in Table 5.1.

5.4. FAILURE LIKELIHOOD

The Musa basic execution time model of Poisson type and exponential class was used to estimate failure likelihood. It was assumed that the model parameters—the mean number of faults in a module μ and the module per fault hazard rate θ (the probability that a fault would cause a failure)—could be described by independent Γ probability distributions with parameters derived from the failure history of similar modules. The Γ prior distributions for μ and θ were chosen because they represent reasonable distributions that describe the mean number of faults and the per fault hazard rate. Empirical evidence points to the reasonableness of this assumption concerning the prior distribution of μ. Bayesian analysis was used to update estimates of these parameters as the CLS was used and failures were recorded and faults corrected.

5.4.1. Estimating Parameters Prior to Test

The data source for parameter prediction was problem report logs for programs maintained by the CLS developer. The number of faults corrected in 693 program modules that had been in use for at least two years was recorded. It was assumed that the location of a fix was the source of a failure. Modules were grouped by size since that was shown to be a predictor of the number of faults in code (see Appendix A).

The Γ distribution for the mean number of faults is implied by a negative binomial distribution for the number of faults. (See Appendix B.2 for proof.) Negative binomial probability distributions were fitted to the data in each of three size categories: small modules of less than 1000 executable lines of code, medium-size modules of 1000 to 5000 executable lines, and large modules exceeding 5000 executable lines. Chi-square tests of fit indicated very strong evidence that these distributions correctly described the number of faults found. Table 5.7 summarizes the results of Chi-square tests for the three size categories of modules. In all cases, results supported the hypothesis that the number of

Table 5.7. Tests for Negative Binomial Distribution

Module size[a]	Number of modules	Chi-square	Degrees of freedom	Significance level
$N < 1000$	489	4.42	4	0.35
$1000 < N < 5000$	187	5.59	8	0.69
$N > 5000$	17	0.51	1	0.47

[a]Executable lines of code.

faults has a negative binomial distribution. Figure 5.7 shows the negative binomial distribution fit to the empirical data for medium-size modules.

The parameters of the Γ distribution for the mean number of faults (a,b) were computed directly from parameters of the negative binomial distributions of the number of faults (r,p) using the relationships derived in Appendix B.2, i.e., $a = r$ and $b/(b + 1) = p$ (see Table 5.8).

Estimated execution times of failure for faults found in these previously tested programs were used to estimate their per fault hazard rates using the Musa software reliability model. Γ distributions were fitted to the per fault hazard rates of the online and batch programs (see Table 5.9). Hence, using information on program size and operation along with the failure data obtained from problem report logs, it was possible to estimate the parameters of prior distributions.

These parameters were then used to predict the mean number of faults and the per fault hazard rate of modules in the CLS based upon a module's size and operational mode.

5.4.2. Updating Parameters with Test Data

Problem reports generated at the savings and loan were then used to indicate failures and location of fixes during the execution of the system. Operational logs were analyzed to evaluate the savings and loan's execution time of a module at the time of failure. A total of 34 corrections were made to 21 modules during the execution of the system, with six being the maximum number of corrections to any one module. In most cases, only one or two corrections were made to any one module. It is interesting to note that, because of the small number of failures due to faults in each module, maximum likelihood estimation would not otherwise have been feasible. Bayesian methodology, developed in Chapter 4, was used to update the parameters, thereby providing an opportunity to use information about the code and its operational performance to estimate the probability of failure.

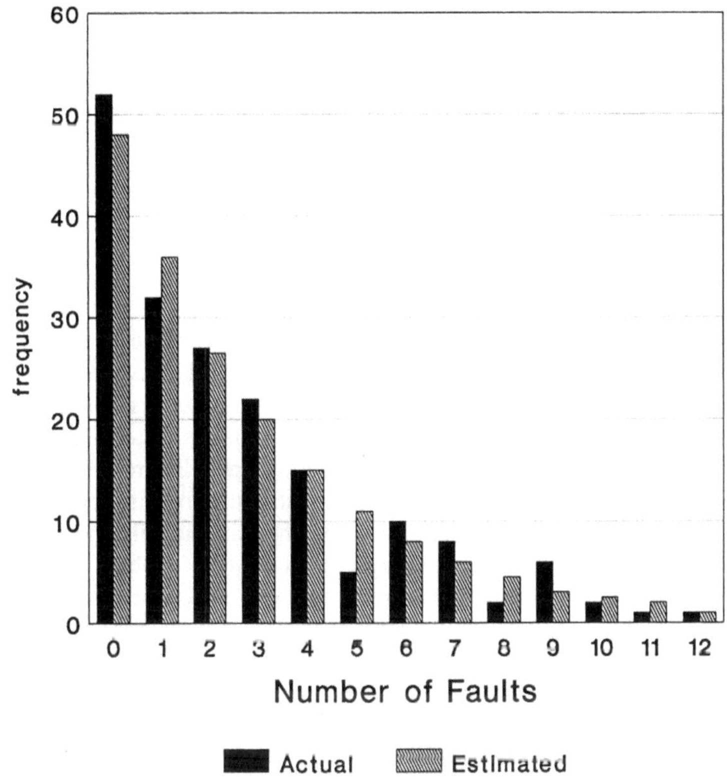

Figure 5.7. Negative binomial fit for medium size modules, between 1000 and 5000 executable lines of code.

Table 5.8. Parameters of Prior Distribution of μ

$$f(\mu) = \frac{b^a \mu^{a-1} e^{-b\mu}}{\Gamma(a)}$$

Module size	a	b	Mean
$N < 1000$	1	1.464	0.683
$1000 < N < 5000$	1	0.344	2.907
$N > 5000$	2	0.106	18.868

[a]Executable lines of code.

Table 5.9. Parameters of Prior Distribution of θ

$$f(\theta) = \frac{d^c \theta^{c-1} e^{-d\theta}}{\Gamma(c)}$$

Module type	c	d	Mean
Online	0.387	149.147	.002595
Batch processing	0.203	176.661	.001149

5.4.3. Results

Figure 5.8 compares the prior probability distributions of the mean number of faults μ and the per fault hazard rate θ for a single module with the distributions after nearly eight months of operation. Two errors found in this module after operation of the software system for approximately $7\frac{3}{4}$ months suggested that prior estimates should be revised upward. Figure 5.8a reflects that the maximum likelihood of the probability distribution of μ is skewed to the right after operation, increasing from 0 to 4.48. The maximum likelihood of the posterior probability distribution of θ also increased (Fig. 5.8b).

Table 5.10 compares a sample of prior mean estimators of μ and θ with posterior mean estimators computed after operation of the system for almost eight months. The failures because of faults in modules 21, 22, and 1120, predicted from the prior estimates of μ and θ were fewer than the actual failures caused by faults in these modules. The original parameters were therefore revised upward for these modules. Conversely, modules 10 and 1070 experienced no failures, and the estimated likelihood of their failure therefore decreased. Changes in μ and θ are a function of the number of faults found in these modules, the sum of the times of the failures recorded, and the amount of execution of the module during this eight-month period. Thus, the one fault found in module 984 increased the posterior estimate of μ more than did the one fault found in module 22, since the execution time of module 984 was less than that of module 22 during this time. Although no faults were found in modules 3740 and 1070, the decrease in the posterior estimates for module 3740 were greater than for module 1070 because module 3740 was executed more frequently during this period.

Table 5.11 compares prior and posterior estimates of the expected number of failures remaining after approximately eight months operation. Both of these estimates were made using mean estimators of the parameters. Table 5.12 compares prior-to-use estimates of the likelihood of failure within one month and the expected number of failures for that period with the likelihood and expected number of failures subsequent to 8 months use. The prior estimate was determined using mean estimators of μ and $e^{-\theta t}$ developed from the characteris-

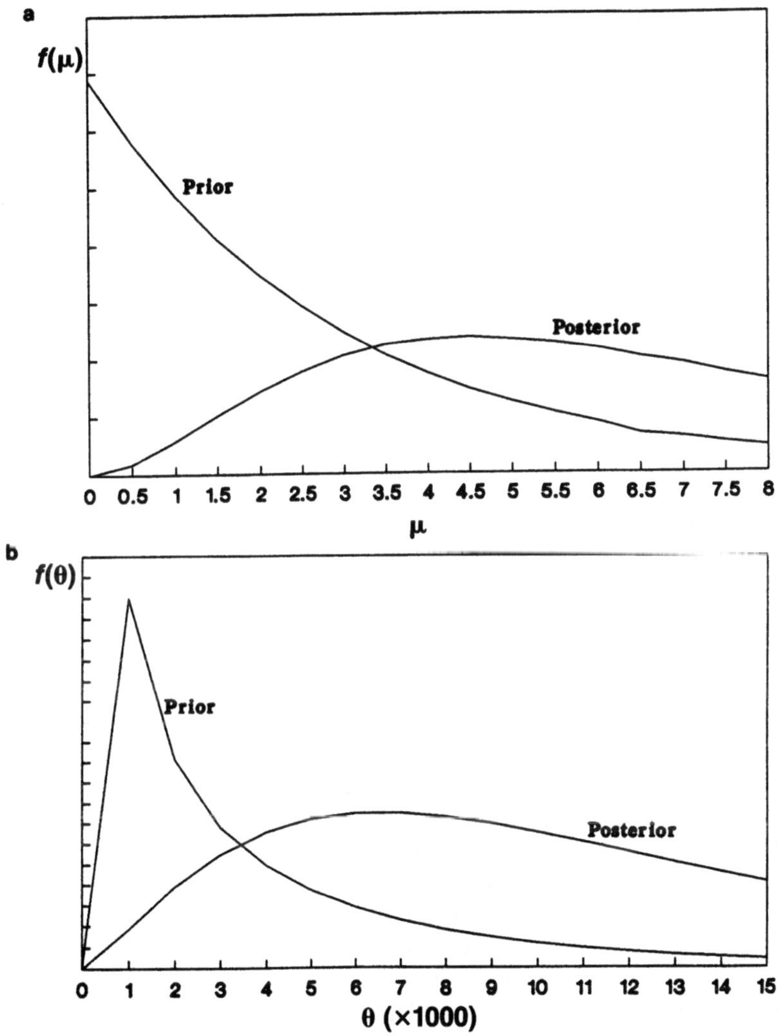

Figure 5.8. Comparison of prior and posterior probability distributions: Prior and posterior estimates, for module 21, of (a) μ and (b) θ.

Table 5.10. Prior and Posterior Estimates of μ and θ

Module	Prior estimates		Estimated execution time per month	Number of failures	Posterior estimates	
	μ	θ			μ	θ
10	2.907	0.0026	1.9400	0	2.699	0.0023
18	2.907	0.0026	0.0040	0	2.896	0.0028
21	2.907	0.0026	1.1800	2	6.781	0.0112
22	2.907	0.0026	0.2000	1	5.486	0.0088
23	2.907	0.0026	0.0140	1	5.657	0.0093
31	2.907	0.0026	0.0060	1	5.665	0.0093
111	2.907	0.0026	0.0200	1	5.651	0.0092
164	0.683	0.0026	0.4000	2	1.912	0.0149
173	0.683	0.0026	0.0004	1	1.342	0.0093
984	2.907	0.0026	0.0004	1	5.671	0.0093
1040	0.683	0.0011	10.2000	1	1.161	0.0045
1070	18.868	0.0011	0.8000	0	17.625	0.0011
1120	18.868	0.0011	0.0200	1	25.922	0.0066
1150	2.907	0.0011	1.2000	2	6.998	0.0090
2300	18.868	0.0011	31.4000	6	23.262	0.0015
2400	18.868	0.0011	49.4000	3	19.333	0.0007
2450	18.868	0.0011	1.0000	2	25.836	0.0062
2530	2.907	0.0011	14.8000	0	2.608	0.0010
3500	18.868	0.0011	21.4000	1	17.277	0.0007
3690	2.907	0.0011	0.7700	1	5.239	0.0058
3720	2.907	0.0011	0.6000	1	5.314	0.0060
3740	18.868	0.0011	34.2000	0	16.502	0.0002
3920	2.907	0.0011	0.4400	1	5.395	0.0061
4600	18.868	0.0011	9.9400	2	19.004	0.0021

tics of the code. Posterior estimates were made conditional upon failure history after eight months of operation, and the expected number of failures was reduced based on the number of failures that occurred.

Other researchers have suggested using locally uniform prior estimates (Musa *et al.*, 1987). If our analysis had used a locally uniform prior estimate, early estimates would be very biased by a few failures. In the example, use of a locally uniform prior estimate results in estimates of θ that would be much higher than historical evidence, resulting in underestimating the mean number of faults. For example, if a locally uniform prior estimate were used for θ of module 21, the updated estimates of μ and θ would be 2.292 and 0.0562, respectively. The first two failures suggest that each fault has a much higher per fault hazard rate, suggesting that most of the errors in this module were found. Previous evidence from programs of this type suggests that a per fault hazard rate of 0.05 is too high, and that, in all likelihood, the two failures found early in

Table 5.11. Prior and Posterior Estimates of Expected Number of Failures Remaining after Eight Months

Module	Prior estimate	Posterior estimate	Module	Prior estimate	Posterior estimate
10	2.801	2.509	1120	18.864	25.896
18	2.907	2.896	1150	2.877	6.449
21	2.841	6.137	2300	15.826	16.762
22	2.895	5.412	2400	14.931	15.445
23	2.906	5.651	2450	18.704	24.647
31	2.907	5.663	2530	2.626	2.382
111	2.907	5.643	3500	16.495	15.532
164	.678	1.826	3690	2.887	5.063
173	.683	1.342	3720	2.892	5.170
984	2.907	5.671	3740	15.665	15.790
1040	.634	.855	3920	2.896	5.284
1070	18.736	17.510	4600	17.531	16.364

the system's operation indicate that more faults would continue to be found in this module. However, the uniform distribution for θ does not permit consideration of any knowledge of typical hazard rates for programs of this type, leading to the hypothesis that this will cause the number of faults to be underestimated.

If the forms of the distributions are valid, but our parameters are incorrect, these prior estimates will dominate with few failures. For example, if θ is overestimated prior to testing, it can be expected that faults will be discovered early in the testing cycle. When this occurs, the estimate of the total number of errors in the module based upon this information is not updated. Overestimation of θ therefore may lead to underestimation of μ early in the testing cycle. For example, if parameters of the prior distribution of θ for module 22 are changed, thereby increasing the mean estimate of θ by 50%, the posterior mean estimate of μ is 2.775 rather than 5.486. In this case, the prior estimates suggest that the one failure recorded does not indicate that more faults exist in this module than originally estimated.

Future research to provide better estimates of the parameters, based upon characteristics of the code and development process, could improve the operational performance of this methodology. As they are developed, they can easily be incorporated within the methodological framework presented here.

5.5. RISK ESTIMATES

Estimated risk was computed for approximately 135 batch and online modules in the CLS. It is interesting to note that only three modules, represent-

Table 5.12. Likelihood of Failure within One Month of Operation

Module	Prior to test: Probability of failure	Prior to test: Expected number of failures	Posterior to use: Probability of failure	Posterior to use: Expected number of failures
10	0.015	0.015	0.012	0.012
18	0.000	0.000	0.000	0.000
21	0.009	0.009	0.084	0.088
22	0.002	0.002	0.009	0.009
23	0.000	0.000	0.001	0.001
31	0.000	0.000	0.001	0.001
111	0.000	0.000	0.001	0.001
164	0.001	0.001	0.011	0.011
173	0.000	0.000	0.000	0.000
984	0.000	0.000	0.000	0.000
1040	0.008	0.008	0.037	0.037
1070	0.017	0.017	0.016	0.016
1120	0.000	0.000	0.003	0.003
1150	0.004	0.004	0.072	0.075
2300	0.460	0.616	0.645	0.747
2400	0.602	0.921	0.455	0.485
2450	0.021	0.021	0.146	0.158
2530	0.046	0.047	0.034	0.035
3500	0.351	0.433	0.231	0.236
3690	0.002	0.002	0.023	0.023
3720	0.002	0.002	0.019	0.019
3740	0.486	0.666	0.101	0.107
3920	0.001	0.001	0.014	0.014
4600	0.188	0.208	0.324	0.337

ing 2% of all modules analyzed, demonstrated substantial risk prior to test and use. Approximately 89% of the modules had negligible estimated risk (less than $1/month), and 98% of the modules had an estimated risk of less than $100/month (Sherer, 1988). This supports our contention that traditional methodologies may not be cost-effective approaches to testing because they do not distinguish between the few high-risk modules and the remainder of the modules when allocating test effort. Expending more test resources on high-risk modules will prove more cost-effective, by reducing those faults that have high consequences of failure.

Some examples of the estimated risk for several of the modules in the CLS are provided in Table 5.13. Our risk assessment may overestimate the true risk because the impact of fault correction techniques was not included. The use of fault correction or fault tolerance techniques in one module to correct or handle faults in another module can reduce the actual risk of failure in a module. These

Table 5.13. Sample Risk Assessments

			Prior		Posterior	
Module	Description	Exposure ($/month)	Expected number of failures within one month	Estimated risk ($/month)	Expected number of failures within one month	Estimated risk ($/month)
10	Online interface	1800	0.015	27	0.012	22
18	Obligor number assignment	8	0.000	0	0.000	0
21	Online data entry	1435	0.009	13	0.088	115
111	Inquiry—payoff	21	0.000	0	0.001	0
162	Inquiry—turndown reference	7	0.000	0	0.000	0
164	Inquiry—transaction history	621	0.001	1	0.011	7
1000	Strip online proof file	1800	0.001	2	0.002	1
1150	Validation and update	1804	0.004	7	0.075	135
2300	Financial posting	1879	0.616	1157	0.747	1404
2400	Create billing extract	2573	0.921	2370	0.485	1248
2450	Billing print	2573	0.021	54	0.158	406
3500	Report extract	1804	0.433	781	0.236	406
3600	Report generator	1804	0.023	42	0.020	36
3960	Statistical history extract	20	0.001	0	0.001	0
4600	Cash flow extract	50	0.208	10	0.337	17

strategies include error detection, fault treatment, damage assessment, and error recovery (Randell *et al.*, 1978).

The methodology for estimation of software failure risk provides the ability to combine information about the software and its use into an assessment of the criticality of a module as it is being developed and used. Software reliability estimates did not provide the ability to include information about the exposure of a module, a very significant contributor to the criticality of a module. For example, in the CLS, if only failure probability were considered, then module 4600 (extracting information for cash flow analysis) would have a much higher probability of failure than module 2450 (prints bills). However, exposure of the latter module is significantly greater. Inclusion of this information makes risk assessment a very useful measure of the criticalness of a module.

REFERENCES

Misra, P. N., "Software Reliability Analysis," *IBM Systems J.* **22**(3), (1983), 262–270.

Musa, J. D., A. Iannino, and K. Okumoto, *Software Reliability: Measurement, Prediction, Application*, New York: McGraw-Hill, 1987.

Randell, B., P. A. Lee, and P. C. Treleaven, "Reliability Issues in Computing Systems Design," *Computing Surveys* **10**(2), (June, 1978), 123–165.

Sherer, S. A., "Analysis of Commercial Loan System," unpublished, March, 1988.

Chapter 6

Applying the Methodology to a Funds-Transfer Security System

This case study demonstrates the application of the risk assessment methodology to a funds-transfer security system. As a result of the high financial exposure involved in funds transfers, several external security measures are used to minimize processing risk. These include callback and verification of wire transfers as well as manual records paralleling the system accounts. Software exposure in this environment is relatively low compared to the potential magnitude of exposure because of the effectiveness of these hazard mitigators.

In addition, variability in system functionality is minimal because the system is used solely to send and receive wires. Hence, estimates of module exposure are more uniform.

6.1. INTRODUCTION

An originator of a wire transfer* issues a payment order to its bank, which in turn instructs an intermediary bank or the bank of the beneficiary to pay or credit a fixed amount to the beneficiary on behalf of the originator. The transfers

*Wire transfers are electronic transmissions of funds, whereas funds transfers in general can include nonelectronic communication.

are made through the Federal Reserve wire transfer network (Fedwire), or the New York Clearing House Interbank Payments Systems (CHIPS) or by some other method.

Due to the efficiency of payments by electronic funds transfer, more than 350,000 funds transfers, with a total value of between $1 and $2 trillion, are processed daily in the United States (Federal Reserve Bank of Philadelphia, 1990). The number of transfers has increased significantly. In 1987 the daily transaction volume in the United States was 24 times greater than the amount that reserve banks had on deposit with the Federal Reserve, up from a multiple of 9.4 in 1980. Electronic linkages make it possible for money to move so quickly that the same money can be used to finance more than seven deals a day (Karmin, 1987).

The sheer magnitude of dollars moved by funds transfer implies large financial exposure for the banks involved. A considerable amount of litigation has arisen regarding fraudulent and erroneous transfers. In one case, a bank that failed to execute a $27,000 payment order was sued for $2.1 million because the originator of the wire transfer claimed it had lost a valuable ship charter as a result. Although the suit was finally resolved in the bank's favor by a federal appellate court, considerable expense and time were involved in the litigation (Brandon, 1990).

An individual bank's role in a wire transfer is routine, involving low-cost processing relative to the potential magnitude of the funds transferred. This has prompted banks to employ several measures to reduce potential exposure, one of which is an automated funds-transfer security system. However, since exposure is so high, the automated system is generally used in conjunction with other external processing procedures to reduce potential risk resulting from software failure. These procedures include setting limits on amounts transferred without approval, limiting approval authority, manual balancing of accounts, and wire verification.

6.2. FUNDS-TRANSFER SECURITY SYSTEM

The funds-transfer security system provides an interface to Fedwire, which maintains daily information on a bank's wires to and from the Federal Reserve. Wires are structured in a format required by the Federal Reserve, and information required for repetitive wires is maintained by the system.* The system directs external verification procedures for the wires by maintaining

*Repetitive wires involve funds sent by the same originator to the same beneficiary. In fully repetitive wires, the fee, date, and amount fields can be changed; semirepetitive wires allow additional changes in transfer instructions.

information that describes and controls wire approval. For example, wires requiring verification can be configured for verification by both a second wire room operator and a second party at a bank branch office. The system contains information about who can verify individual wires. Special procedures are available for processing changes, exceptions, rejections, and holds. This processing is controlled by limits maintained in control files. A communication link is provided with the Federal Reserve Bank. This link not only sends and receives wires but also processes functional requests to the Federal Reserve and provides recovery procedures. The system also interfaces with the bank's host computer to verify and post account and general ledger transactions. Reporting capabilities and customer mailings are provided by the system.

6.3. EXTERNAL EXPOSURE ASSESSMENT

External exposure assessment began by reviewing the environment in which the funds system would operate. Procedures used by bank personnel have substantial impact on exposure.

6.3.1. Risk Identification

Risk identification requires an understanding of the environment in which the software will operate to analyze the nature and impact of software failure on the current and potential future activities of the organization. When identifying risk, it is necessary to first bound the study.

The study boundary in this case was based on the fact that risk is being analyzed for a single installation of the software. While this system will be used by many banks, in different Federal Reserve districts, this risk analysis was limited to one specific operations center that had recently purchased the software. This center would initially provide information-processing services to four banks which transmit wires through the Third District's Federal Reserve Bank in Philadelphia. While the use and potential exposure of the system could differ from one installation of the software to another, the basic methodology for assessing its risk would remain unchanged, hence easily applicable to each location, thereby providing individual risk estimates. Alternatively, if this analysis were to be done primarily for the software developer (which may be more concerned with expected failure risk at all locations), expected values might have been selected to define use and exposure, developing single risk estimates for all potential installations.

The analysis focused on risk that could arise from software failure. While external actions were considered to measure external exposure, the hazards that were ultimately analyzed were limited to those that could result from software failure. Several sources of risk in the funds-transfer application were not measured. For example, while the system provides for personal identification number (PIN) access to the system, poor external procedures for maintaining the security of these numbers, such as allowing unauthorized access to the wire room, can be a source of risk that is not a result of software failure. This risk can be minimized by developing strict procedures for access to the wire room, for original authorization of wires at the bank, and for processing procedures. Hardware failures in the Fedwire communications systems are also a source of risk. While this study considered risk that could result from failure of the software to adequately recover data when hardware failed, it did not specifically focus on hardware failure risk.

6.3.2. Hazard Identification

To identify hazards that might arise from the use of this software, preliminary discussions were held with the users, including the executive of the bank operations center, the wire room supervisor, and the operations manager for the wire room system. These discussions were guided by the focus questions cited in Chapter 4. User documentation for the system was reviewed to compare the new system's use with the current processing of wires at the operations center. A preliminary list of hazards was identified and reviewed with the users as well as the software developers. The list was refined based upon these discussions. The major hazards identified with the use of the funds-transfer security system at this location are shown in Table 6.1.

Table 6.1. Major Hazards and Consequences

Hazard	Daily consequence
1. Outgoing wires not sent	$35
2. Incoming wires not received	75
3. Outgoing wires sent but not posted	25
4. Incoming wires received but not posted	25
5. Wire sent with insufficient funds	50
6. Outgoing wires posted to wrong account	75
7. Incoming wires posted to wrong account	125
8. Outgoing wires posted from wrong account	75
9. Fees not charged	32
10. Incorrect amounts wired (outgoing)	35
11. Incorrect amounts received	75
12. Outgoing wires duplicated	35
13. Unauthorized receipts	200
14. Customer service problems	40
15. Extra clerical work	25

The hazards arising from use of this system are all financial. Since the system would be used to relay information to the Federal Reserve, *failure to send wires* and *failure to receive wires* were identified as two of the hazards. The system would be used to verify account balances; hence, another hazard was *sending the wire when insufficient funds exist* in the originator's account. The system posted wire amounts to customer accounts, possibly leading to hazards related to improper posting, such as *wires not posted*, *posted to/from the wrong accounts*, and *posting incorrect wire amounts*.

User discussions revealed that the funds-transfer security system was not the sole source of wire information. Several manual checks would be imposed on the system; for example, wire room personnel would maintain a hardcopy Order for Wire Transfer form to document the information called in to the wire room. An adding-machine tape of the totals on these forms would be verified twice each day against the totals provided by the system. In addition, all incoming and outgoing calls would be tape-recorded to provide an additional reference in case of questionable accuracy. The wire-transfer initiation request forms, completed at the branch offices, would be faxed or delivered by courier to the wire room the same day as the request was authorized. Most wires would be verified by a second wire room operator calling a second branch office employee (other than the one who called in the wire). Daily totals would be verified by comparing totals provided by the system with the general ledger account records. All of these external checks affected the external risk and were considered in the development of the expected exposure.

In defining hazards, changes that were expected to arise when the new system was installed were also considered, requiring a thorough understanding of both the "current" and the "new" systems for processing wires at the operations center.* Since improper attention to new processing techniques can lead to hazards, significant procedural changes that would be required with the "new" system were identified. Some of the identified changes included new wire-verification procedures and direct posting to accounts. How analysis of these changes was used to identify system hazards will be described subsequently.

In the "current" system, a wire verifier input the dollar amount of the wire twice so that the system could verify the amount. The "new" system did not require re-input of the amount; rather, it asked the verifier to review the amount shown on the screen. Wire-transfer personnel required careful training to review the dollar amount and to make changes if an error in the amount occurred. Their failure to do so could contribute to the hazard of *sending a wire for the wrong amount*.

A second change required by the "new" system was that the wire room

*The "current system" is the one that was replaced. The funds-transfer security system whose failure risk was evaluated in this study is referred to as the "new" system.

verifier called bank office personnel *after* the information had been entered into the system. Using the "current" system, a callback was made *before* the wire was entered. Thus, in the "new" system, wire room personnel had to learn how to delete or modify a wire in which a discrepancy arose. Otherwise, an *invalid wire could be sent.*

Automatic generation of wire notices was a new feature. Discussion with users indicated that beneficiaries would be notified by phone before receiving the wire notice so that the hazards resulting from improper wire notices would be limited to *additional clerical work* or *customer dissatisfaction*.

Automatic posting of wires by the funds-transfer security system decreased the number of external checks on this function. In the "current" system, the sending of wires was a separate task from that of posting the wires. Thus, the totals of the general ledger system could be compared with the totals on the funds-transfer system as a security check. Since different systems performed these tasks, software failure risk was minimized. However, while external risk might decrease with the "new" system, software failure risk increases because discrepancies would not be as readily apparent without additional checks on the system.

In order to understand and identify all hazards, it is important to understand how the use of the system could change in the future. One major processing change was the inclusion of wires for more than one bank. The operations center had processed wires for only one bank. However, since the operations center is the basis of operations for four banks, the center wanted to incorporate all wire transfers for these banks. In addition, if the scope of the center widens (assuming bank operations consolidation continues), the system will need to process wire transfers for additional banks. The inclusion of more banks could lead to several hazards. First, if a processing problem arose, funds could be *wired to/from wrong accounts* if bank identification was improperly maintained. Second, the funds-transfer security system must relay wires for individual banks through individual data communication terminals.* Invalid routing of wires with different bank numbers could result in *wires not sent/received.*

6.3.3. Accident Scenarios

As hazards were identified, accident scenarios were developed to describe the series of external events that could lead to these hazards. This was critical in the analysis of this case because of the considerable amount of external wire validation that could minimize the occurrence of some hazards. Analysis

*This is due to data encryption requirements.

revealed which hazards had reduced exposure due to the significant amount of external validation.

For each hazard, personnel and procedures were identified that could contribute to hazard occurrence or mitigate the effect of a hazard initiating event. Conditional event trees were developed to describe how each validation step could influence the accident scenarios.

The following example describes some of the scenarios involved in the hazard *outgoing wire not sent*. Consider Fig. 6.1, which represents the event tree for a nonrepetitive wire requiring verification. When a customer wishes to send a wire, a wire transfer initiation request form is completed and approved by authorized branch office personnel. A branch office employee who is authorized to handle wires of the amount requested must call the wire room and relay the information. The wire room operator completes the Order for Wire Transfer form (via a tape-recorded phone call). Failure at any of these events can lead to the wire not being sent, even before the software enters the picture.

Several external checkpoints arise once the wire information is entered into the software system. The wire is verified when a wire room verifier calls a bank verifier. If the wire is not in the system or if it is not verified, the bank verifier is one person who can reverse the accident sequence, thereby mitigating the hazard. The bank verifier, who has a copy of the wire transfer initiation request form, may realize that he or she has not been called to verify the wire and can inquire as to its status, causing the wire to be re-input, reviewed, or sent nonelectronically (via telephone) to the Federal Reserve bank. The wire verifier, who has a copy of the Order for Wire Transfer form, can also recognize that a wire is missing, or has not been verified, and can respond by insuring that the wire is sent. The wire room supervisor, who checks wires before end-of-day processing (to release holds or wires on pending status) can also send a wire or submit the wire to be reprocessed in the wire room. If a wire is not received by the Federal Reserve, wire room audit should uncover this fact when the wire room totals are balanced (twice each day), comparing the adding-machine tape developed from the wire request forms with the balance from the Federal Reserve.

Figure 6.2 illustrates some accident sequences for posting an incoming wire to an incorrect account number. This hazard can be initiated when the wire reviewer receives a wire with incorrect account information (Fig. 6.2a). The wire reviewer can then correct the account number. But even if the wire reviewer fails to do so, bank personnel may recognize the error. Finally, little chance of any loss exists if one of the customers recognizes the error immediately. Note that this hazard can also result if the wire reviewer posts an account number incorrectly (Fig. 6.2b).

Examination of the external processing at the operations center and the resulting event trees for each of the hazards revealed two interesting facts:

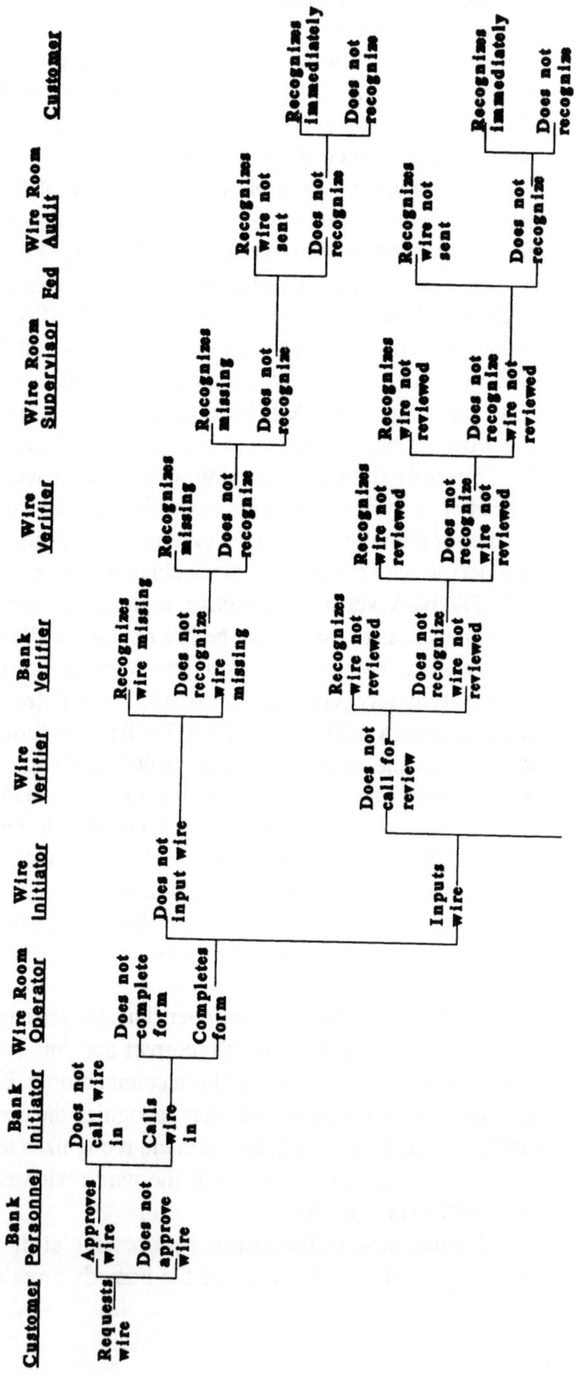
Customer
Bank Personnel
Bank Initiator
Wire Room Operator
Wire Initiator
Wire Verifier
Bank Verifier
Wire Verifier
Wire Room Supervisor
Fed
Wire Room Audit
Customer
Requests wire
Approves wire
Does not approve wire
Does not call wire in
Calls wire in
Does not complete form
Completes form
Does not input wire
Inputs wire
Recognizes wire missing
Does not recognize wire missing
Recognizes missing
Does not recognize
Recognizes missing
Does not recognize
Recognizes wire not sent
Does not recognize
Recognizes immediately
Does not recognize
Does not call for review
Recognizes wire not reviewed
Does not recognize wire not reviewed
Recognizes wire not reviewed
Does not recognize wire not reviewed
Recognizes wire not reviewed
Does not recognize wire not reviewed
Recognizes wire not sent
Does not recognize
Recognizes immediately
Does not recognize

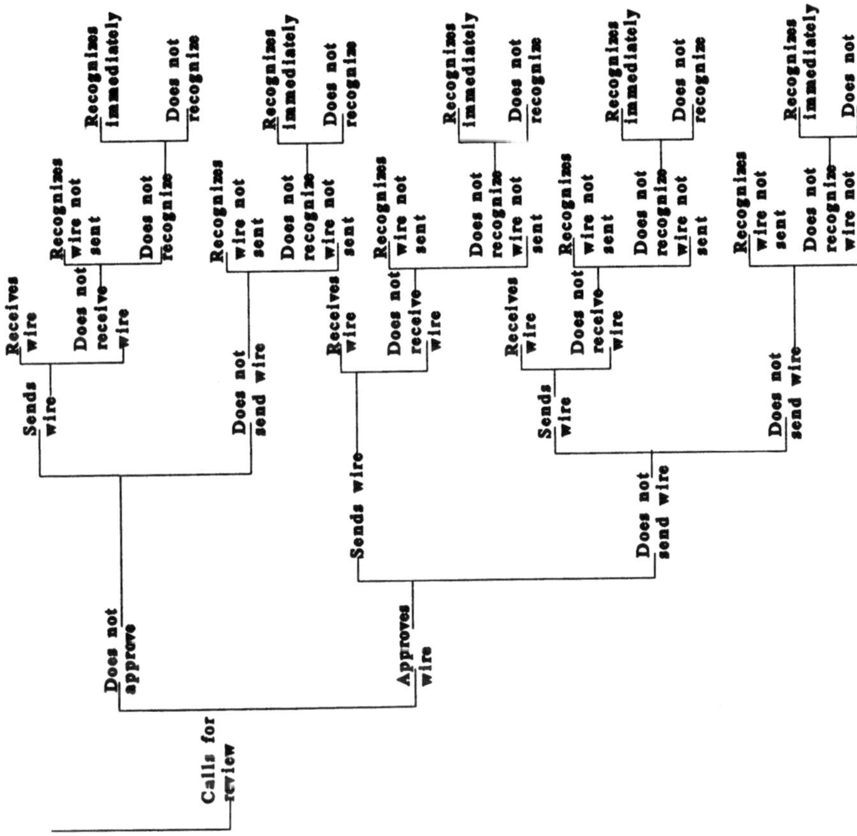

Figure 6.1. Event tree for the hazard *outgoing wire not sent.*

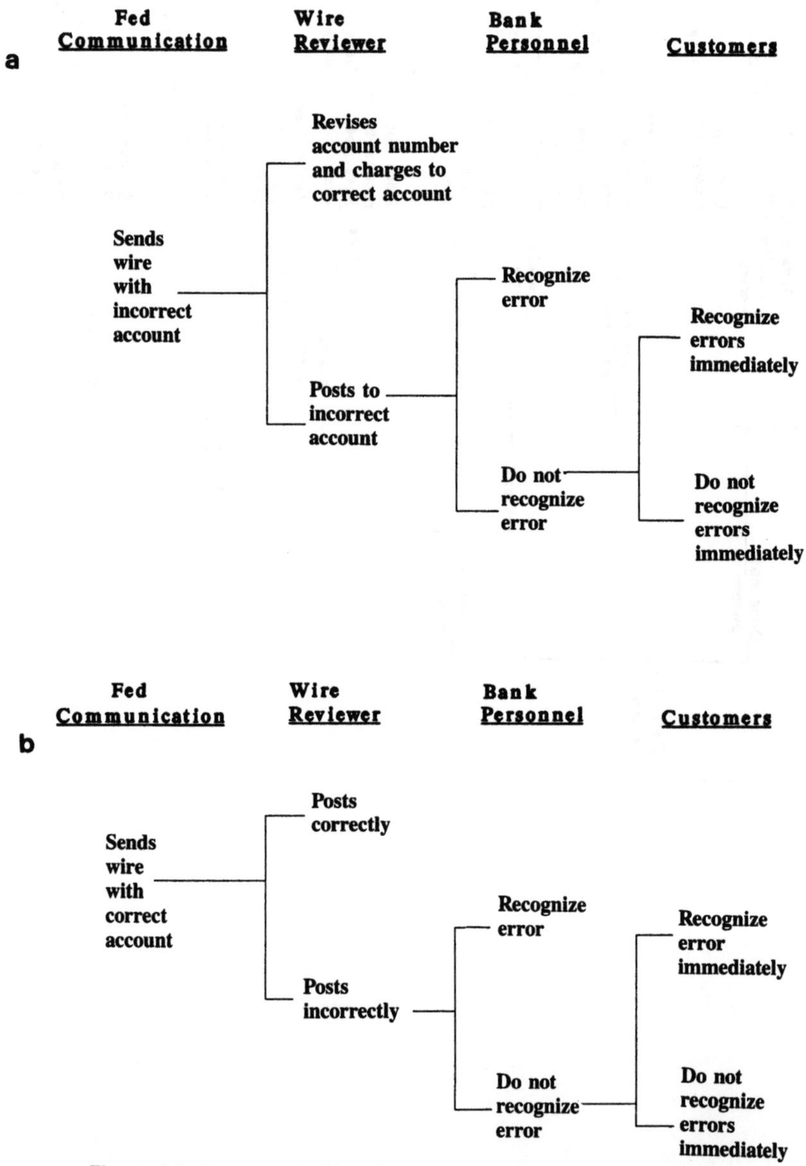

Figure 6.2. Event tree for the hazard *posts incoming wire to wrong account.*

- More external validation of outgoing wires exists compared to incoming wires.
- More external validation of the amount sent or received exists than the account information. (The twice-daily check on totals reveals errors only in amounts, not in accounts.)

It is therefore expected that, if a software failure exists, there would be less probability of detecting errors associated with incoming wires and less probability of detecting errors that would result in posting to/from incorrect accounts as compared to not sending/receiving wires or sending/receiving wires with wrong amounts.

6.3.4. Failure Modes Analysis

Failure modes analysis considers external events leading to a hazard to determine where and how erroneous or missing information that can result from software failure can contribute to the failure scenario.

The analysis began by reviewing the event trees to determine which external events might result from erroneous information. Until a wire is entered in the funds-transfer security system, the software cannot contribute to the accident scenarios. Hence, failure modes of external events preceding the entry of the data into the system were not considered. For the remaining events, fault trees were developed to analyze the relationships among human actions, hardware failure, and erroneous information.

Two fault trees in Fig. 6.3 illustrate how the contribution of erroneous information to an accident sequence can be determined. Fig. 6.3 has fault trees for some of the events in the accident scenario shown in Fig. 6.1, events that can lead to the hazard of not sending wires. One event, the wire room verifier not sending a wire after it has been approved by the bank verifier, can result from any of three different scenarios. (1) the wire verifier does not know that a wire needs to be sent, (2) the wire cannot be memo posted, or (3) the wire verifier cannot gain access to send a wire. In the first case, the wire verifier may not be aware that a wire must be sent if he or she does not check the system—a human error. However, he or she may be unaware that a wire is ready to be sent due to invalid status information in the system. Erroneous information can also contribute to the inability to post, as well as the inability to gain access to the system. Diamond shapes in the figure indicate where erroneous information can contribute to the failure mode.

The second fault tree illustrates how erroneous information can affect the event *bank verifier does not approve a wire*. If invalid information is on the wire or if the personnel information regarding who can verify a wire is incorrect, then the bank verifier may be unable to approve a wire.

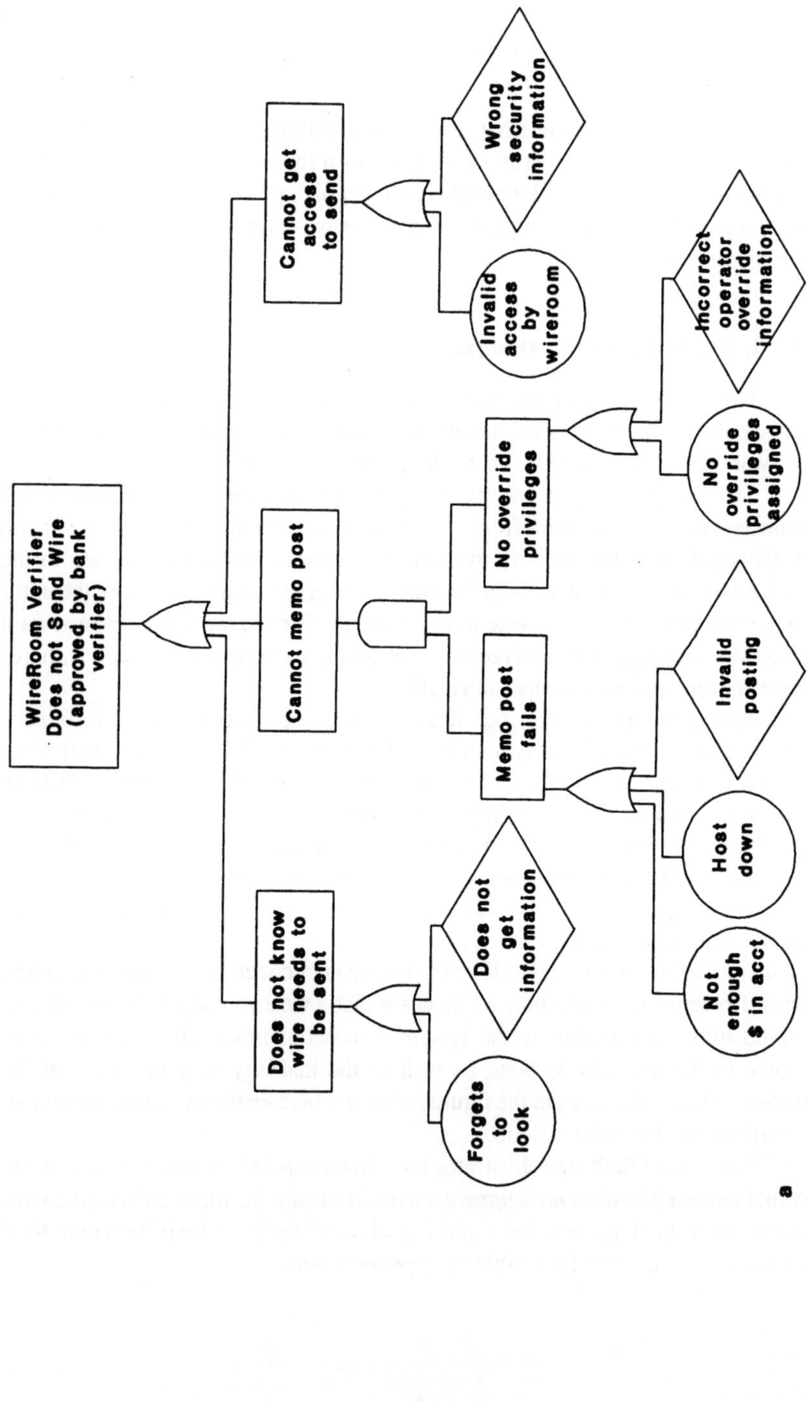
WireRoom Verifier Does not Send Wire (approved by bank verifier)
Cannot get access to send
Cannot memo post
Does not know wire needs to be sent
Wrong security information
Invalid access by wireroom
No override privileges
Memo post fails
Incorrect operator override information
No override privileges assigned
Invalid posting
Host down
Not enough $ in acct
Does not get information
Forgets to look

a

b

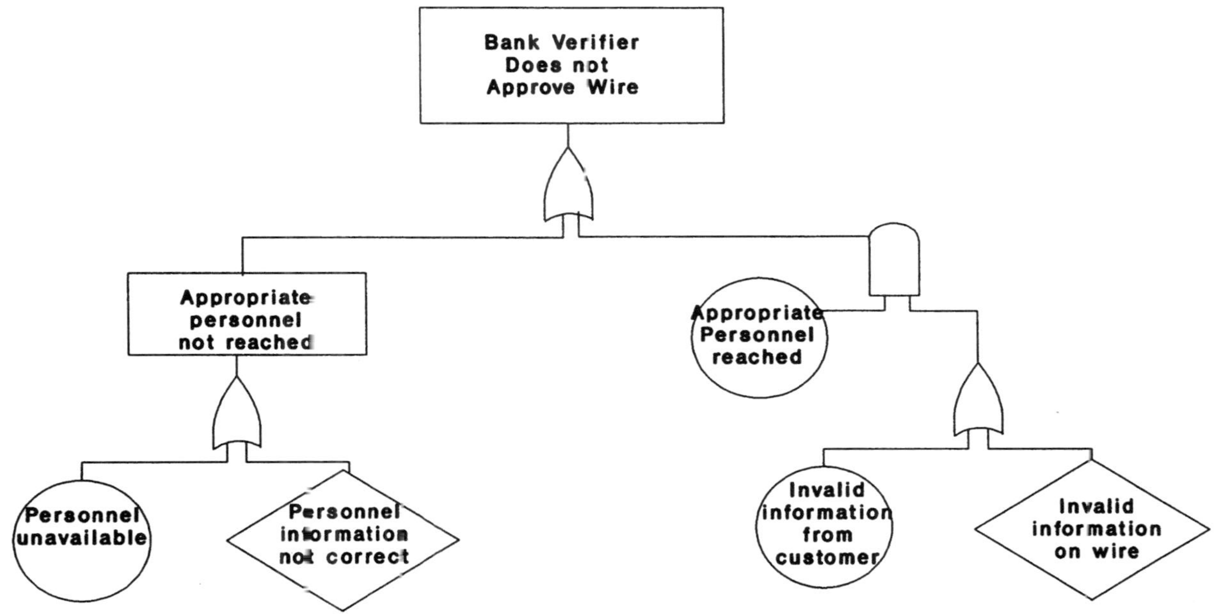

Figure 6.3. Sample fault trees for the hazard *outgoing wire not sent*: (a) Fault tree for the event "wire room verifier does not send approved wire". (b) Fault tree for the event "bank verifier does not approve wire."

The objective of each fault tree is to depict in detail where erroneous information can contribute to various accident scenarios. Such information and configuration is critical and lies at the heart of determining software failure modes that may be related to each hazard.

6.3.5. Consequence Analysis

The consequence of each hazard was estimated by weighing the magnitude of potential loss for each accident scenario by the likelihood of the external events in the failure modes and accident scenario analysis. A list of the consequence estimates for each of the hazards is given in Table 6.1. (Underlying assumptions are reported in Appendix C.2.)

To assess the potential magnitude of loss associated with each hazard, the magnitude of funds transferred by this operation was evaluated first. This was based upon forecasted business for each of the four banks processed by this center. Total expected daily processing was projected to involve approximately 100 incoming and 100 outgoing wires, averaging about $20,000 per wire. These wires included corporate, bank, and personal transfers (see Table 6.2). While a separate analysis could have been accomplished for each type of wire, the expected value of wires was used. If results of the study had indicated high exposure or very different processing methods, the study would have been further partitioned with separate risk estimates for each type of account being developed.

The potential magnitude of loss for each hazard depends on the bank's liabilities in each case. These liabilities include both nonrecoverable and recoverable losses. Nonrecoverable losses include additional clerical effort required in the event of a failure, possible loss of business resulting from erroneous wire processing, and potential bank liability if the bank is responsible for erroneous or fraudulent funds transfer. In some cases, losses due to processing errors could eventually be recovered from bank customers, e.g., if the bank inadvertently wired funds that were not in the originator's account.

To determine the cost of additional clerical effort, the amount of additional effort that would be required in the event of each hazard was estimated,

Table 6.2. Distribution of Wires by Customer

Customer	Proportion of wires	Average value ($)
Corporate	0.5	10,000
Bank	0.3	50,000
Personal	0.2	200

multiplied by the unit cost of clerical work. Daily exposure estimates were used since the system was reviewed each evening.

The consequence of a possible loss of business was estimated at 0.001% of the average daily wire business ($4 million). While this consequence is difficult to estimate, $40/day seemed a reasonable approximation of the opportunity cost of lost business.

Estimates of the bank's liability for a nonrecoverable loss were based upon new regulations defining rights of the parties to wire transfers.* These regulations limit the scope of recoverable damages to payment of interest, thereby prohibiting consequential damages. Furthermore, these regulations state that the originator of the loan must notify a receiving bank of an unauthorized, erroneous, or erroneously executed payment order within a reasonable time, not exceeding 90 days from receipt of the notice. Therefore, the consequence assessments for the hazards related to these types of liabilities (e.g., *outgoing wire not sent*, *incoming wire not received*) were limited to 90 days' interest on an average wire.

Several hazards, such as sending a wire with insufficient funds or crediting the wrong account, can lead to recoverable losses. For example, if the bank errs by sending a wire with insufficient funds, the bank may need to credit the originator's account until the funds can be recovered. If the bank posts a wire to the wrong account and that account subsequently uses the funds before the error is recognized, the bank may have to credit the correct originator's account while waiting to recover funds posted to the wrong account. Even though the bank will recover these monies eventually, hazards such as this subject the bank to immediate financial exposure. These losses were incorporated in this study by measuring exposure in terms of interest on these possible "loans."

Accident scenarios were used to determine the probability of a particular consequence, based on estimates of the probability of all external actions. Here is where detailed external accident scenarios proved most helpful in the analysis because they indicated the affect of external security checks on software exposure. For example, as shown in Fig. 6.1, a considerable number of checkpoints exist at which sending wires is verified. Reasonable estimates of the probability that a wire not sent would remain unnoticed were included at each of the external checkpoints illustrated in the event tree. For example, the probability that an unsent wire would go unnoticed by a bank verifier, wire verifier, wire room supervisor, and wire auditor was estimated to be only one in a thousand ($p = 0.001$). (See Appendix C.2.) A greater probability exists that a wire

*The regulations regarding commercial wire transfers were incorporated in Amendment 4A of the Uniform Commercial Code (adopted by 12 states by 1990 and expected to be adopted by most of the other states within the next few years) (Brandon, 1990). These regulations are pursuant to the revision to subpart B of Federal Reserve Regulation J (Federal Reserve Bank, 1991).

debited/credited to the wrong account by the software would go unnoticed because there is no external check on this processing. In fact, if a wire were posted to the wrong account, the probability that this error would not be recognized immediately was estimated to be greater ($p = 0.01$) than that of not recognizing wires not sent, because there would be no wire room audits using external information to verify account posting activities.

Likelihood estimates were used to weight the loss estimates. The consequence assessment for the first hazard, not sending wires, illustrates the process. Since liability resulting from not sending wires is limited to 90 days' interest, the liability for this hazard was assessed by multiplying 90 days' interest on the average daily value of outgoing wires—\$2,000,000 (0.1/4) = \$50,000—by the probability that wires not sent would result in loss.* The latter is equal to the probability that a wire not sent would be unnoticed ($p = 0.001$) times the probability that the customer would not recognize the error in time to avoid financial loss ($p = 0.2$), or $p = 0.002$. Thus, the expected liability is \$10/day. In addition, if the error were recognized, further wires would be sent nonelectronically, resulting in additional clerical effort estimated at \$25/hr. Hence, total consequence was estimated to be \$35/day (\$10 liability + \$25 clerical effort).

Note that these exposure estimates involve some likelihood estimates for which there may be few sources of objective data. However, reasonable approximations incorporated in the analysis provide exposure estimates that can be used to provide relative software failure risk information. If the software failure risk analysis reveals unusual degrees of risk, these estimates can be reviewed, thus providing a sensitivity analysis for these variables, and suggesting how external processing could be modified to reduce software failure risk.

6.4. STRUCTURAL EXPOSURE ANALYSIS

Software structure was reviewed and related to the external exposure. Both fault potential and module use were determined and incorporated into an estimate of exposure for each module.

6.4.1. The Software

The funds-transfer security system consists of 109 Pascal modules. The average module consists of 750 lines of code, with the largest module having 3500 lines. Table 6.3 summarizes the modules by function. Risk assessment was limited to modules that would be used routinely at the operations center and did not, therefore, include utilities and installation routines.

*The assumed interest rate was 10%.

Table 6.3. Summary of Modules by Function

Processing functions	Number of modules
Outgoing wires	11
Incoming wires	6
Federal Reserve communication	10
Reports and mailings	16
Control file maintenance	9
Supervisory processing[a]	22
Host interface	3
General processing	16
Utilities[b]	10
Installation[b]	6
Total	109

[a]Includes system audits and end-of-day processing.
[b]Not included in the risk study.

6.4.2. Software Failure Modes

Erroneous information (uncovered in developing the fault trees) that could be involved in accident scenarios for each hazard was considered. The objective was to determine how software failure could contribute to any erroneous information.

For example, failure to send an outgoing wire could be due to a number of different software failure modes. A fault tree that relates to failure of the wire room verifier to send a wire is shown above in Fig. 6.3a. Note that software can contribute to this event in several ways. The operator may be unable to access the system due to invalid operator security information or validation routines. Memo posting may not be possible because of errors in the memo posting routines. Finally, the processing of outgoing wires may lead to invalid wire status information so that wire room personnel may not recognize that wires need to be sent. All fault trees related to each of the external events in the accident scenario were considered, e.g., *wire initiator cannot input wire to system*, *bank verifier does not approve wires*, or *Federal Reserve does not receive wires*. These yield additional software failure modes related to this hazard, such as failure in the Federal Reserve communications modules.

6.4.3. Module Fault Potential

Module fault potential is determined by reverse engineering the system, identifying all modules that could process information related to the software failure modes. The hope was to review design documentation that would detail the function of each module, but detailed structure charts were available for only a portion of the modules, (those that had been revised in the last major revision of the system). To complete this task, the programmer supplied the module call relationships and complete descriptions of each module.

Results of the mapping of the modules to hazards are shown in Table 6.4. Each hazard was found to be related to more than half of the modules, reflecting the fact that this system provides little variability in function. The system is used primarily to process incoming or outgoing wires, with limited alternative uses. Since most modules are related to one or the other of these functions or to both, they are related to most of the hazards.

Table 6.4 shows hazards that were identified as related to several of the modules in the system. The first module shown, CALLCHLD is a calling routine used throughout the system, hence it is identified with all hazards. The OWSEND module sends outgoing wires to the Federal Reserve and is related only to

Table 6.4. Module Fault Potential

Hazard	Number of modules with fault potential	Module/hazard map			
		CALLCHLD[a]	OWSEND[b]	IWMISC[c]	R45DAY[d]
Outgoing wire not sent	55	Yes	Yes	No	No
Incoming wire not received	46	Yes	No	Yes	No
Outgoing wire sent but not posted	48	Yes	Yes	No	No
Incoming wire received but not posted	45	Yes	No	Yes	No
Wire sent with insufficient funds	46	Yes	Yes	No	No
Post outgoing wire to wrong account	50	Yes	Yes	No	No
Post incoming wire to wrong account	45	Yes	No	Yes	No
Post outgoing wire from wrong account	50	Yes	Yes	No	No
Fees not charged	43	Yes	Yes	No	No
Incorrect amount wired (outgoing)	55	Yes	Yes	No	No
Incorrect amount received	47	Yes	No	Yes	No
Outgoing wire duplicated	45	Yes	Yes	No	No
Unauthorized receipts	63	Yes	Yes	Yes	No
Customer service problems	64	Yes	Yes	Yes	No
Extra clerical work	88	Yes	Yes	Yes	Yes

[a] CALLCHLD is a calling routine used throughout the system.
[b] OWSEND sends wires to the Federal Reserve.
[c] IWMISC creates screens for processing incoming wires.
[d] R45DAY creates the inactive account report.

hazards involved with outgoing wires. Conversely, IWMISC provides screens to review incoming wires and is related only to hazards involved in processing incoming wires. The R45DAY module creates a report of all accounts that have been inactive for more than 45 days. As a result of the information in this report, wire room personnel may decide to remove an inactive account from the account mailing address file. While invalid information in this report can result in additional clerical work to reinstate the account mailing information and in customer dissatisfaction with mailings, it will not lead to hazards such as not sending, receiving, or posting wires.

6.4.4. System Use Distribution

Estimates of the expected use of the system were based upon analysis of the forecasted number of wires for all four banks whose transactions were processed by the operations center. Assumptions were made concerning the expected use of the new features such as supervisory review and PIN updates. The main menu of functions provided by the system proved to be a good basis to begin the functional use breakdown. Table 6.5, showing the estimated number of daily transactions, provided the basis for the expected system use distribution. Because of the processing of different types of outgoing wires, it was found necessary to further subdivide the use distribution for outgoing wires as shown in Table 6.6.

6.4.5. Module Use Distribution

Module use distribution was developed by determining which modules could be invoked for each system use. For example, when sending outgoing wires, any of the following modules could be utilized: outgoing wire modules,

Table 6.5. Number of Transactions

	Number of transactions	
Type of transaction	Daily	Monthly
Outgoing wires	102	
Incoming wires	106	
Supervisor inquiries	2	
PIN updates		1
Reports	1	
Control files		1/3
Account mailing updates		2/3
FED link requests	3–5	

Table 6.6. System Use Distribution

System	Probability
Outgoing wires[a]	0.47429
Incoming wires	0.49289
Supervisor inquiries	0.00930
PIN updates	0.00014
Reports	0.00465
Control file updates	0.00005
Account mailing updates	0.00008
Federal Reserve requests	0.01860
Total	1.00000

[a]Outgoing wires include 10% nonaccounting wires, 20% repetitive wires, and 70% nonrepetitive wires. Changes are made 15% of the time and wires are rejected 0.1% of the time.

e.g., modules that enter, change, verify, or send wires; Federal Reserve communication modules, such as status routines and functional request modules; and general data processing modules such as calling and global routines.

Module probability use distribution was based upon the system use distribution. Table 6.7 reflects the probability of use by function for several modules in the system. For example, OWCHANGE, a module that changes original wires, is used only when changes are made in outgoing wires. The expected probabil-

Table 6.7. Sample of Module Use Probability

	Module				
Use	CALLCHLD	OWCHANGE	OWSEND	IWMISC	R45DAY
All outgoing wires	0.47429		0.47429		
Nonaccounting wires					
Repetitive wires					
Nonrepetitive wires					
Changes		0.071			
Rejections					
Incoming wires	0.49269			0.49289	
Supervisor inquiries	0.00930				
PIN updates	0.00014				
Reports	0.00465				0.00465
Control file updates	0.00005				
Account mailing information	0.00008				
FED link requests	0.01860				
Total probability of use	1.00000	0.071	0.47429	0.49289	0.00465

ity of such changes is 0.071. OWSEND is used with all outgoing wires, with a probability of use = 0.47429. CALLCHLD is used all the time. Its probability use distribution is equal to the system use distribution.

6.4.6. Use/Hazard Map

External hazards were mapped against system uses to determine which hazards could result from various uses of the system (see Table 6.8). If a problem occurs when the system is being used to request information from the Federal Reserve, any of the hazards could result. Since the supervisor can obtain information to alter any accident scenario, problems with supervisory inquiries are also related to any of the hazards. However, when an outgoing wire is being sent, only the subset of hazards related to outgoing wires might result. If a problem occurs when the system is being used to enter information for account mailings, resulting hazards would be limited to customer service problems, extra clerical work, or unauthorized system access.

6.4.7. Module Exposure Estimates

To estimate module exposure, the expected exposure of all hazards for each module use was determined. This was then weighted by the use distribution of the module. A description of how this was accomplished is outlined below by building and analyzing a decision tree for failure of one of the modules in this system, WTHOST. This module performs host interface functions, pulling account information from the host computer.

First, branches are developed for each use of the module. WTHOST is used when processing all outgoing wires or when receiving incoming wires,* as well as for maintaining account mailing information. The probability of each branch (shown in Figure 6.4) is determined from the module use distribution.

Second, hazards that can result were determined for each module use. A hazard can result for a particular use if

- The module is in the fault potential set defined for this hazard, and
- The hazard has been mapped to this use.

For outgoing wires, the faults in WTHOST can lead to any outgoing wire hazard. For account mailings, the only hazards are customer service problems, extra clerical work, and invalid access. The consequence of each hazard is based upon the external exposure assessment.

Third, the hazard probability distribution for each use was assigned. It was believed appropriate to use a ratio of 6:3:1 for the relative probability of losses

*Wires were assumed to be processed only for host accounts.

Table 6.8. Use/Hazard Map

Use	Hazards
Outgoing wires (except nonaccounting)	Outgoing wires not sent
	Outgoing wires sent but not posted
	Wire sent with insufficient funds
	Outgoing wires posted to wrong account
	Outgoing wires posted from wrong account
	Fees not charged
	Incorrect amounts wired (outgoing)
	Outgoing wires duplicated
	Unauthorized receipts
	Customer service problems
	Extra clerical work
Incoming wires	Incoming wire not received
	Incoming wire received, not posted
	Incoming wires posted to wrong account
	Incorrect amounts received
	Unauthorized receipts
	Customer service problems
	Extra clerical work
Federal Reserve requests	All hazards
PIN updates	Outgoing wires not sent
	Incoming wires not received
	Outgoing wires sent but not posted
	Incoming wires received but not posted
	Wire sent with insufficient funds
	Outgoing wires posted to wrong account
	Incoming wires posted to wrong account
	Outgoing wires posted from wrong account
	Fees not charged
	Incorrect amounts wired (outgoing)
	Incorrect amounts received
	Unauthorized receipts
	Customer service problems
	Extra clerical work
Supervisory inquiries	All hazards
Reports	Unauthorized receipts
	Customer service
	Extra clerical work
Control file	Outgoing wires not sent
	Incoming wires not received
	Outgoing wires sent but not posted
	Incoming wires received but not posted
	Wire sent with insufficient funds
	Outgoing wires posted to wrong account
	Incoming wires posted to wrong account
	Outgoing wires posted from wrong account
	Fees not charged

Table 6.8. (*Continued*)

Use	Hazards
Control file (*continued*)	Incorrect amounts wired (outgoing)
	Incorrect amounts received
	Unauthorized receipts
	Customer service problems
	Extra clerical work
Account mailings	Unauthorized receipts
	Customer service problems
	Extra clerical work

associated with additional clerical work, recoverable losses, and other nonrecoverable liabilities, respectively. This distribution reflects the fact that software developers generally pay more attention to portions of the code that have nonrecoverable consequences.* The probability distributions shown in Fig. 6.4 for each of the hazards reflects this relative assessment. Outgoing wires not sent can result in nonrecoverable losses with a probability of occurrence of 0.0385, which is only 1/3 that of wires sent with insufficient funds, because these funds can be recovered. Since an outgoing wire sent but not posted leads only to extra clerical work, its probability of occurrence as a result of software failure is six times greater than that of outgoing wires not sent.

Finally, expected exposure is estimated by evaluating the decision tree. For this module, expected exposure was computed for each use by summing the probability of each hazard multiplied by its consequence. The expected module exposure is then equal to the sum of the expected exposure for each use multiplied by the probability of each use of the module.

Module exposure estimates for a sample of modules in this system are included in Table 6.9. More than 40% of the modules in this system had exposures of less than $1/day. These were modules that generally performed specific functions related to few hazards or are expected to be used infrequently. Approximately 20% of the modules had the highest exposure, between $40 and $50/day. These were modules that were used all the time such as CALLCHLD or modules used for both outgoing and incoming wires such as posting modules. Modules involved in processing either incoming or outgoing wires (but not both) had exposure varying from $20 to $25/day, with the exposure of modules processing incoming wires being slightly higher than those processing outgoing wires. This is because external exposure for incorrect processing of incoming

*If it were not believed that developers would be more careful when developing this code, a uniform distribution could be assigned.

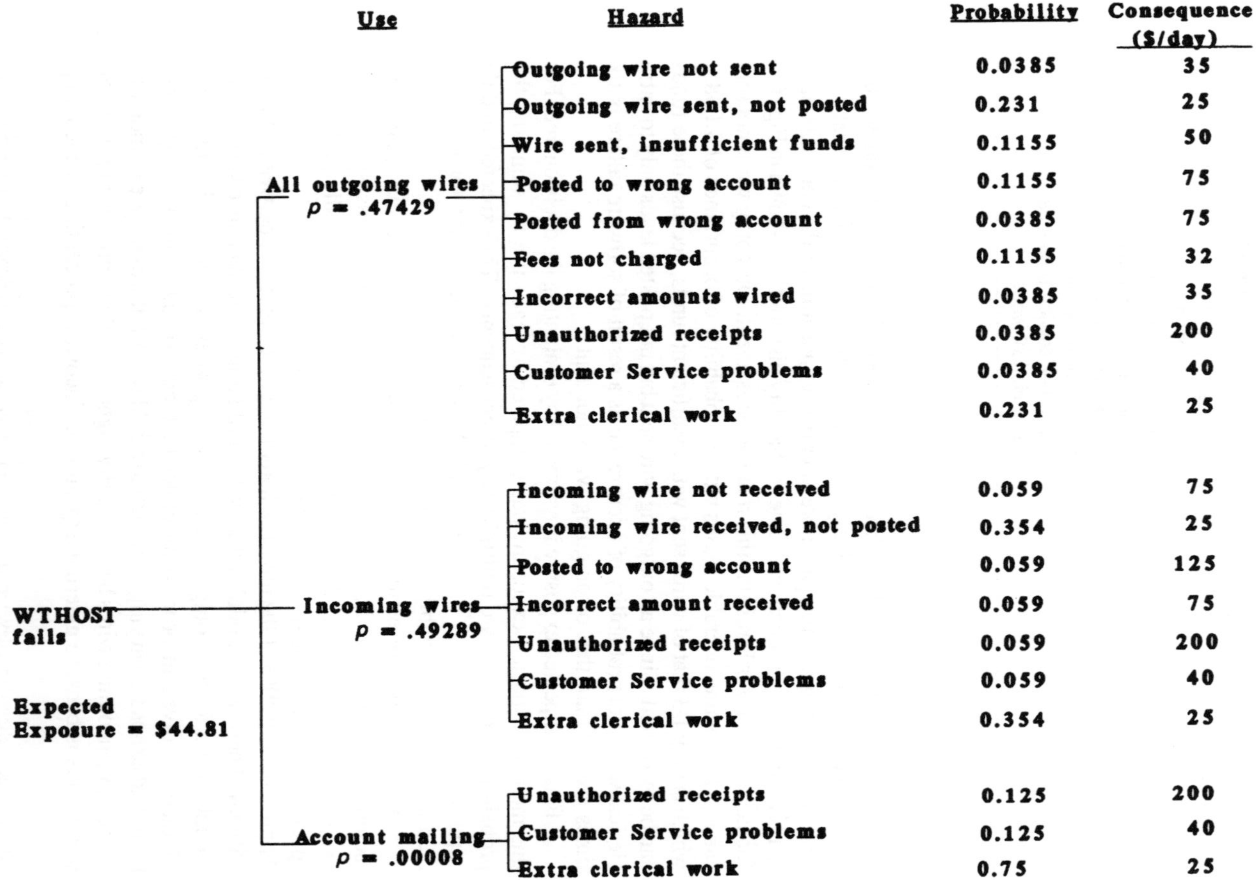

Figure 6.4. Exposure assessment for module WTHOST.

Table 6.9. Sample Module Exposure Estimates

Module	Exposure ($/day)
CALLCHLD	45.73
CTRLTYPE	44.25
IWENTER	23.63
OWCHANGE	3.09
OWENTER	20.62
R45DAY	0.13
WTMPOST	44.72

wires is greater than for outgoing wires—fewer external manual checking procedures exist to verify information in incoming wires compared to those for outgoing wires.

6.5. FAILURE LIKELIHOOD

The Musa software reliability model (Musa *et al.*, 1987) was used to estimate the failure likelihood of the modules prior to use at the operations center. This required prior estimates of the average number of faults in a module and the module per fault hazard rate. While it would have been preferable to develop estimates based on failure data from similar modules developed in a similar environment, it was discovered that the developer's historical failure records were incomplete. Hence, failure data on inherent faults found in more than thirty systems (Musa *et al.*, 1987) were used initially, adjusted for the operational life of this software. While it is recognized that these early estimates of failure likelihood would not be as accurate had the data been obtained in the same environment, this data at least provides a basis upon which to make some initial predictions, predictions that would be updated as testing continued at the operations center.

An alternative approach, in the absence of data, would have been to use subjective estimates from the development team to adjust these forecasts. For example, the development team could have been asked to rank the modules in terms of their perceived difficulty (assuming that more difficult modules have more errors) or degree of effort (assuming more effort might result in fewer errors). This approach would be similar to the use of qualitative forecasting tools in conjunction with quantitative tools—the use investigated in the next case study.

To determine the expected number of failures prior to operation at this center, the prediction procedures from Musa *et al.* (1987) were used, as

Table 6.10. Sample Computations for Failure Likelihood Estimates

Module	OWSTRUCT
Module description	This module, which had just been implemented in the latest revision of the software, handles processing to structure wires as required for the Federal Reserve.
Module information[a]	I_s = size = 1324 source lines of code
Module use	N_m = number of times used per month at each location = 1800 N_p = number of months in use = 3
General assumptions	K = fault exposure ratio = 0.00000042 failures/fault[b] r = execution rate = 3333333 object instructions/CPU sec[b] Q_x = average expansion ratio = 3.5 object/source instructions[c] N_l = faults/kloc before operation = 1.48[b]
Computations	1. f = linear execution frequency = $r/(I_s \times Q_x)$ = 719.32 cycles/CPU sec 2. θ = per fault hazard rate = fK = 0.00029 failures/fault/CPU sec 3. μ = inherent fault density = $N_l \times I_s$ = 1.96 4. t_p = total use prior to operation at this center $(1/f)N_mN_p$ = 7.51 sec 5. $F_p(t_p)$ = expected number of remaining failures at this operations center = $\mu \exp(-\theta t_p)$ = 1.95

[a]Source of data: system developer.
[b]Musa *et at.* [87].
[c]Jones [86].

illustrated in Table 6.10. An explanation of each of the five computational routines is outlined below:

1. The linear execution frequency, the number of times the program would be executed per unit time if it had no branches or loops, was estimated by dividing an average instruction execution rate by the number of object instructions in the program. The number of object instructions was estimated by multiplying an estimate of the average expansion ratio for Pascal programs (Jones, 86) by the number of source instructions per module.
2. The per fault hazard rate was estimated by multiplying the linear execution frequency by the fault exposure ratio. The fault exposure ratio, the fraction of time that a passage results in failure, was estimated from other programs (Musa *et al.*, 1987). The fault exposure ratio accounts for the fact that programs have branches (so that they are not executed linearly) and that there are different machines states (so that the program may not be executing with the same information each time) (Musa *et al.*, 1987).
3. The inherent fault density (the mean number of faults per module prior to any operation of a module) was estimated by multiplying the number of

source lines of code in a module by an estimate of the average number of faults per line of code found in other systems prior to operation.*

4. To estimate the use of the module prior to installation of the software at this operations center, the life of the module and its daily expected use were considered. Some modules had more extensive prior use because they had been in production for a longer time period, provided functions used by more banks, or were executed more frequently at any particular location. A recent revision of the system resulted in a few new modules with little prior use and some revised modules whose changes had been used only for a short while. Most modules had been used without revision for several years.
5. To determine the expected number of remaining failures at this operations center, the software reliability model was applied, using the estimated prior operation of each individual module. This estimate reflects the assumption that newer modules would have more initial failures because they had not been used as much as the older modules.

Table 6.11 reflects some estimates of the remaining number of failures in a module as well as estimates of the expected number of failures within the first month of operation. WTMPHOST had one of the highest failure likelihoods. It was not only one of the larger modules, but it was also a new module that had little prior use at other installations, although it would be used often at this center to post all incoming and outgoing wires. While OWSEND is also a large module, it had more prior use at other locations. It would be used less than WTMPHOST at this center because it would be used only when sending outgoing wires. While FIFIAPI is only half the size of OWSEND, its execution time is approximately the same since it handles communication for all incoming and outgoing wires. IWRCVD is a small module and has a smaller failure likelihood than the other modules shown.

6.6. MODULE RISK

Daily risk during the first month of operation was estimated as the product of the daily exposure and the expected number of failures within the first month of operation. In general, software failure risk is minimal for this system due to several factors:

*Note that these estimates were based on faults found in systems, not individual modules. If a constant inherent fault component in modules exists that is unrelated to size (Shen *et al.*, 1985), these estimates may be low. However, since the inherent fault component in modules was contested by Card *et al.* (1986), estimates of faults found in other systems were used to begin this analysis.

Table 6.11. Module Failure Likelihood Estimates

Module	Size (loc)	Degree of prior use	Execution time per month (CPU sec)	Per fault hazard rate	Expected failures at this center	Expected failures within first month
CALLCHLD	575	High	2.50	0.00069	0.799	0.001
FLFIAPI	923	Medium	3.88	0.00043	1.34	0.002
OWSEND	1896	Medium	3.98	0.00021	2.78	0.002
IWRCVD	410	Medium	0.86	0.00043	0.60	0.0005
OWSTRUCT	1324	Low	2.50	0.00029	1.95	0.001
WTMPHOST	2103	Low	8.92	0.00019	3.10	0.005

- The external exposure is very low because of the external verification procedures used at the operations center.
- Modules are fairly small and cohesive.
- Most of the modules have been used prior to this installation at other locations.

Table 6.12 shows the risk assessments for the modules whose daily risk exceeds \$0.01/day for the first month of operation. The remainder of the modules exhibited negligible risk (<\$0.01/day). Modules with the greatest risk (in order) are:

- Large modules used all the time, such as data retrieval, IO, and global modules
- Modules that interface with the host computer
- Audit routine modules
- Federal Reserve communication modules

Among the modules that handle outgoing and incoming wire processing, the modules with the largest risk send outgoing wires and provide outgoing wire screens. While incoming wire modules generally have slightly greater exposure, they are smaller and less complex than outgoing wire processing modules and exhibit less failure likelihood.

It was suggested that the operations center concentrate the testing in four areas:

- Host information
- Posting transactions
- Audit trail
- Federal Reserve communications

Information derived from the host should be verified against host data. All posting transactions should be examined very closely during the initial opera-

Table 6.12. Risk Assessments for Highest-Risk Modules

Module	Daily risk within the first month of operation	Daily exposure	Expected failures within first month
General processing			
WTIO	$1.37	$45.73	0.0300
MISC	0.38	45.73	0.0084
GLOBAL	0.21	45.73	0.0047
WTBTRV	0.19	45.73	0.0042
WTMISC	0.15	45.73	0.0032
WTMENU	0.09	45.73	0.0020
CALLCHLD	0.06	45.73	0.0014
WTINIT	0.05	45.73	0.0011
WTXREF	0.04	45.87	0.0009
WTENCRPT	0.02	45.73	0.0005
WTMAIN	0.01	45.73	0.0003
Host interface			
WTMPHOST	0.23	44.72	0.0052
WTHOST	0.21	44.72	0.0048
TMPOST	0.04	44.72	0.0008
Audit modules			
DANOCTRL	0.14	50.00	0.0028
WTFAUDIT	0.13	50.00	0.0027
DAMISC	0.11	50.00	0.0022
Federal Reserve communications			
FLFIAPI	0.08	33.73	0.0023
FLWSTAT	0.03	32.41	0.0011
FLFIPX	0.02	13.80	0.0013
Incoming wire processing			
IWINFORM	0.03	23.63	0.0014
IWMISC	0.02	23.63	0.0007
IWMAIN	0.02	23.62	0.0008
IWRCVD	0.01	23.63	0.0005
Outging wire processing			
OWMISC	0.05	20.62	0.0022
OWSEND	0.05	20.62	0.0023
OWSTRUC	0.03	18.56	0.0015
OWREVCAL	0.02	18.56	0.0010

tion of this system at this center. Since audit information is to be used to monitor daily transactions, it was suggested that audit documents be carefully reviewed to insure correctness and completeness. Federal Reserve communications should be tested, especially for the processing of the four different banks' wires.

Since minimal software failure risk occurs in this system because of the external verifications, it is extremely important that attention be paid to these procedures. It was suggested that specific instructions for sending and receiving wires be developed for each branch office as well as for wire room personnel. These procedures should pay particular attention to wire room security and manual processing tasks, such as the verification of wire totals. Recovery procedures should also be developed. Training should focus on the external use of this system to insure compliance with these procedures. Since potential exposure is very high, if the external exposure of this system were to increase due to improper external processing with this software, the software failure risk could dramatically increase.

6.7. COMPARISON WITH COMMERCIAL LOAN SYSTEM: LESSONS LEARNED

Risk estimates for the modules in the funds-transfer security system are less than those in the commercial loan system. In addition, much less variability in risk exists among the modules in the funds system as compared to the loan system. While some differences are due to changes in the application of the methodology, most result from differences in the processing environment and the software.

The first major difference between the analyses is the time basis for exposure estimation. Monthly exposure was computed for the commercial loan system, daily exposure for the funds system. This choice was based on the processing function and review procedures. The major function of the CLS was the production of monthly bills. If bills are sent improperly (or not sent at all), it may take a month to recognize and fix this problem since many significant reports are produced and reviewed on a monthly basis. In the funds-transfer security system, all processing and verification for wires is accomplished in one day and, since the reporting cycle is also one day, it is more reasonable to expect that system errors would be recognized more quickly.

Note that if risk estimates are used solely to rank module risk for modules within a single system, the ranking will be consistent as long as the time basis is consistent. Thus, the choice of a time basis will be inconsequential for most uses of the analysis. However, when comparing two different processing systems, as is done here, it is important to recognize differences in time estimates. The funds transfer system will have lower risk because its output is verified on a more timely basis.

Not only is the funds system software verified on a more timely basis, but external verification of the data in this system is more extensive than in the commercial loan environment. Processing wire transfers involves more manual checks on the information produced by the software than occur in the commercial loan application. In the funds-transfer system, external activities were regulated to a greater extent to reduce the expected magnitude of risk. The commercial loan system is reviewed by verifying audit reports produced by the system itself. Thus, the system rather than external sources is relied on for verification of data accuracy. If a software failure is propagated throughout the system, it would not be recognized as quickly. This is reflected in much higher probability estimates for the failure events in the fault and event trees in the CLS compared to the funds-transfer system. These differences demonstrate how failure risk assessment methodology accounts for differences in external risk management techniques. Managers can use failure risk assessment analysis to make trade-offs regarding the use of different external risk management techniques. The method can demonstrate the impact of different risk management techniques on software failure risk mitigation.

The funds-transfer security system contains no module with an expected number of failures as great as that of some modules in the CLS. The funds system is an online system with fairly small modules, whereas the CLS contains some large batch-processing modules with diverse processing functions. These have a much higher failure likelihood.

Another contributor to the difference in exposure estimates between these systems is differences in the way exposure was estimated. In the CLS, the total value of loss was included in the exposure estimate even if the loss was eventually recoverable. For example, if bills were not mailed, exposure was estimated based on the total value of bills expected to be mailed. In the second study, exposure was limited to the interest lost on recoverable losses, in the belief that this would more accurately reflect true loss. Again, as long as the analysis is consistent, the ranking of modules will be unaffected. This fact is significant only when comparing analyses for different systems.

Finally, considerably less variability was found in the risk estimates of the modules in the funds system compared to those of the loan system. The funds system provides much less diversity in function. It is basically used to send or receive wires. While differences in exposure exist, they are not significant. Moreover, module size did not vary greatly. The CLS provides many different functions, ranging from maintenance of account billing information to collateral deposit tracking, and customer inquiries. Many modules each provided several types of inquiries and reports. Exposure as well as module size varied greatly. The differences in exposure variability are reflected in differences in external exposure of the hazards as well as smaller module fault potential sets. In the funds-transfer system, the module fault potential set of each hazard included more than 50% of the modules, whereas in the loan system, the module fault potential set averaged about 37% of the modules. The use of failure risk assessment methodology to guide development is expected to be more helpful when there is wide variation in module risk such as existed in the loan system.

REFERENCES

Brandon, G., "What You Should Know About Your Wire-Transfer Liabilities," *Financial Executive*, November–December 1990, pp. 39–43.

Card, D. N., V. B. Church, and W. W. Agresti, "An Empirical Study of Software Design Practice," *IEEE Trans. Software Engrg.* **SE-12**(2), (February, 1986), 264–271.

Federal Reserve Bank of Philadelphia, Circular Letter 4567, June 15, 1990.

——Operating Circular No. 10, January 1, 1991.

Jones, C., *Programming Productivity*, New York: McGraw-Hill, 1986.

Karmin, M., "Risky Moments in the Money Markets," *U.S. News & World Report*, March 2, 1987, p. 44.

Musa, J. D., A. Iannino, and K. Okumoto, *Software Reliability: Measurement, Prediction, Application*, New York: McGraw-Hill, 1987.

Shen, V. Y., T. Yu, S. Thiebaut, and L. Paulsen, "Identifying Error-Prone Software—An Empirical Study," *IEEE Trans. Software Engrg.* **SE-11**(4), (April, 1985), 317–323.

Chapter 7

Applying the Methodology to a Payables Processing System

This case study involved software developed by an internal systems group of a Fortune 200 manufacturing company. The study provided several unique opportunities. First, it enabled development guidelines to be provided to the project team as the software was being developed rather than waiting until testing at a specific installation. Second, the system was developed with a more advanced software language. Finally, because the system is fairly small, a complete report of the results could be included.

7.1. INTRODUCTION

The Voucher Input Processing System (VIPS) is an online entry system for payable transactions not covered by specific purchase orders. It was developed solely for internal use by a single organization. The payable transactions processed by this system include

- Utility bills
- Invoices processed via check requests
- Field invoices
- Payment of patent fees
- Manual releases against blanket purchase orders
- Payments against manual purchase orders

The number and the dollar value of these transactions vary widely. The vast majority of the approximately 18,000 transactions per month involve small amounts, averaging $300. However, approximately fifty large utility payments average $2.7 million per transaction.

The system includes online screens and the processing necessary to insure the integrity, completeness, accuracy, and security of the data. VIPS accesses vendor, accounts payable, and employee data bases.

The data processed by this system feed into batch accounts payable and material distribution systems. The accounts payable system maintains an open item file and generates checks from this file at the appropriate time after taking steps to prevent duplicate payments. It also performs status and disbursement reporting and generates the accounts payable distribution journal voucher at the end of the month. The material distribution system is concerned with validating account charge information, distributing the source charge to the final designated charge, and reporting. It generates the general ledger journal voucher for all types of material details. These batch systems were not included in the initial risk assessment, and their failure risk was assumed to be minimal.*

7.2. EXTERNAL EXPOSURE ASSESSMENT

External processing flows were first reviewed for all transaction types. This information was used to identify risk and accident scenarios. Since dissimilar transaction types involved different processing flows and amounts of money, unique external exposure assessments were developed.

7.2.1. Risk Identification

To identify risk in the environment in which this software was to operate, it was necessary to first understand the external processing flow. Since VIPS would be used to enter data for different payable transactions, it was important to understand if this fact would indicate differences in the external processing flow.

This study was initiated just subsequent to the development of a design report by the corporate systems project team. After review of this design report, a meeting was held with the users, the accounts payable manager and another staff member, to learn how the system would be used.

Three distinct external processing flows were identified as depicted in Figs. 7.1, 7.2, and 7.3. Standard external processing flow includes check

*This assumption was made to bound the study to a reasonable context. It is expected that the batch system may exhibit failure risk that would increase the risk of the VIPS system.

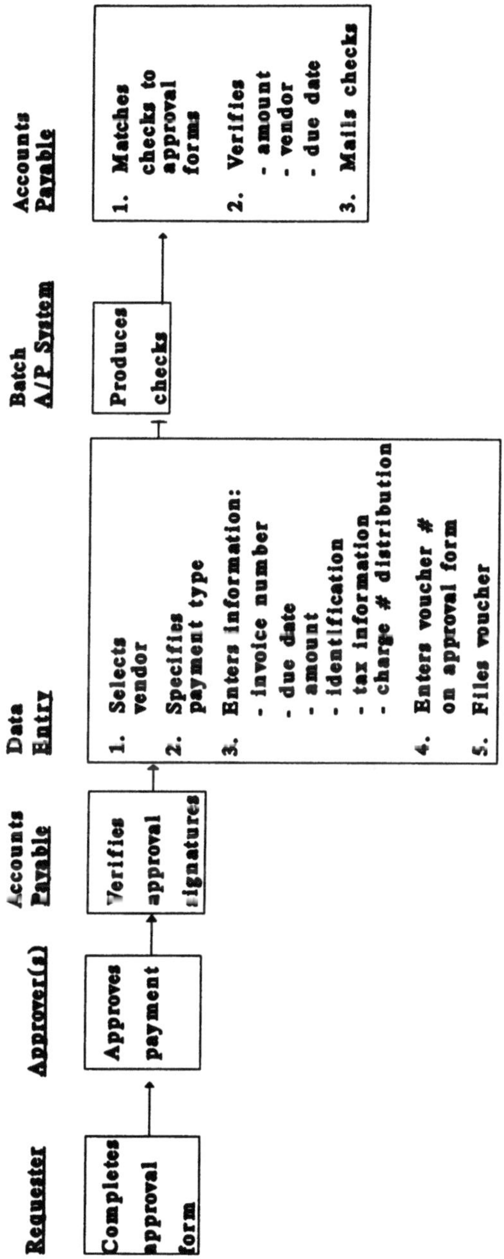

Figure 7.1. Standard processing flow.

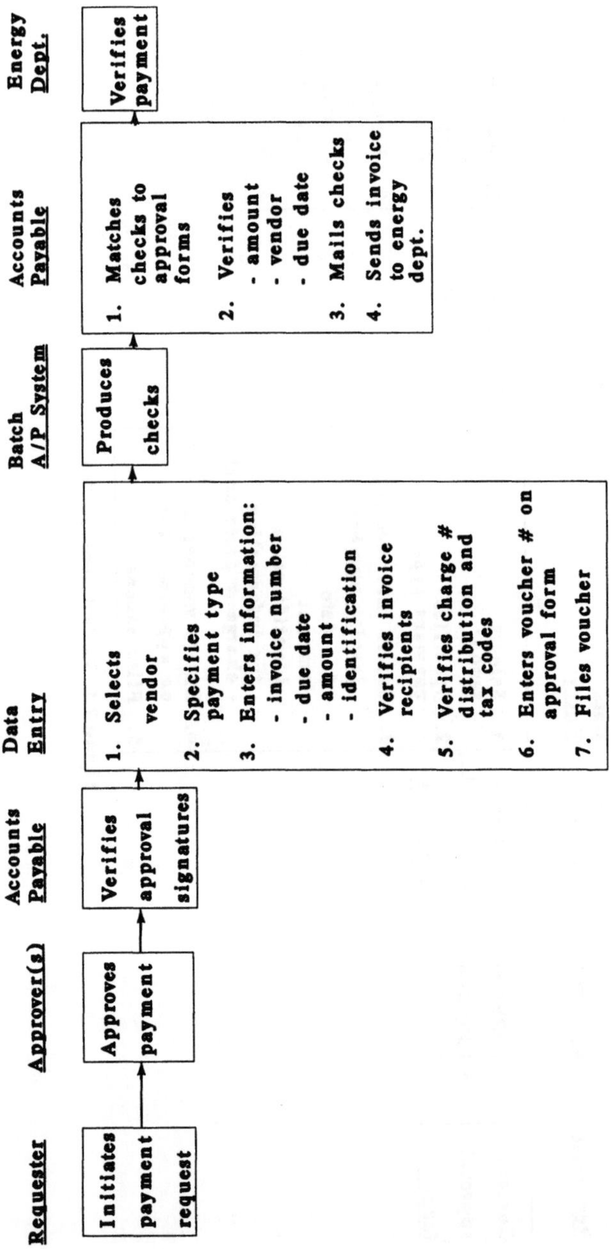

Figure 7.2. Utility payments processing flow.

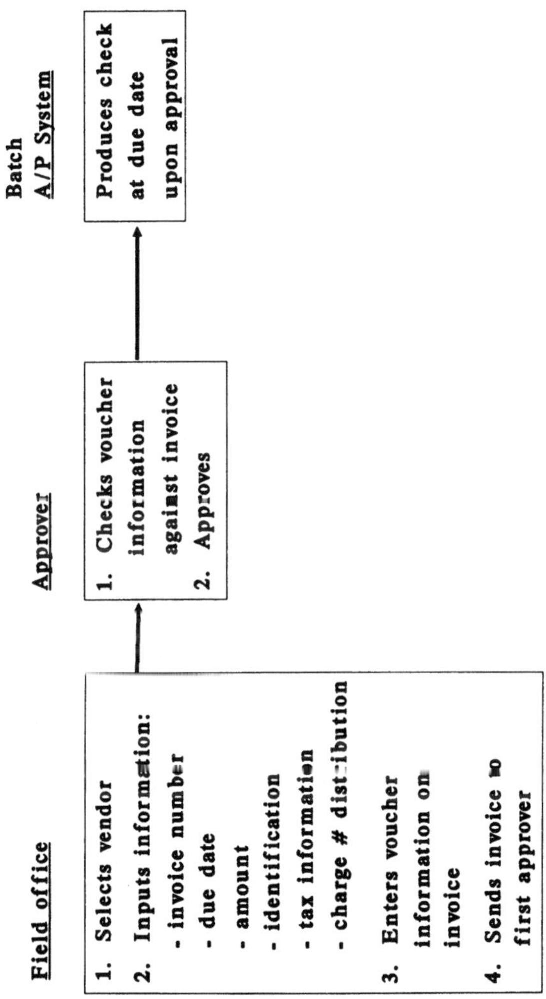

Figure 7.3. Field invoice processing flow.

requests (payroll, subscriptions, seminars, company dues, luncheons, etc.), patent fees, manual releases against blanket purchase orders, and payments against manual orders. Utility bills and field invoices have unique external processing sequences.

For standard processing (Fig. 7.1), accounts payable would receive an approval form, usually accompanied by an invoice,* and then manually verify the approval against signature files. The system would then be accessed to

- Choose the correct vendor
- Specify type of payment†
- Enter invoice information including amount, due date, tax codes, identification information (invoice number, date, purchase order number, liability authority, etc.), and charge number distribution.

When the system assigns a voucher number, the accounts payable clerk enters it on the approval form, which is then filed.‡ When the due date arrives, the batch system produces the check. It then goes to accounts payable, where it is manually verified against the approval form with respect to such items as vendor, address, and amount. The check is then mailed.¶

External processing of utility payments differs from standard processing (Fig. 7.2). First, the accounts payable clerk does not need to input the charge number distribution since the standard distribution for utility accounts is maintained in the system. Second, the voucher can be created after receipt of a late billing notification produced by the system. Third, copies of some invoices are sent to appropriate members of the Energy Department, who in turn administer these contracts by checking the amount against utility usage.

Payment of field invoices by VIPS eliminates check writing in 350 different field locations (Fig. 7.3). Invoice information is entered at the field location. The voucher is then put in an approval queue as specified by the system. The package of invoices for approval is sent to the approver, who then calls up the respective vouchers for approval with respect to vendor, amount, and distribu-

*Invoices are not received for payroll and tax department transactions.

†While most payments are made with checks produced by the batch accounts payable system, some are made with manual checks, bank transfers, or bank drafts. These payments cover single or multiple invoices. In each case, VIPS is used mainly to record information such as check number, bank transfer number and code, and draft number. In addition, foreign currency is converted to liability authority currency for charge number distribution.

‡At any time prior to the due date, the date can be changed, the voucher voided, or a discrepancy removed. A discrepancy becomes set if the payment causes the total value of a blanket order to be exceeded.

¶Checks are normally mailed directly to the vendor, although in some cases they are sent to the requester.

tion. Once the invoice is approved at all required levels, it goes to the batch accounts payable system, where a check is produced as the due date approaches. When these checks are sent to accounts payable, they are coded as field invoices and not reviewed thereafter by the accounts payable clerk.

Analysis of processing flows shows how users interact with the system and answers three questions:

- Who are the users who interact with this system?
  In this case, they are accounts payable personnel, field office personnel, and the energy department.
- What are all the outputs from this system?
  They are checks, the report of "Late Utility Bills," the report of "Unapproved Vouchers Awaiting the Assignment of an Approver," and a data base of vouchers.
- What does the organization do with the outputs?
  It sends out checks.
  It reviews late billing notification to determine what utility bills are missing.
  It assigns approvers for field invoices.
  It voids or changes vouchers that have not been paid.
  It uses the data base to inquire about vouchers, payments, distribution, check request, and/or utilities.
  It tracks hazardous waste.
  It determines tax liability.

As in any risk identification study, it is necessary to develop reasonable boundaries for the analysis. Several factors bounded this analysis. First, it was decided to analyze only the online portion of the system. The client organization wanted to determine how the analysis would work by evaluating its effectiveness on a small system. Batch programs and description were unavailable for this study. To proceed with the analysis, it was assumed that the batch system had no failure risk. Although it was expected that this assumption would yield somewhat optimistic estimates of failure risk, the batch system could eventually be analyzed to adjust estimates.

It was assumed that all vouchers would eventually be paid. It is reasonable to expect a vendor to send a duplicate bill if payment is not received; hence the hazard of not sending checks at all was excluded from this analysis.

7.2.2. Major Hazards

External processing sequences were reviewed to determine the major hazards resulting from failures of this system. Study of the proposed system's use indicated the following system functions:

- Send checks
- Verify blanket order totals
- Distribute charges
- Obtain approvals
- Void vouchers
- Supply voucher information
- Maintain identification information

The analysis considered hazards that could result if a problem arose with one or more of these functions. For example, the main objective of the system was to enter data needed to produce checks when due. A major hazard, therefore, is *not producing checks by the due date*.* Second, these checks may be invalid either because of *wrong vendor information* or *incorrect amount*. The system would also be used to distribute charges. A major hazard in this regard is *invalid distribution of charge numbers*. The system would also be used to archive invoices for hazardous waste as well as to maintain inventory valuation codes and quantities for certain classes of raw-material purchases. Hazards involving these functions are *invalid records for hazardous waste* and *invalid inventory records*.

Also considered was how the environment might change. The company would be distributing the data input to many field offices; some might have personnel who are not sufficiently experienced with the accounts payable systems. This disparity may contribute to *wrong vendor* or *duplicate payments*. In addition, the approval process can contribute to *not paying by due date* because of the time it may take to complete the required levels of approvals.

A summary of the ten major hazards is shown in Table 7.1. These hazards were reviewed with the users and system developers to insure completeness. Generally, these hazards can occur for each type of transaction and have different consequences for each.

7.2.3. Accident Scenarios

Once the external processing sequences were understood, accident scenarios were developed to describe how hazards could occur. Operator actions that could cause (hazard initiators) or alter (hazard mitigators) the occurrence of these hazards were identified. In this case, the accident sequence varied for different transactions because external processing differed. These differences resulted in unique external exposure of each hazard for each transaction type. For example, Figs. 7.4, 7.5, and 7.6 show accident sequences related to the

*Several months prior to the adoption of this system, the company had incurred a $25,000 penalty on a utility bill that had been paid late.

Table 7.1. Major Hazards

1.	Do not pay vendor by due date
2.	Pay wrong amount
3.	Charge wrong accounts
4.	Tax information incorrect
5.	Pay wrong vendor
6.	Invalid records for hazardous waste
7.	Invalid inventory records
8.	Clerical work—low (e.g., manual input of information)
9.	Clerical work—high (e.g., lose track of trail: payments, check numbers)
10.	Duplicate payments

hazard of *paying the wrong amount* for each of three processing sequences. For standard processing and utilities (Figs. 7.4 and 7.5), hazard initiation is similar but hazard mitigation differs. Some utility bill amounts are verified twice when checks are produced, by accounts payable personnel and by the energy department. Check requests and other vouchers that involve standard processing are verified only once, by the accounts payable department. It is expected that the probability of sending bills for the wrong amount will be smaller for utility bills than for other checks.

For field invoices (Fig. 7.6), hazard initiation and mitigation are very different. First, field invoices involve different personnel (field versus internal accounts payable) who are usually not as familiar with the system. Second, the hazard can be initiated by invalid initial input or approval using the system. Finally, hazard mitigation is very different. Since checks produced are not verified externally before they are sent out, the external probability of sending checks with the wrong amount (given system error) is expected to be much higher for field invoices than for any other processing type.

7.2.4. Failure Modes

Failure modes analysis pinpoints how erroneous system information contributes to the accident sequences. For example, Fig. 7.7 shows the fault tree for *accounts payable entering a late utility payment*, one of the events contributing to the hazard, *not paying on time*. Erroneous system processing can contribute to this event in two ways when paying utility bills. First, a system problem can contribute to the inability to accept the information necessary to produce checks. Second, accounts payable may not be aware that the bill is missing, possibly because of a system failure in producing the late billing notification report. For standard processing of check requests, only the prior event of system inability to accept information is a potential system contributor to the hazard.

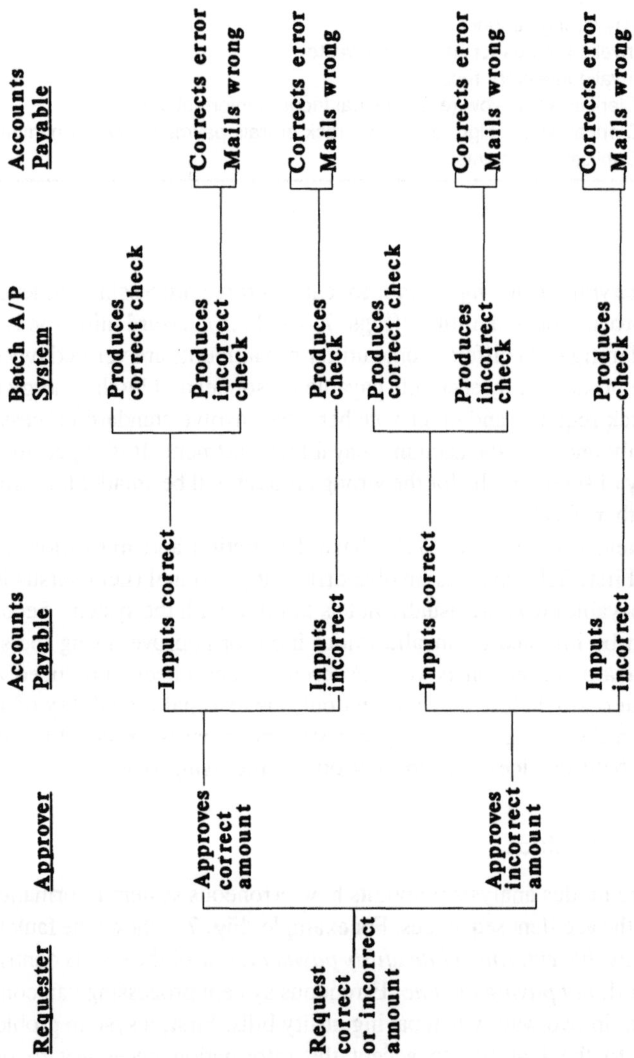

Figure 7.4. Sample event tree: Pays wrong amount with standard processing.

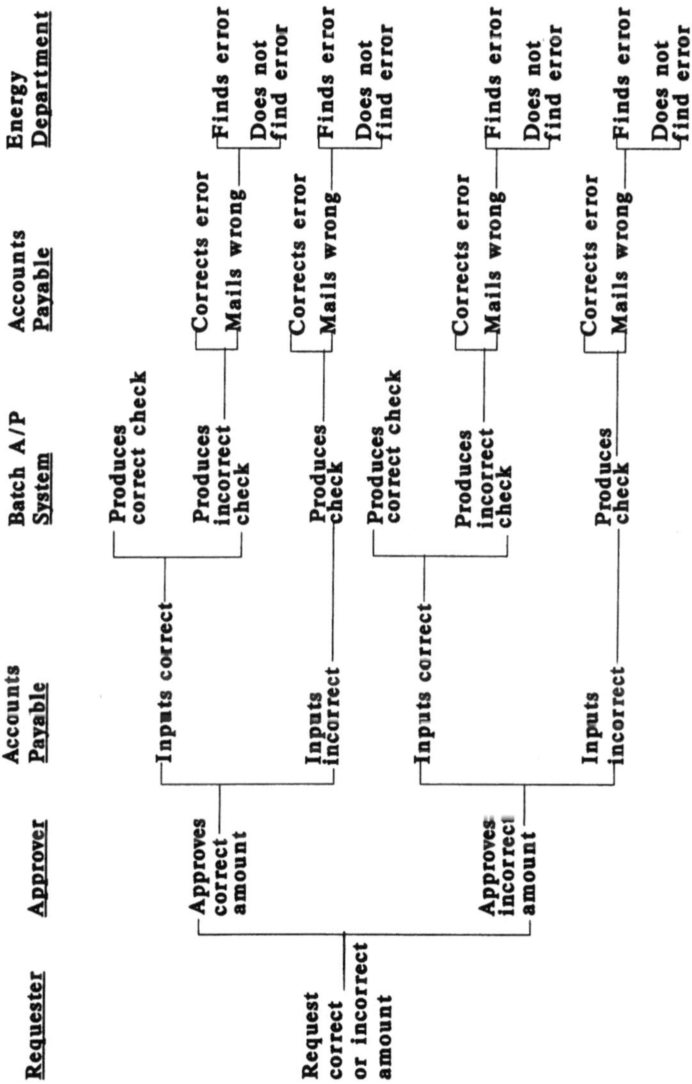

Figure 7.5. Sample event tree: Pays wrong amount to utilities.

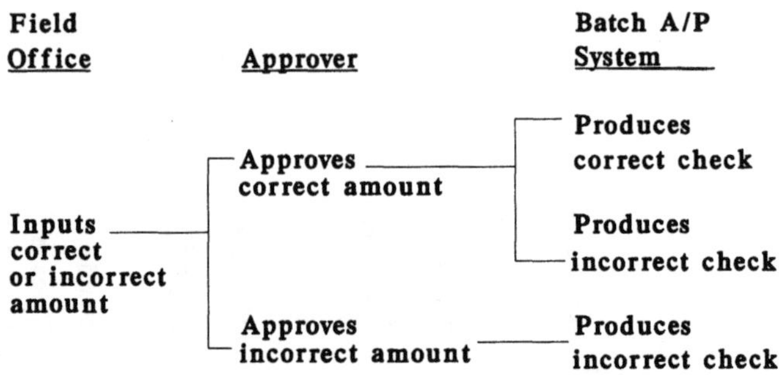

Figure 7.6. Sample event tree: Pays wrong amount on field invoices.

The latter event, notification of late bill, can not be caused by information from the system because the system does not keep track of late billings for check requests and other types of vouchers.

7.2.5. Consequence Assessment

The expected consequence of each hazard differs for each transaction type. The liability of each hazard for each type of processing is adjusted by its external probability of occurrence.

First, liability is determined. If a payment is not received by the due date, the liability is late penalties. If a payment is sent to the wrong vendor, the money can be lost completely, or it can be returned with only interest lost. In addition, a late penalty can be charged by the correct vendor. If the wrong amount of money is sent, overpayment can result in loss of the money or loss of interest on any repayment. Underpayment can result in penalty charges. In many cases, a failure results only in additional clerical work, which can involve the need to enter voucher data directly to the payable system, bypassing VIPS. It could also involve additional effort to search for and correct invalid information maintained by the system.

Both the number and the amount of transactions were considered in computing the value of the transactions processed per month. The expected value of utility transactions, for example, is equal to \$136,051,200 per month (50 bills averaging \$2.7 million and 1752 bills averaging \$600). The expected value of check requests equals \$1,430,100, and the expected value of local invoices is \$1,714,800. Table 7.2 summarizes the monthly dollar value of each type of transaction.

To determine the expected consequence, accident scenarios were reviewed to estimate the external probability of hazards. These scenarios indicate events that can mitigate a hazard. Hazards with many external hazard mitigators

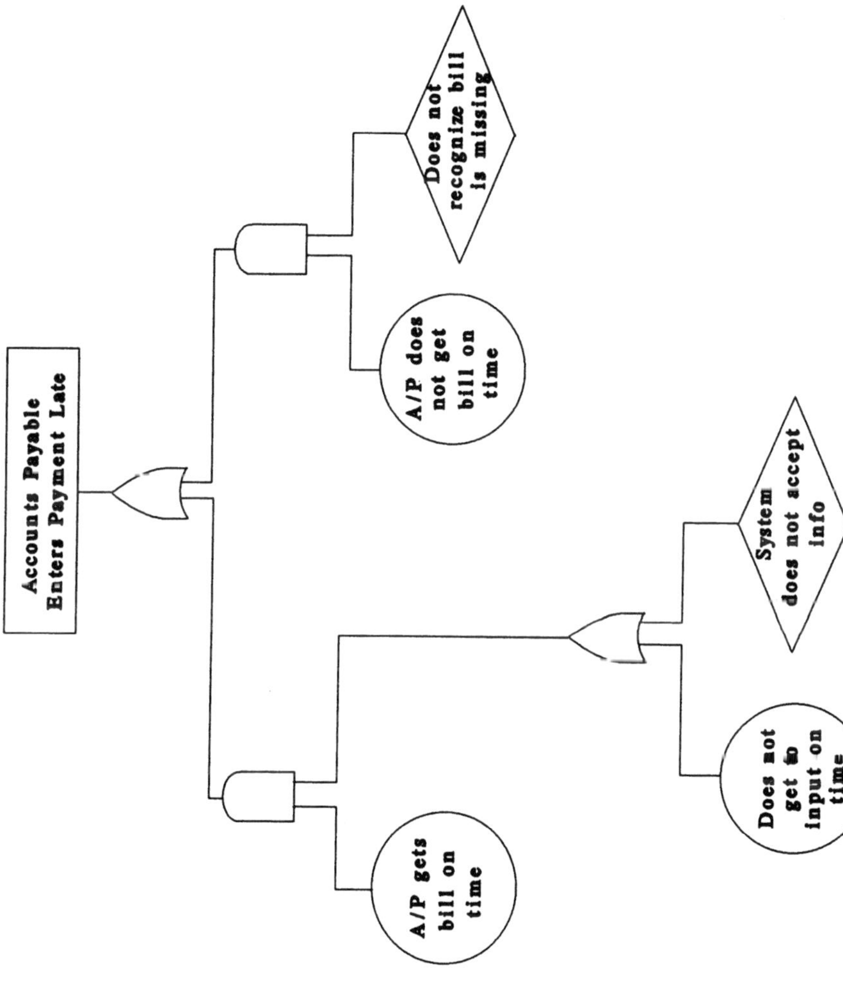

Figure 7.7 Sample fault tree leading to the hazard *does not pay utilities by due date.*

Table 7.2. Transaction Volumes

Processing type	Monthly volume	×	Average value per transaction ($)	=	Monthly value of transaction ($)
Check requests	4,767		300		1,430,100
Manual releases—blanket orders	5,355		300		1,606,500
Utility bills—large	50		2,700,000		
—small	1,752		600		
—total	1,802				136,051,200
Patent fees	140		200		28,000
Local invoices	5,716		300		1,714,800
Generic	145		300		43,500
Distribution only	350		None		—
Total	18,275				140,874,100

generally have smaller external probabilities of occurrence and therefore less external exposure.

To illustrate the consequence assessment, consider the hazard *paying the wrong amount*. General liability is assessed for a specific type of transaction and then adjusted by the probability of occurrence of the hazard based upon the external processing sequence. To compute the liability, assume there is an equal chance of overpayment or underpayment. Payment error generally involves either transposed digits (899 instead of 989) or slipped decimal point (e.g., 9000 instead of 900). While it is difficult to anticipate the amount of the error, the average amount of underpayment was estimated at 50% of the value of the voucher, whereas the average amount of overpayment was estimated at five times the value of the voucher.* Underpayments incur a late penalty charge of 1.6% per month. An overpayment liability can either be loss of the total amount of the overpayment (if not repaid) or interest on the overpayment estimated at 1% per month (if the vendor returns the overpayment). The average time for return was estimated to be three months, and the probability of an overpayment being returned is 0.7. Therefore, the liability is equal to 81% of the value of the transactions processed per month (see Fig. 7.8).

The external probability that checks will be mailed for the wrong amount is 0.001—relatively low because accounts payable personnel review these payments before they are mailed. This probability represents the probability that

*While it is recognized that slipped digits of more than one place could result in larger losses, it is expected that these will be recognized more quickly.

Liability = Probability of underpayment × Loss due to underpayment + Probability of overpayment × Loss due to overpayment

Loss due to underpayment = Penalty on average amount underpaid (1.6%/month × 0.5 × $ value of transaction)
Loss due to overpayment = (Probability payment is returned × average loss of interest) + (Probability payment is not returned × average loss of payment)
Loss due to overpayment = (0.7 × 1%/month × 3 months × 5 × average value of transactions) + (.03 × 5 × average value of transactions)

Liability = $ value of transactions × [(0.5 × 0.008) + (0.5 × 1.605)]
= $ value of transactions × 0.8065

External probability = Probability of mailing payment for wrong amount (given software failure)

External exposure = Expected consequence of hazard given software failure

	Check requests	Blanket orders	Patent fees	Generic payment	Local invoices	Utility payment
$ value of transaction	1,430,100	1,606,500	28,000	43,500	1,714,800	136,045,200
Liability	1,153,376	1,295,642	22,582	35,083	1,382,986	109,720,450
External probability	0.001	0.001	0.001	0.001	0.005	0.0001
External exposure	1,153.38	1,295.64	22.58	35.08	6,914.93	10,972.05

Figure 7.8. Consequence assessment for the hazard *pay wrong amount*.

personnel fail to correctly identify errors in the amount.* The accident scenarios in Figs. 7.4 and 7.5 show additional external hazard mitigators for sending utility payments for the wrong amount compared to check requests and other vouchers.† The probability of mailing a check for the wrong amount (given system error) was smaller for utilities compared to other processing. On the other hand, the probability was estimated to be five times greater for local invoices because these are verified only when approved rather than before mailing (see Fig. 7.8). Although subjective, these estimates appeared reasonable, having been developed from analysis of the external environment in conjunction with the system users.

Probability estimates were multiplied by total liability estimates to determine the expected consequence, or external exposure. The external exposure resulting from *paying the wrong amount* when the software fails to provide correct information is shown for each transaction type. Utility bills reflect the highest external exposure. Even though the probability that the incorrect amount would not be noticed was low, the high dollar value of these transactions increased exposure. The external exposure of this hazard for local invoices is very high. Although the dollar value of these transactions was considerably less than in the case of utilities, the probability that the incorrect amount would go unnoticed was higher because these payments would not be verified prior to mailing. The external exposure for patent fees and generic payments is quite low, involving lower transaction values plus being verified before mailing.

Table 7.3 provides the complete list of consequence assessments for each hazard and transaction type. (The liability and probability assumptions involved in these assessments are summarized in Appendix C.3.)

7.3. MODULE EXPOSURE ASSESSMENT

The system structure was analyzed to determine the fault potential and use of each module. Since the voucher system was small and modular, this was a fairly straightforward task.

7.3.1. Description of System

This online system consisted of 31 modules. Most of these modules form the new Voucher Input Processing System, providing menu access, database queries, processing for each of the different types of vouchers, and updating of

*Note that exposure estimates were based upon proposed plans for external validation of checks by accounts payable personnel before mailing. Should accounts payable decide not to perform this task, the external exposure would increase.

†This is because they are reviewed twice after production of checks by the system.

Table 7.3. Consequence Assessments ($/Month)

Hazard	Check requests	Blanket orders	Patent fees	Ge-neric	Invoices with approval	Utilities
Do not pay vendor by due date	2.29	25.70	0.05	0.07	27.44	2,176.82
Pay wrong amount	1,153.38	1,295.64	22.58	35.08	6,914.93	10,972.52
Charge wrong accounts	7,150.50	8,032.50	210.00	217.50	3,429.60	2,776.50
Tax information incorrect	514.84	578.34	0.00	15.66	617.32	489.73
Pay wrong vendor	40.90	45.95	0.80	1.24	245.22	972.77
Invalid records for hazardous waste	0.00	1,363.75	0.00	0.00	1,454.00	0.00
Invalid inventory records	2,432.50	535.00	0.00	220.00	0.00	125.86
Clerical work—low	715.05	803.25	21.00	21.75	857.40	270.30
Clerical work—high	2,383.50	2,677.50	70.00	72.50	2,858.00	901.00
Duplicate payments	4.59	5.16	0.09	0.14	0.55	218.36

the data base. Several modules involved new processing in the Accounts Payable system that was needed to maintain utility information as well as provide information for invoice approvals. Table 7.4 enumerates each of these modules.

These modules were developed using an application development system that was marketed as fourth generation. This classification is somewhat questionable. Considerable controversy surrounds the definition of a 4GL (Martin, 1985). According to one recent definition, 4GL encompasses nonprocedural programming languages as well as all tools for the design of application systems that incorporate prototyping-oriented transaction development, standardized interface to a relational data base, and a report generator (Lehner, 1990). While

Table 7.4. Module Description and Exposure

Module	Description	Type	Difficulty[a]
VP01	Master menu	Menu	High
VP02	Processing submenu	Menu	Low
VP04	Maintenance submenu	Menu	Low
VP11	Voucher summary	Processing[b]	Medium
VP21	Request for check	Update	Medium
VP22	Utility payment	Update	High
VP23	Patent fee payment	Update	Low
VP24	Invoice with approval	Update	High
VP25	Blanket order payment	Update	High
VP32	Utility distribution	Update	Low
VP34	Generic distribution	Update	High
VP37	Chemical freight distribution	Update	High
VP41	Invoice processing	Update	Low
VP42	Utility account inquiry	Query	High
VP61	Invoice approval	Processing	High
VP62	Vendor name select	Processing	Medium
VP65	Special handling window	Processing	Low
VP66	Remit-to-select	Processing	Medium
VP67	Payments options	Processing	Medium
VP68	Change voucher	Update	Low
VP83	Payment inquiry	Query	High
VP84	Distribution inquiry	Query	Medium
VP86	Voucher inquiry	Query	Medium
VP87	Check request inquiry	Query	Medium
AP85	Utility account maintenance	Update	High
AP86	Utility account parameters	Update	Low
AP93	Approver/backup	Update	Low
AP94	Approver level	Update	Low
AP95	Approver maintenance	Update	Low
AP97	Backup maintenance	Update	Low
AP98	Approver maint submenu	Update	Low

[a]Difficulty estimates were based upon the developer's perceptions.
[b]Processing modules do not update any files.

this application system did include a series of screen-driven development tools that provided screen prototyping as well as a standardized interface to a relational data base, programmers still wrote procedural code similar to COBOL.

7.3.2. Module Fault Potential Set

Assigning modules to hazards was relatively straightforward due to the system's small size and modularity. Table 7.5 completely maps modules to hazards for this system.

Failures due to faults in menu modules, such as VP01, VP02, and VP04, generally lead to extra clerical work, possibly requiring data entry to the batch system by manual means. Menu modules do not process any data that could result in other hazards. Faults in inquiry modules generally lead to additional clerical work, such as tracking down vouchers, payments, or invoices. However, since these modules do not modify any data, faults in these modules generally do not lead to any other hazard. The voucher summary module, VP11, provides the user with the voucher number and updates the database with vendor name and code, payment amount, invoice number, date, location, purchase order number, and discrepancy information. Processing faults in this module can lead to *not paying on time*, *paying the wrong amount*, *wrong vendor*, *duplicate payments*, or simply *additional clerical work*. The check-request processing module, VP21, verifies all of this data as it is input by the user and processes tax information. Faults here could lead to *invalid tax information* in addition to the hazards identified for module VP11.

7.3.3. Use Distribution

System use distribution was based on the expected number of transactions of each processing type, as shown in Table 7.6, based on projections from historical processing.

Each module's use distribution was developed from the system use distribution based on the module's function. Table 7.7 outlines some module use distributions. Module VP11 (voucher summary) is used for all data entry except distribution. Module VP21 is used to enter data for check requests, whereas module VP22 is used for data entry for utility bills only. Module VP34 (generic distribution) is used to enter charge information for all data except utilities. It was assumed that Module VP01 (master menu) would be used 26% of the time for all VIPS functions, based on the assumption that similar transactions would be entered by the same people so that users need to access the menus only once each day.*

*The system does not require return to the main menu when processing a similar transaction. It was expected that users would sign on to a particular function once per day, the only exception being field invoices, which are expected to be entered individually.

Table 7.5. Module/Hazard Map

Module	Not on time	Wrong amount	Wrong accounts	Tax information	Wrong vendor	Hazardous waste	Inventory record	Clerical—low	Clerical—high	Duplicate payment
VP01								×		
VP02								×		
VP04								×		
VP11	×	×			×				×	×
VP21	×	×		×	×				×	×
VP22	×	×		×	×				×	×
VP23	×	×			×				×	×
VP24	×	×		×	×	×			×	×
VP25	×	×		×	×	×			×	×
VP32			×	×	×				×	
VP34			×	×					×	
VP37							×		×	
VP41	×	×		×	×				×	×
VP42									×	
VP61	×	×	×		×	×			×	×
VP62					×			×		
VP65	×	×							×	×
VP66					×			×		×
VP67									×	×
VP68	×							×		
VP83									×	
VP84			×						×	
VP86								×	×	
VP87									×	
AP85			×	×					×	
AP86	×								×	
AP93	×							×		×
AP94	×							×		×
AP95	×							×		×
AP97	×							×		×
AP98	×							×		×

Table 7.6. System Use Distribution

Processing type	Transactions per month	Probability of use
Data entry	18,275	0.349
Check requests	4,767	0.091
Manual releases against blanket purchase orders	5,355	0.102
Utility bills	1,802	0.034
Patent fees	140	0.003
Local invoices	5,716	0.109
Other	145	0.003
Distribution only	350	0.007
Void/change/release[a]	1,795	0.034
Invoice approvals[b]	8,002	0.152
Inquiries[c]		
Payments	7,170	0.136
Distribution	7,310	0.139
Voucher	7,310	0.139
Check requests	1,907	0.036
Utility payments	721	0.014
Accounts payable maintenance		
Utility maintenance	15	0.0002
Approval maintenance	15	0.0002
Special processing		
Automated checks	17,361[d]	
Know vendor code	9,137[e]	
Know remit to code	3,655[f]	

[a]Assumes 10% of vouchers require void/change/release processing.
[b]Assumes 70% require one approval, 20% two approvals, and 10% three approvals.
[c]Assumes inquiries are 40% of transactions.
[d]Assumes 5% of the payments are not automated checks.
[e]Assumes accounts payable knows vendor code 50% of the time.
[f]Assumes accounts payable knows remit to code 20% of the time.

7.3.4. Module Exposure

Module exposure was estimated by considering the expected consequences of each hazard for each module use, since consequence is a function of module use. It was assumed that should a failure occur, its consequence would most likely result in hazards involving additional clerical work—primarily because developers generally pay more attention to the more critical code. Other hazards were assumed to be only 1/3 as likely. Figs. 7.9 and 7.10 illustrate the exposure analysis exposure assessments for Modules VP21 and VP11.

Only one use branch is involved with module VP21 because it is used only for check requests. The probability of each of the six hazards was based on the assumption that clerical work will most likely result. The expected consequence is that of the hazards for check requests, from Table 7.3. The expected exposure was computed by finding the product of probability and consequence for each

Table 7.7. Module Use Distribution

Module	Description	Probability
VP01	Master menu	0.26[a]
VP11	Voucher summary	0.342
	Check requests	0.091
	Blanket orders	0.102
	Utility bills	0.034
	Patent fees	0.003
	Local Invoices	0.109
	Other	0.003
VP22	Utility payment	0.034
VP34	Generic distribution	0.315
	Check requests	0.091
	Blanket orders	0.102
	Patent fees	0.003
	Local invoices	0.109
	Other	0.003
	Distribution only	0.007

[a]This probability was derived from analysis of the expected use of this module, the main menu. For accounts payable data entry and inquiries, it is assumed that this menu will be accessed only once per day for each type of transaction. For field invoices, it is assumed that this module will be accessed once for each transaction.

hazard, adding those products, and multiplying the sum by the use probability of the whole module.

Module VP11 has several uses. The identified hazards for this module are shown for each use, along with their probability of occurrence should the module have a fault resulting in failure. The expected consequence is the external exposure for the type of processing. Thus, the expected consequence is $2.29 when the system contributes to failure to pay a check request by the due date. However, if utility bills are not paid by the due date, the expected consequence is $2176.72 because of the larger magnitude of these bills and their external processing (see Table 7.3). The exposure for each use is equal to the external probability of the hazard times its consequence. These exposures are then multiplied by the probability of each use. The sum of these products for the various uses is the total module exposure, $574.

7.4. MODULE FAILURE LIKELIHOOD

In the first two case studies (Chapters 5 and 6) actual code size was used to develop initial estimates of module failure likelihood. Since the VIPS study was

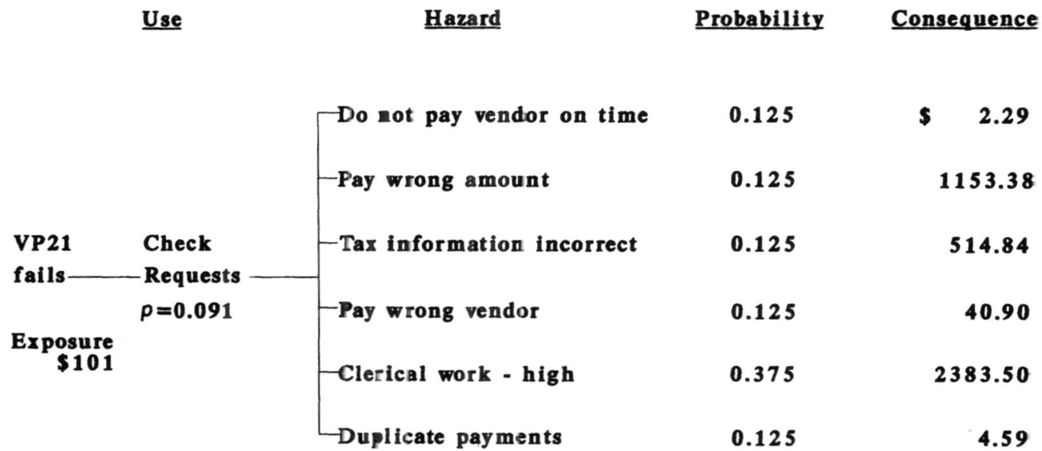

Figure 7.9. Exposure analysis of module VP21.

VP11 fails

Exposure $574

Use	Hazard	Probability	Consequence
Check Requests $p=0.091$	Do not pay vendor by due date	0.143	$ 2.29
	Pay wrong amount	0.143	1153.38
	Pay wrong vendor	0.143	40.90
	Clerical work - high	0.428	2383.50
	Duplicate payments	0.143	4.59
Blanket Orders $p=0.102$	Do not pay vendor by due date	0.143	25.70
	Pay wrong amount	0.143	1295.64
	Pay wrong vendor	0.143	45.95
	Clerical work - high	0.428	2677.50
	Duplicate payments	0.143	5.16
Utilities $p=0.034$	Do not pay vendor by due date	0.143	2176.72
	Pay wrong amount	0.143	10972.52
	Pay wrong vendor	0.143	972.77
	Clerical work - high	0.428	901.00
	Duplicate payments	0.143	218.36
Patent fees $p=0.003$	Do not pay vendor by due date	0.143	0.05
	Pay wrong amount	0.143	22.58
	Pay wrong vendor	0.143	0.80
	Clerical work - high	0.428	70.00
	Duplicate payments	0.143	0.09
Field Invoices $p=0.109$	Do not pay vendor by due date	0.143	27.44
	Pay wrong amount	0.143	6914.93
	Pay wrong vendor	0.143	245.22
	Clerical work - high	0.428	2858
	Duplicate payments	0.143	0.55
Other $p=0.003$	Do not pay vendor by due date	0.143	0.07
	Pay wrong amount	0.143	35.08
	Pay wrong vendor	0.143	1.24
	Clerical work - high	0.428	72.50
	Duplicate payments	0.143	0.14

Figure 7.10. Exposure analysis of module VP11.

Table 7.8. Hours of Development Effort by Module Type and Degree of Difficulty

	Difficulty		
Type	Low	Medium	High
Menu	12	—	18
Update	56	70	100
Processing	36	60	92
Query	56	70	86

performed prior to the development of the code, however, estimates of the code size had to be used. These estimates were developed using the anticipated programming effort predicted by the developer. Table 7.4 lists the modules by type and level of difficulty, and Table 7.8 summarizes the estimated effort for developing each type of module. VP41, an update module of low difficulty, was completed first and found to have approximately 940 executable lines of code. Estimates of the code size of the other modules were based on their relative development effort compared to this module.

To determine the initial number of errors per line of code, failure data were reviewed for a similar system that had been developed in the same environment using the same application development system.* All problem reports generated during $3\frac{1}{4}$ years of operation of this system were reviewed. Approximately 14 errors were found in eight online modules. These modules were all update or processing modules with medium to high difficulty. The average number of errors per 1000 lines of code varied from 1.0 to 1.5. Musa *et al.* (1987) summarized errors found in complete systems (generally developed with third-generation tools) ranging up to 11,000 lines of code. In Musa's study, the average number of faults found in operation was 1.48 per 1000 lines. Little research has examined differences between the number of errors found in systems developed using third- versus fourth-generation software languages. One study found little difference in the maintenance life cycles of third- versus fourth-generation software, leading the author to conclude that actual maintenance costs arise from actual use of the application system. The major factor is not the programming language, but the dynamism of the environment and the experience and acceptance of the user (Lehner, 1990).

To estimate the number of faults in the VIPS modules prior to operation, an average estimate of 1.3 errors/kloc was applied to the estimated module size. Table 7.9 presents a complete array of estimated numbers of faults by module.

*Errors per line of code was believed to be a reasonable measure since the application development system involved a procedural language requiring coding lines of code.

Table 7.9. Estimated Number of Faults

Module	Estimated size	Estimated number of faults prior to operation
VP01	565	0.735
VP02	565	0.735
VP04	565	0.735
VP11	950	1.235
VP21	1093	1.421
VP22	1420	1.846
VP23	950	1.235
VP24	1420	1.846
VP25	1420	1.846
VP32	950	1.235
VP34	1420	1.846
VP37	1420	1.846
VP41	950	1.235
VP42	1420	1.846
VP61	1420	1.846
VP62	950	1.235
VP65	807	1.049
VP66	950	1.235
VP67	950	1.235
VP68	950	1.235
VP83	1420	1.846
VP84	1093	1.421
VP86	1093	1.421
VP87	1093	1.421
AP85	1420	1.846
AP86	950	1.235
AP94	950	1.235
AP97	950	1.235
AP98	950	1.235

Adequate execution information or sufficient failure data on the operational system was not available to determine the distribution of the per fault hazard rate. Hence, this information was estimated using the same procedure as for the funds system. The per fault hazard rate was estimated as

$$\theta = (r/I_s Q_x)k$$

where θ = per fault hazard rate, r = execution rate (estimated at 3,333,333 object instructions per CPU sec) (Musa *et al.*, 1987), I_s = estimated lines of source code (see Table 7.9), Q_x = average expansion ratio (estimated at 3) (Jones, 1986), k =fault exposure ratio (estimated at 4.2×10^{-7} failures/fault (Musa *et al.*, 1987).

Table 7.10. Initial Estimates of Failure Likelihood

Module	Estimated number of faults	Per faults hazard rate (failure/fault/sec)	Execution time per month (CPU sec)	Expected number of failures within first month of operation
VP01	0.735	0.000786	6.939	0.0040
VP02	0.725	0.000786	2.963	0.0017
VP04	0.735	0.000786	0.015	—
VP11	1.235	0.000467	15.326	0.0088
VP21	1.421	0.000406	4.689	0.0027
VP22	1.846	0.000312	2.303	0.0013
VP23	1.235	0.000467	0.119	0.0001
VP24	1.846	0.000312	7.305	0.0042
VP25	1.846	0.000312	6.844	0.0040
VP32	1.235	0.000467	1.541	0.0009
VP34	1.846	0.000312	21.052	0.0121
VP37	1.846	0.000312	3.508	0.0020
VP41	1.235	0.000467	0.124	0.0001
VP42	1.846	0.000312	0.921	0.0005
VP61	1.846	0.000312	10.227	0.0059
VP62	1.235	0.000467	7.812	0.0045
VP65	1.049	0.000550	0.036	—
VP66	1.235	0.000467	12.500	0.0072
VP67	1.235	0.000467	0.766	0.0004
VP68	1.235	0.000467	1.535	0.0009
VP83	1.846	0.000312	9.163	0.0053
VP84	1.421	0.000406	7.191	0.0041
VP86	1.421	0.000406	7.191	0.0041
VP87	1.421	0.000406	1.876	0.0011
AP85	1.846	0.000312	0.019	—
AP86	1.235	0.000467	0.013	—
AP93	1.235	0.000467	0.013	—
AP94	1.235	0.000467	0.013	—
AP95	1.235	0.000467	0.013	—
AP97	1.235	0.000467	0.013	—
AP98	1.235	0.000467	0.013	—

Initial estimates of the number of faults, per fault hazard rate, and failure likelihood are given in Table 7.10.

7.5. INITIAL MODULE RISK ESTIMATES

Initial module risk estimates are shown in Table 7.11. Only three modules have risk of greater than $1/month during the initial month of operation. The generic distribution module (VP34) had the highest risk because distribution information is not externally verified once it is entered. Thus, there is a high

Table 7.11. Initial Assessments of Module Risk

Module	Description	Module exposure ($/month)	Expected number of failures within one month	Module risk ($/month)
VP01	Master menu	95.19	0.0040	0.38
VP02	Processing submenu	94.24	0.0017	0.16
VP04	Maintenance submenu	0.29	—	—
VP11	Voucher summary	574.41	0.0088	5.05
VP21	Request for check	100.65	0.0027	0.27
VP22	Utility payment	75.24	0.0013	0.10
VP23	Patent fee payment	0.09	0.0001	—
VP24	Invoice with approval	215.78	0.0042	0.91
VP25	Blanket order payment	115.76	0.0040	0.46
VP32	Utility distribution	53.62	0.0009	0.05
VP34	Generic distribution	1,158.17	0.0121	14.01
VP37	Chemical freight distribution	84.75	0.0020	0.17
VP41	Invoice processing	0.09	0.0001	—
VP42	Utility acct inquiry	1.24	0.0005	—
VP61	Invoice approval	381.19	0.0059	2.25
VP62	Vendor name select	102.36	0.0045	0.46
VP65	Special handling window	2.55	—	—
VP66	Remit-to-select	132.43	0.0072	0.95
VP67	Payments options	31.31	0.0004	0.01
VP68	Change voucher	16.59	0.0009	0.01
VP83	Payment inquiry	16.66	0.0053	0.09
VP84	Distribution inquiry	16.66	0.0041	0.07
VP86	Voucher inquiry	16.66	0.0041	0.07
VP87	Check request inquiry	8.66	0.0011	0.01
AP85	Utility account maintenance	56.51	—	—
AP86	Utility account parameters	41.89	—	—
AP93	Approver/backup	79.28	—	—
AP94	Approver level	79.28	—	—
AP95	Approver maintenance	79.28	—	—
AP97	Backup maintenance	79.28	—	—
AP98	Appr maint submenu	79.28	—	—

probability of financial exposure resulting from clerical effort to fix these errors. In addition, because the module is an update module of high difficulty, it may be more prone to error. Finally, it is used frequently each month since it is required for all transactions except utility payments. The voucher summary module (VP11), while of only medium difficulty, had high exposure since it provided the information to the batch system for all transaction types. The invoice approval module (VP61) had high risk because no external review of the payment information occurs after the module provides information to the batch system.

Although the module is used only for field invoices, it is a module of high difficulty.

Twelve modules had risk lower than $0.01 per month, and an additional seven had risk below $0.10 per month. The results indicate the importance of considering both components of risk, exposure and expected number of failures. In some cases risk was low even if the expected number of failures was fairly high because financial exposure was low. For example, the payment inquiry had low exposure since failure usually leads only to some additional clerical work. In other cases, exposure was high but the expected number of failures was low. For example, the utility distribution screen had some financial exposure but little probability of failure. It was an update module of low difficulty with use limited to utility payments. Again, the results support the contention that focused testing proves most efficient since modules have very different degrees of financial risk.

7.6. UPDATING MODULE RISK ESTIMATES

The module risk estimates were supplied to the software development team as they began programming and testing. Payment modules were developed chronologically in order of increasing risk. Modules with the lowest risk were used for test and debugging purposes. It was hoped that this practice would reduce the probability of failure in higher-risk modules with similar functions.

Table 7.12 shows the number of faults found when testing each module as well as the prior classification of the module's type and degree of difficulty. These original classifications appeared to predict faults fairly well, except for four modules that had higher than anticipated numbers of faults for their classification: the payment options module (VP67), the change voucher module (VP68), the generic processing module (VP41), and the check request module (VP21).

Two update modules of high difficulty, VP24 and VP25, the field invoice and blanket order payments modules, did not have any faults even though they were high-difficulty update modules. Since these were the final payment modules developed, they were neither tested nor used as frequently as the other modules. It is hypothesized that their faults have not yet been found.

The absence of parameters for the prior distribution of the per fault hazard rate prevented the parameter distributions from being updated in the manner described in Chapter 4. However, test information was used to revise estimates of the number of faults in the four modules identified above. In addition, the amount of test time was considered in recalculating failure likelihood estimates since more testing is assumed to reduce operational failure likelihood.

Table 7.13 displays all modules whose estimated risk was revised with the

Table 7.12. Faults Found during Test

Module			
Type	Number	Level of difficulty	Faults
Menu	VP02	Low	0
	VP04	Low	0
	VP01	High	0
Query	VP84	Medium	0
	VP86	Medium	0
	VP87	Medium	0
	VP42	High	0
	VP83	High	1
Processing	VP65	Low	0
	VP62	Medium	0
	VP66	Medium	0
	VP11	Medium	1
	VP67	Medium	2
	VP61	High	2
Update	AP86	Low	0
	AP93	Low	0
	AP94	Low	0
	AP95	Low	0
	AP97	Low	0
	AP98	Low	0
	VP23	Low	0
	VP32	Low	0
	VP65	Low	0
	VP68	Low	1
	VP41	Low	4
	VP21	Medium	2
	VP24	High	0
	VP25	High	0
	VP22	High	1
	VP37	High	2
	VP34	High	3

test information. Estimated risk was reduced for six modules because they had been well tested and the number of failures during testing had been lower than would be expected with the prior estimates. These reductions were, however, generally insignificant: less than 6% in all cases. In three cases (modules VP21, VP67, and VP68), risk estimates increased because the number of failures during testing exceeded the number anticipated by use of the prior estimates. Test information indicated no need to revise risk estimates for the other modules. In fact, while the number of faults found in module VP41 was greater than anticipated, the operational risk remained insignificant due to the great amount of testing of this module as well as its limited operational use.

Table 7.13. Risk Estimates Revised by Means of Test Information

Module		Module risk estimates ($/month)	
Number	Description	Original	Revised
VP01	Master menu	0.38	0.36
VP11	Voucher summary	5.05	4.79
VP21	Request for check	0.27	0.35
VP24	Invoice with approval	0.91	0.90
VP25	Blanket order payment	0.46	0.45
VP34	Generic distribution	14.01	13.32
VP61	Invoice approval	2.25	2.23
VP67	Payments options	0.01	0.02
VP68	Change voucher	0.01	0.02

7.7. COMPARATIVE SUMMARY OF CASE STUDIES AND RESULTS

Each of these three case studies involved financial data processing systems that collected information used to generate financial transactions. All systems had substantial potential financial exposure. However, actual failure risk was found to vary among systems according to two factors:

- external environment
- software and its development

Many organizations use other risk management techniques, with software often being only one element in the risk management plan. Risk associated with manually managing commercial loan transactions, transferring funds by wire, or initiating voucher payments was expected to greatly exceed software failure risk. Software failure risk measurement provides the opportunity to decrease risk and broaden organizational capabilities.

The environment in which the software is installed plays a significant role in establishing software failure risk. Software failure risk is reduced if opportunities exist to verify software output externally. Organizations often use external risk mitigators when exposure is high. In the funds system, high exposure prompted verification of wires not only by callback but through checks against manual logs. In the voucher system, when exposure was high (for example, in processing utility payments), payments were reviewed twice—by accounts payable and by energy department personnel. In the CLS, however, while billing information was reviewed, it was verified against audit reports produced by the system. Hence, software failure risk is a more significant component of its risk profile.

Risk assessment methodology includes the impact of these external risk mitigators on software failure risk. The methodology not only accommodates external risk mitigation but can also be used to determine how and where to include such mitigation. Exposure assessment indicates where exposure is high. The failure likelihood analysis determines where failure is more probable. Users can incorporate different external methods to reduce exposure and manage risk, and different strategies can be evaluated before the system becomes operational.

Software can itself be a significant source of risk. Poorly structured and developed software has a large failure likelihood, which can contribute to high risk. Large noncohesive batch-processing modules in the CLS had high failure likelihood. Failure risk assessment can indicate which modules may require restructuring and more extensive testing because of high exposure.

In all three systems, only a few modules were found to have large failure risk compared to other modules within the system. In fact, a large difference in failure risk generally exists between these few modules and the other modules in the same system. Differences were most pronounced in systems that provided the most varied functionality and software. The CLS, for example, provided a wide variety of functions and consisted of several software components, ranging from the online CICS modules and small report modules to large noncohesive batch-processing modules that served several functions in a single module. On the other hand, the voucher-processing system had more uniformity in the software modules. However, module exposure had a wide range due to differences in function because of the processing of different types of payment. The funds-transfer system had the least variation in risk because the number of different functions was minimal. Thus, while software failure risk varied in all three case studies, the method demonstrated that modules within a system possess varying degrees of risk. Traditional testing methodologies which assume uniform risk are not cost effective.

REFERENCES

Jones, C., *Programming Productivity*, New York: McGraw-Hill, 1986.

Lehner, F., "Cost Comparison for the Development and Maintenance of Application Systems in 3rd and 4th Generation Languages," *Information and Management* **9**, (1990), 131–141.

Martin, J., *Fourth Generation Languages: Volume 1, Principles*, Englewood Cliffs, NJ: Prentice-Hall, 1985.

Musa, J. D., A. Iannino, and K. Okumoto, *Software Reliability: Measurement, Prediction, Application*, New York: McGraw-Hill, 1987.

Part III

Software Failure Risk Management

Chapter 8

Software Requirements and Design

Managing the software development process is a difficult task. It is an art, requiring skillful integration of software technology, economics, and human relations (Boehm and Ross, 1989). The software project manager simultaneously satisfies several constituencies (users, customers, developers, maintainers, and management) whose desires frequently create fundamental conflicts that often result in functional, project, political, financial, technical, or systemic risk. Managing these components of risk involves identifying, measuring, and prioritizing them and developing and implementing plans to manage them. Software failure risk management techniques include modification of the development process to reduce the magnitude or frequency of loss, incorporation of controls to reduce vulnerability, development of recovery procedures, transference of risk to another party by subcontracting or purchase, and avoidance when risks are simply too high. Software failure risk assessment can provide the information to analyze functionality, financial, and project risks associated with failure due to faults in software. This information can modify the development process or suggest changes to system use that will reduce vulnerability.

Project managers generally have distinct but often conflicting cost, schedule, and performance objectives. Labor and computer costs and schedules must be controlled in order to complete projects within budget and on time. When managing large projects that do not involve software, budget and schedule objectives often conflict. If a project is behind schedule, more project personnel are added at an additional cost. However, this strategy is dangerous in software development. Adding more people lengthens, not shortens, the schedule, because software construction involves a great deal of communication (Brooks, 1982). Cost increases generally accompany schedule increases. On the other hand, performance objectives frequently require trade-offs with both schedule and cost. For example, allocating more time to requirements development can reduce errors but adversely impact achievement of early schedule goals. Development and evaluation of alternative designs provides information to improve quality but increases design costs. While additional testing insures that software has minimal errors, this testing increases both cost and schedule. Many trade-offs are required during development, because it is rarely possible to predict performance, schedule, and cost requirements accurately before the start of the project. Software failure risk assessment can help project managers evaluate these trade-offs so that software failure risk is effectively managed.

The software development process defines and translates a problem or need into a set of logical instructions. The first step—problem definition—determines feasibility and requirements; it is often the most difficult phase of the project. Next, requirements are translated into software design, which is in turn implemented into code.

This chapter presents key management decisions in the initial development of software, that is, defining the problem and designing a system to meet requirements. The chapter begins by describing two software process models: the traditional stagewise or waterfall model and the more iterative spiral model. Traditional management decision methods and trade-offs involved in definition, design, and programming phases are reviewed. Software failure risk provides a theoretical basis for project management decisions during the entire software development process. Examples illustrating use of failure risk estimates are drawn from the three case studies introduced in Part II. While risk was actually assessed after the design of all these systems, the use of the failure risk assessment methodology before design is suggested with some examples from these studies.

8.1. SOFTWARE PROCESS MODELS

The software process is the set of actions required to efficiently transform a user's needs into an effective software solution (Humphrey, 1989). A software process model determines the order of these actions and the transition criteria from one stage of action to the next (Boehm, 1988).

During the past two decades, the most widely used software process model has been the waterfall model, in which development proceeds in stagewise fashion with formal elaborated documents often used as completion criteria for entering successive stages, as illustrated in Fig. 8.1. Key project management considerations include the determination of completion criteria and resource assignments. Completion criteria are frequently based on schedule milestones and reviews, whereas resource allocation is based on subjective observations regarding the effectiveness and efficiency of management decisions. A theoretical basis for consideration of the consequence of failure has been lacking in both types of decisions. Software failure risk provides information to determine the cost effectiveness of phase completion (or extension) and the information to allocate resources cost effectively so that failure risk is effectively managed.

The late 1980s saw the evolution of a new software process model made possible by technological advances that rendered prototyping cost effective. The spiral model incorporates the same development phases as the stagewise or waterfall model but differs in the order of stages and the transition criteria from one to the next (Boehm, 1988). Detailed design, coding, and testing commence after several requirements, prototypes, and design cycles are completed and risks are assessed. Each cycle proceeds from overall concept to detail, as shown in Fig. 8.2. The radial dimension in Fig. 8.2 represents cumulative cost, whereas the angular dimension represents progress in each cycle of the spiral. A

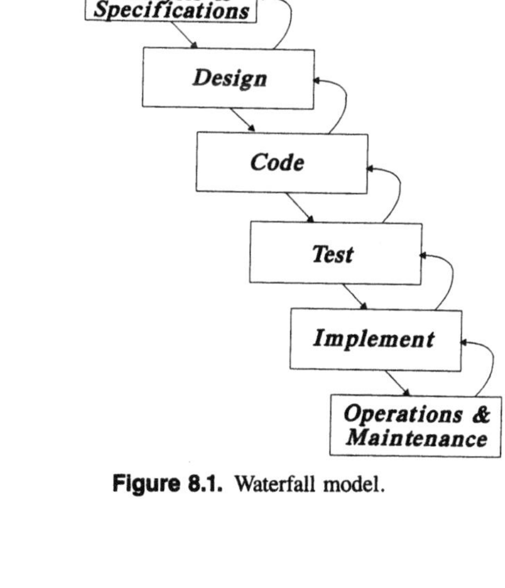

Figure 8.1. Waterfall model.

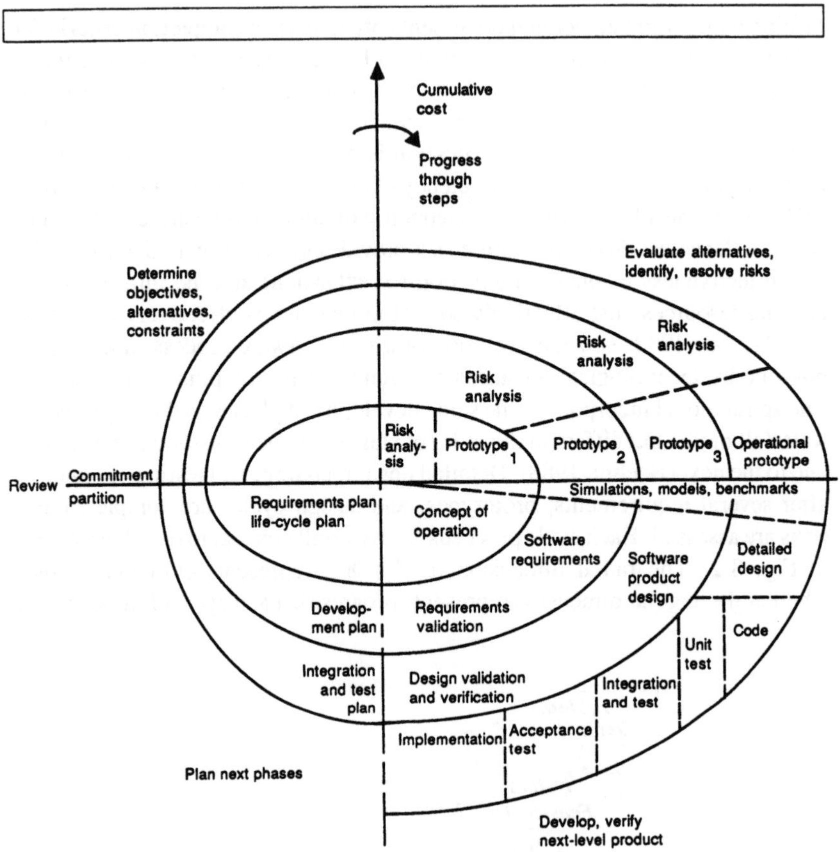

Figure 8.2. Spiral model (Boehm, 1988). ©1988 IEEE.

cycle begins with the identification of the objectives of the portion of the product being elaborated, such as performance and functionality goals; alternative implementation strategies, such as design, reuse, or buy; and constraints on application of alternatives. Alternatives are evaluated relative to objectives, and areas of uncertainty and risks are identified. Risk identification drives the next step of the cycle. For example, if performance or user interface risks strongly dominate program development, evolutionary development may be necessary, beginning with general prototypes and eventually moving to more detailed prototypes. If, on the other hand, interface control risks dominate, the next step would be to write detailed specifications. Key management tasks in the spiral model include identifying risk elements, making plans to manage these elements, and deciding how to proceed.

Advantages of the spiral model include the following (Boehm, 1988):

- It provides guidance on the best mix of existing approaches to a problem, including specifying, prototyping, and evolutionary development.
- It provides a mechanism for incorporating software quality objectives into software product development.
- It focuses early on eliminating errors or poor alternatives.
- It accommodates life cycle evolution, growth, and changes of the software product.
- It focuses on risk.

The spiral process model depends upon risk assessment expertise. It relies on the ability of the developer to identify and manage different sources of project risk. For example, risk-driven specifications provide detailed information on high-risk elements but leave low-risk elements to be elaborated in further stages. This requires the analyst to properly distinguish between high-risk and low-risk elements. The methodology presented in Part II can help the analyst identify and measure software failure risk so that each cycle can properly proceed with strategies to manage this risk.

8.2. PRODUCT DEFINITION

Product definition includes feasibility and requirements analysis. Risk considerations are crucial in this phase. External exposure assessment achieves its greatest benefit from guiding product definition.

8.2.1. Feasibility Analysis

Product definition includes a feasibility analysis of a project or cycle, which evaluates whether the system or subsystem's gains will warrant development and use costs. Using the waterfall model, an entire system's feasibility is generally investigated before development proceeds; in the spiral model, each cycle's feasibility is evaluated in turn.

Feasibility analyses frequently involve surveys, analyses, and structured interviews that focus on a proposed system's accomplishments relative to its development costs. Feasibility analyses should also review external hazards in the proposed environment so that benefits are evaluated relative to the expected costs of both development and failure. Failure cost is one component of financial risk that can significantly impact feasibility. For example, software recovery was not deemed feasible in the Boeing 737-300 and the Airbus 310 because of the considerable cost should recovery fail. Instead, a nondigital backup system immediately receives control if systems fail (Leveson *et al.*, 1990).

8.2.2. Requirements Analysis

Requirements analysis assesses needs to be fulfilled and determines why a system is needed and what features will serve this need. Analyses of the technical, operational, and economic feasibility of a system form boundary conditions for system construction (Ross and Schoman, 1977).

> The hardest single part of building a software system is deciding precisely what to build. . . . No other part of the work so cripples the resulting system if done wrong. No other part is more difficult to rectify later. . . . For the truth is, the client does not know what he wants. The client usually does not know what questions must be answered, and he has almost never thought of the problem in the detail necessary for specification. (Brooks, 1987)

Poor communication and documentation provide roadblocks to successful requirements analysis. Not only is it difficult for developers to determine what users really need, but it is frequently difficult for users to understand what developers plan to produce.

Historically, these difficulties were addressed by developing tools and methodologies that improve communication and documentation. In the 1970s, graphical and diagrammatic methods were introduced to structure thinking and enhance communication. Tools that sought to manage risks associated with poor communication included data flow diagrams, data structure diagrams, data dictionaries, structured English, decision tables and trees, structured walk-throughs, and structured analysis (DeMarco, 1979; Gane and Sarson, 1979; Jackson, 1975; Myers, 1975; Orr, 1977; Ross, 1977; Yourdon and Constantine, 1979). Automated tools like PSL/PSA (Problem Statement Language, Problem Statement Analysis) (Teicherow and Hershey, 1977) and HOS (Higher Order Software) (Hamilton and Zeldin, 1976) were developed to document requirements reliably. However, these tools were often not readily understood by users; requirements frequently were incorrect or missing.

The requirements analysis tools focus on what the system is supposed to do, how it is supposed to operate. Specifications are considered complete if the project manager is satisfied that all functions are included and the system will do what users want. But functionality is often missing. "Omissions are particularly pernicious and difficult to discover" (Adrion *et al.*, 1982) and have been reported to be the most persistent and expensive types of errors (Glass, 1981). One study found that over one-third of all errors resulted from omissions (Basili and Perricone, 1984). For example, review of the Navy's Aegis combat system programs (which process ships' radar information in order to decide whether to use weapons) showed that the support software had no category for reporting system-wide errors (although errors could be reported for any subsystem) (Enfield, 1987).

Prototyping became a viable option for requirements analysis in the 1980s because of technological advances such as online interactive systems, database management systems, high-level languages, generalized input and output software, and modeling facilities (Naumann and Jenkins, 1982). Prototypes are systems that capture the essential features of a proposed system and thus allow users to understand more easily how a system will work. Prototyping is built on the proposition that users can tell you what they want changed in an existing system more easily than they can tell you what they want developed (Necco *et al.*, 1987). Prototyping has reportedly been used most frequently to develop online transaction processing systems and *ad hoc* systems (Necco *et al.*, 1987).

Prototyping improves communication but does not necessarily eliminate functionality risk resulting from omissions—it depends on how prototypes are used. In the waterfall model, prototyping can be incorporated by a "build it twice" step that runs in parallel with requirements analysis (Boehm, 1988). The analysis should explore not only how the prototype operates, but what can go wrong when the system is used in its operational environment. External exposure analysis can provide this information in order to minimize failure risk.

Prototyping is incorporated in each cycle of the spiral model of development. Detailed design and development are not initiated until performance and user–interface risks are resolved. The external exposure analysis provides a basis for identifying and measuring these risks and determining when to move forward in the cycle. Prototypes should be evaluated to consider what could go wrong with their use. The identification of high-exposure areas indicates where to focus efforts in subsequent cycles. For example, perhaps additional requirements or prototypes are needed if failure risk is high.

Performing external exposure analysis, as described in Part II, can minimize functionality risk resulting from omissions. By focusing on actions in the environment that can cause loss, the analysis may reveal design requirements not initially considered. This should reduce errors of omission in the requirements phase. In fact, external exposure analysis provides its greatest benefit if accomplished during requirements analysis.

8.2.3. Examples from Case Studies

Examples from the case studies introduced in Part II illustrate how software failure risk assessment can improve requirements analysis and suggest risk management techniques for the use of the software.

8.2.3.1. Commercial Loan System

The design of the CLS allows a loan officer to initiate a loan without a billing schedule. No bills are sent until the officer subsequently remembers to add a schedule. External exposure assessment indicated that the hazard of not billing had very high consequence. The application of this analysis prior to design would probably have suggested that the system set a default date to begin billing in the event a loan officer neglected to enter a schedule.

Invalid interest accruals had substantial consequence to the savings and loan institution. Exposure assessment indicates that interest accrual procedures and amounts computed by the software should be monitored by individuals within the organization. In fact, this system's high external exposure suggests that external monitoring be instituted for several critical functions.

8.2.3.2. Funds-Transfer Security System

A major hazard in the funds-transfer security system involved posting to and from incorrect accounts. The likelihood of this hazard increases when this system processes wires for several banks at a single location, as was the case in the application presented in Chapter 6. This fact was not considered when the system was originally designed. In fact, a system modification was developed to incorporate this requirement after the failure risk assessment was completed.

The funds-transfer application demonstrates the effect of extensive external verification procedures. Recognizing the risk associated with the large increase in the amounts of transactions, banks minimize software failure risk with techniques such as limiting amounts transferred without approval, limiting approval authority, manual balancing of accounts, and wire verification. External exposure assessment indicates the effect of different strategies so that alternatives can be compared and evaluated.

8.2.3.3. Payables Processing System

In the voucher input processing system, the large external exposure for charging wrong accounts suggests the incorporation of additional account number validations. In addition, the external exposure analysis suggests and evaluates external risk management procedures. For example, since the processing of utility payments involved the largest transactions, more external procedures were warranted here than for other types of payment. Exposure for some types of transactions, such as patent fees, was small enough to suggest that external verification of these payments might not be warranted. Of course, a cost–benefit analysis would be required in order to make this decision, but the software failure risk methodology can measure the failure cost.

8.3. PRODUCT TRANSLATION

Once a system is defined, it is translated into code. Proper attention to risk during design and development can minimize failures during operation.

8.3.1. Design

Software design encompasses partitioning and elaboration of activities, functions, objects, and data specified in product definition. Output is a complete system definition in formal or semiformal notation. This design is subsequently programmed into machine instructions—a task that is increasingly automated.

Because requirements provide a blueprint for design, errors introduced during product definition generally translate into errors in design and code. The design phase can also introduce errors when requirements are misunderstood, further supporting the need for understandable requirements documentation. Moreover, the design may be so complex that errors are introduced when code based on this design is developed. A study analyzing software errors in three different development projects reported that 81% of all errors were somehow related to design (Weiss and Basili, 1985). Other published figures indicate that design errors range from 55 to 85% of all software errors (Card and Glass, 1990).

System architectural design methodologies include functional decomposition, object-oriented design, and data-structure design (Wasserman *et al.*, 1990). Functional decomposition partitions the system according to functions, whereas the other techniques focus on data. While object-oriented design uses classes or objects as building blocks, the data-structure method emphasizes the development of logical data structures.

The most widely used design methodology is structured design, which is based on the principles of functional or modular decomposition (Card and Glass, 1990). Structured design activities include functional allocation, systems design, and unit design.

Functional allocation collects related requirements into functional groups, identifies dependencies among functions, and defines external interfaces. Data flow diagrams, HIPO diagrams, high-level structure charts, or simple lists of requirements by subsystem are used.

Systems design uses partitioning to define the architecture. Data and functions are allocated to units or design parts and internal interfaces are designed. Strategies include functional decomposition, information hiding, and data abstraction. Structure charts are frequently used in this design phase.

Finally, unit design defines algorithms and data structures that will convert input into output. These are often represented as prologs or pseudocode.

Both understandability and complexity determine programmers' propensity to err. How the work is divided into modules affects complexity. This in turn influences ultimate produceability, or the ability to develop a design that is implementable and maintainable. Three types of complexity exist—structural, data, and procedural—which increase interface, data, and logic errors, respectively. Attempts to minimize simultaneously all three types of complexity may seemingly conflict. For example, reducing data complexity by producing smaller modules can increase structural complexity because the number of interfaces increases.

Designers often consider alternative design strategies. How can the "best" design be chosen? Software exposure can guide this decision. Structural exposure of alternative designs can be compared. The complexity of high-exposure modules should be minimized, even at the expense of other, lower-exposure modules.

All modules have uniform amounts of design in the waterfall model. This may not be a cost-effective approach to design because failure risk varies among modules. The spiral process model, on the other hand, proposes that risk be used to determine the necessary amount of design detail (Boehm, 1988). The exposure analysis can measure the degree of exposure to support this decision.

In safety critical applications, it was suggested that noncritical functions be separated from critical functions so that failures of the former do not affect the latter (Leveson, 1986). Similarly, designers may wish to separate functions of extremely high exposure from low-exposure functions. Modules involving high- exposure functions would receive more stringent development and testing. External exposure assessment helps identify which functions to separate, and structural exposure assessment provides information on the resulting exposure of a proposed design.

8.3.2. Programming

A design is programmed into a particular compiled programming or database language. Historically, the first major advance toward the reduction of programming errors was the development of structured programming techniques. These techniques should be considered prior to coding when the system is designed.

Program coding is becoming highly automated. High-level languages and code generators decrease the number of errors introduced by humans in this translation process.

Not only can the designer use exposure analysis to determine an appropriate design and the level of design detail, but the project manager can use that analysis to determine design and programming assignments. Personnel experience influences error rate (Card and Glass, 1990; Takahashi and Kamayachi,

1989). For example, a comparative experiment in (Brown and Lipow, 1973) indicated a 10:1 difference in error rates between personnel. Hence, more experienced developers should be assigned higher- exposure functions. Furthermore, more design and programming tools, such as CASE technology and code generators, may be warranted for high-exposure modules.

8.3.3. Examples from Case Studies

Once again, examples from the case studies presented in Part II depict the potential application of the exposure analysis—in this case to the design and programming phase.

8.3.3.1. Commercial Loan System

The financial posting module had one of the highest exposures in the CLS described in Chapter 5. This module performs several functions, has high data and procedural complexity, is the lengthiest module in the system (over 11,000 executable lines of code), and has very high failure probability. Specific knowledge of the magnitude of exposure during design would have suggested that alternative designs be used to lower the failure probability of this module as well as other high-exposure modules in this system.

Moreover, programming assignments in the CLS could have been based on relative exposures. Assignment of more experienced programmers would have been indicated, for example, for the payoff inquiry module (111) than for the turndown reference inquiry module (162) since the former's exposure was $21/month compared to $7/month for the latter.

8.3.3.2. Funds Transfer Security System

Exposure did not vary as much in the funds-transfer system as in the CLS because the funds system provides less variability in functionality. This would suggest that all modules be designed more uniformly in terms of complexity and size. In fact, this was the case: modules had fairly uniform size and exposure. Only two functions had slightly higher exposure than the remainder—incoming wire processing and posting. Design trade-offs should have considered this information so that the likelihood of failure of modules providing these functions would be minimized. In fact, incoming wire modules were smaller and less complex than most modules and exhibited lower failure likelihood. However, the posting modules were larger and more complex. Application of the risk assessment methodology prior to design would have suggested that these modules be re-evaluated in order to minimize complexity.

8.3.3.3. Payables Processing System

Modularization in the voucher processing system was driven by interface considerations: unique modules were developed for separate screen displays. Account distribution was separated from financial information in order to facilitate data entry and minimize failure risk. The exposure assessment could have determined the necessary amount of design detail. Modules with high exposure, such as the voucher summary module, would require greater design detail than low exposure modules, such as the check request inquiry module. Moreover, more experienced designers and programmers should have been assigned to develop these high-exposure functions and modules.

REFERENCES

Adrion, W. R., M. A. Branstad, and J. Cherniavsky, "Validation, Verification and Testing of Computer Software," *Computing Surveys* **14**(2), (June 1982), 159–192.

Basili, V. R. and B. T. Perricone, "Software Errors and Complexity: An Empirical Investigation," *Comm. ACM* **27**(1), (January 1984), 42–52.

Boehm, B., "A Spiral Model of Software Development and Enhancement," *IEEE Computer*, May, 1988, pp. 61–72.

Boehm, B. and R. Ross, "Theory-W Software Project Management: Principles and Examples," *IEEE Trans. Software Engrg.* **SE-15**(7), (July, 1989), 902–916.

Brooks, F. P., *The Mythical Man-Month*, Reading, MA: Addison-Wesley, 1982.

——"No Silver Bullet: Essence and Accidents of Software Engineering," *IEEE Computer*, April, 1987, pp. 10–19.

Brown, J. R. and M. Lipow, "The Quantitative Measurement of Software Safety and Reliability," TRW Report QR 1776, August, 1973.

Card, D. N. and R. L. Glass, *Measuring Software Design Quality*, Englewood Cliffs, NJ: Prentice-Hall, 1990.

DeMarco, T., *Structured Analysis and System Specifications*, Englewood Cliffs, NJ: Prentice-Hall, 1979.

Enfield, R. L., "The Limits of Software Reliability," *Tech. Rev.*, April, 1987, pp. 36–43.

Gane, C. and T. Sarson, *Structured Systems Analysis: Tools and Techniques*, Englewood Cliffs, NJ: Prentice-Hall, 1979.

Glass, R. L., "Persistent Software Errors," *IEEE Trans. Software Engrg.* **SE-7**(2), (March 1981), 162–168.

Hamilton, M. and S. Zeldin, "Higher Order Software—A Methodology for Defining Software," *IEEE Trans. Software Engrg.* **SE-2**(1), (March 1976), 9–32.

Humphrey, W., *Managing the Software Process*, Reading, MA: Addison-Wesley, 1989.

Jackson, J. A., *Principles of Program Design*, London: Academic Press, 1975.

Leveson, N. G., "Software Safety: Why, What, and How," *Computing Surveys* **18**(2), (June 1986), 125–163.

Leveson, N. G., S. S. Cha, J. C. Knight, and T. J. Shimeall, "The Use of Self Checks and Voting in Software Error Detection: An Empirical Study," *IEEE Trans. Software Engrg.* **SE-16**(4), (April 1990), 432–443.

Myers, G. J., *Reliable Software Through Composite Design*, New York: Van Nostrand and Reinhold, 1975.

Naumann, J. and M. Jenkins, "Prototyping: The New Paradigm for Systems Development," *MIS Quarterly*, September, 1982, pp. 29–44.

Necco, C. R., C. L. Gordon, and N. W. Tsai, "Systems Analysis and Design: Current Practices," *MIS Quarterly*, December, 1987, pp. 460–475.

Orr, K, *Structured Systems Development*, New York: Yourdon Press, 1977.

Ross, D. T. and K. E. Schoman, Jr., "Structured Analysis for Requirements Definition," *IEEE Trans. Software Engrg*. **SE-3**(1), (January 1977), 6–15.

Takahashi, M. and Y. Kamayachi, "An Empirical Study of a Model for Program Error Prediction," *IEEE Trans. Software Engrg*. **SE-15**(1), (January 1989), 82–86.

Teicherow, D. and E. Hershey, "PLA/PSA: A Computer-Aided Technique for Structured Documentation and Analysis of Information Processing Systems," *IEEE Trans. Software Engrg*. **SE-3**(1), (January 1977), 41–48.

Yourdon, E., and L. Constantine, *Structured Design: Fundamentals of a Discipline of Computer Program and Systems Design*, Englewood Cliffs, NJ: Prentice-Hall, 1979.

Wasserman, A. I., P. A. Pircher, and R. J. Muller, "The Object-Oriented Structured Design Notation for Software Design Representation," *IEEE Computer*, March, 1990, pp. 50–63.

Weiss, D. M. and V. Basili, "Evaluating Software Development by Analysis of Changes," *IEEE Trans. Software Engrg*. **SE-11**(2), (February 1985), 157–168.

Chapter 9

Software Testing

One of the most important applications of software failure risk assessment is the management of testing to minimize project risk. Since there are currently no methods for proving system correctness, testing is necessary to find inherent faults in the code and gain confidence in the software's reliability prior to release. Software testing decisions require implicit trade-offs between software quality and cost. Software development managers recognize that expenditure of additional test effort generally improves quality and reliability. Nevertheless, software development costs are decreased when the testing effort is minimized; at the same time, this reduces software backlogs. Implicit assumptions are often made concerning the "value" of additional testing. However, little theory has been developed to aid this decision because testing "value" has not previously been measured in economic terms. Testing effort can be cost effectively allocated to the individual modules, or components, of a software system when the "value" of testing is measured by the reduction in software failure risk.

This chapter illustrates the limitations of traditional testing theory and describes how software failure risk assessment can guide testing. A decision model is developed that determines the optimum amount of test time to allocate to a module by considering the trade-off between testing cost and the risk of failure. The model's application to the CLS introduced in Chapter 5 is illustrated.

9.1. TRADITIONAL TESTING THEORY

Traditional software testing theory has not addressed the implicit trade-off between testing cost and the operational risk of failure. Testing procedures generally attempt to "cover," or exercise, as much of the software and/or its functions as possible to detect as many errors as possible. There are several methodologies for accomplishing this task. These can be classified as

- White-box testing
- Black-box testing
- Random-input testing

White-box, or structural, testing, uses the internal structure of the program to develop test cases. It is concerned with the degree to which test cases exercise or cover the logic of the program. Coverage criteria include statement coverage, decision coverage, condition coverage, and combinations of these (Adrion *et al.*, 1982; Chusko, 1987; Goodenough and Gerhart, 1977; Howden, 1976; Huang, 1977; Myers, 1979; Prather and Myers, 1987; Redwine, 1983; Schneidewind, 1979).

Black-box, or functional, testing, is largely data driven. The testing process involves partitioning the input space into equivalence classes. These are sets of input states that appear to be similar, so that a test of a representative value in a class should yield results equivalent to a test of any other value in that class (Howden, 1986; Myers, 1979; Richardson and Clarke, 1985). Boundary values of these classes, in particular, are usually tested (Howden, 1976; Myers, 1979; Redwine, 1983).

Random-input testing chooses test cases by randomly selecting inputs from the input space, using the same probabilities of selection of input states as occur during operation (Musa *et al.*, 1987). Thus, test cases are chosen based upon expected use of the system rather than upon consideration of what uses have been found to fail most frequently, i.e., boundary values. In many cases, more efficient testing is accomplished if it is recognized that once an input state has been selected, it does not have to be repeated. In this case, the *failure intensity** must be divided by a *test compression factor*, or ratio of execution time required in operation to execution time required in test phase, to obtain the corresponding failure intensity expected in operation (Musa *et al.*, 1987).

Software testing is a major component of systems development, typically accounting for as much as one-half of the development effort (Yourdon and Constantine, 1979; Zelkowitz, 1978). The testing process generally includes several phases, each of which will be described below:

**Failure intensity* has been defined as failures per unit time (Musa *et al.*, 1987).

- module test
- integration test
- function test
- systems test
- acceptance test

Module, integration, and function testing are typically performed by the systems development group. These phases verify the code against the design and specification. They typically consume 45% of the total development effort (Kubat and Koch, 1983). Systems and acceptance testing are generally performed by an independent group, which verifies the system against the user's objectives. These phases typically consume only a small part of the total systems development effort (Kubat and Koch, 1983).

The purpose of module testing is to compare the code to the module specification. The objective is to show how the module contradicts the specification, i.e., to find faults in the code. Typically, module testing involves a combination of white-box and black-box tests. The test manager is faced with many decisions, such as how to allocate test time among the modules, what test data are necessary, and how to allocate personnel. In many cases, test resources are constrained. Commonly, test time is limited. Personnel may also be limited. Thus, the manager must decide how to allocate test effort to each module so as to locate as many errors as possible. Typically, this is done on an *ad hoc* basis based upon the logic in the code (white-box tests) and the equivalence partitions (black-box tests).

During integration testing, the parts of the code are put together and the integrated code is compared to the program structure and systems design. White-box and black-box testing may be used. The integration strategy chosen and the testing sequence affect the form in which module test cases are written, the types of test tools used, the cost of generating test cases, and the cost of debugging errors (Myers, 1979).

Function testing is the comparison of the system to the requirements specification, a description of the system from the user's point of view. Thus, the system is not tested against the design but against the user's specifications. Function testing is typically a black-box process. During this test phase, management must decide how to allocate test effort to various data categories so as to uncover as many errors as possible. Typically, time and personnel constrain testing efforts.

The function of the systems test is to compare the system or program to its requirements (Myers, 1979). Its purpose is to assess the system against its original objectives, as opposed to the specifications. The objective of the systems test phase is to produce a reliable software product. During this phase, testing generally proceeds by randomly choosing inputs based upon the user objectives. Software is tested until the deadline for system release is reached or the test team feels that the software is reliable enough for release. Several models have been developed to determine when desired reliability levels have been attained (Forman and Singpurwalla, 1977; Kruger, 1988; Okumoto and Goel, 1980; Ross, 1985).

9.2. LIMITATIONS OF TRADITIONAL TESTING THEORY

The theory supporting coverage testing does not consider the consequence of an error, implicitly assuming that all failures have the same consequence. It does not address the fact that the magnitude of potential loss resulting from a software failure can have a wide range of values, depending upon how the software is used and the type of fault leading to failure. Traditional testing theory has not adequately addressed the trade-off between quality and cost because a basis for measuring the impact of testing on the risk of failure has previously been unavailable.

During the module test phase, management should be guided by a theory that assesses the differential failure risk of each module. Efforts can then be allocated on the basis not only of the structure of the code and the equivalence partitions but of the different consequences of failure in different modules as well. The assessment of module risk can be used to determine how much test effort should be allocated to testing that module. The allocation of test effort where it can most effectively reduce risk can result in more cost effective software development while still reducing failure risk. The optimum amount of module testing depends upon the characteristics and expected use of a module, testing costs, and most important, the potential impact of failure due to faults in the module.

The test manager during integration must decide how to combine and test modules. In some cases, this choice is based on the availability of test tools. Software failure risk can help identify which combinations of modules have the greatest risk, thus aiding in the integration decision.

During function and systems testing, management typically decides how to allocate test efforts to various equivalence classes developed from the external specifications and requirements. During systems testing, inputs are often chosen at random from the operational distribution, the probability distribution of inputs in operation. Software failure risk analysis can identify which modules have the greatest risk. The risk associated with a particular equivalence class depends on the expected risk of failure in the modules invoked when input from that class is tested.

As testing proceeds, management must finally decide when to release the software. Since reliability models do not measure the economic significance of failure, only the likelihood of failure, these models are inadequate for addressing the economic impact of testing. When the cost of failure has been included in testing-decision models, all faults have been assumed to have a single cost of failure (Brown *et al.*, 1989; Dalal and Mallows, 1988; Koch and Kubat, 1983; Okumoto and Goel, 1980); the differential risk of failure in different modules has not been considered. Since software failure risk measures the differential risk of failure in modules, a cost–benefit analysis can compare the expected loss with the cost to continue testing as well as the benefits from releasing the software.

9.3. USING RISK ASSESSMENT TO GUIDE TESTING

Software development managers can be provided with decision procedures based upon theory that will support the minimization of failure risk in computer software. Instead of randomly testing a system until the likelihood of system failure is judged to be small enough for release, systems can be tested until the magnitude of the operational risk of failure no longer justifies the cost of testing. This should improve the quality of software while controlling the rapidly increasing costs of software development.

The risk assessment procedures can be applied to measure the impact of testing on the components of risk, the magnitude of exposure, and the likelihood of failure. Testing generally reduces the failure likelihood of a module. Its impact, however, is a function of the magnitude of the module's exposure, the characteristics of the module, and its expected use.

Although it is usually more beneficial to test higher-exposure modules, additional testing generally does not change exposure, but only reduces the likelihood of failure. The reduction in the expected number of failures that results from testing must be measured so that the resulting impact on risk can be evaluated. Equal allocation of test time to the modules may not produce equivalent reductions in the expected number of failures. The magnitude of the potential decrease in the expected number of failures depends upon the number of faults in the module, the probability that a fault will cause a failure, the amount of prior testing of the module, and the expected operational use of the module.

The parameters of the reliability model incorporated in the risk estimates—the mean number of faults and a module's per fault hazard rate—as well as the amount of prior testing determine the effectiveness of additional testing in reducing failure intensity. Well-tested modules typically require larger increments of additional test time to reduce failure intensity than do poorly tested modules, as shown in Fig. 9.1. Modules with many faults possess greater failure likelihood in a short test period as compared to modules with few faults, as is also illustrated in Fig. 9.1.

The impact of testing on failure intensity is, however, not the only factor

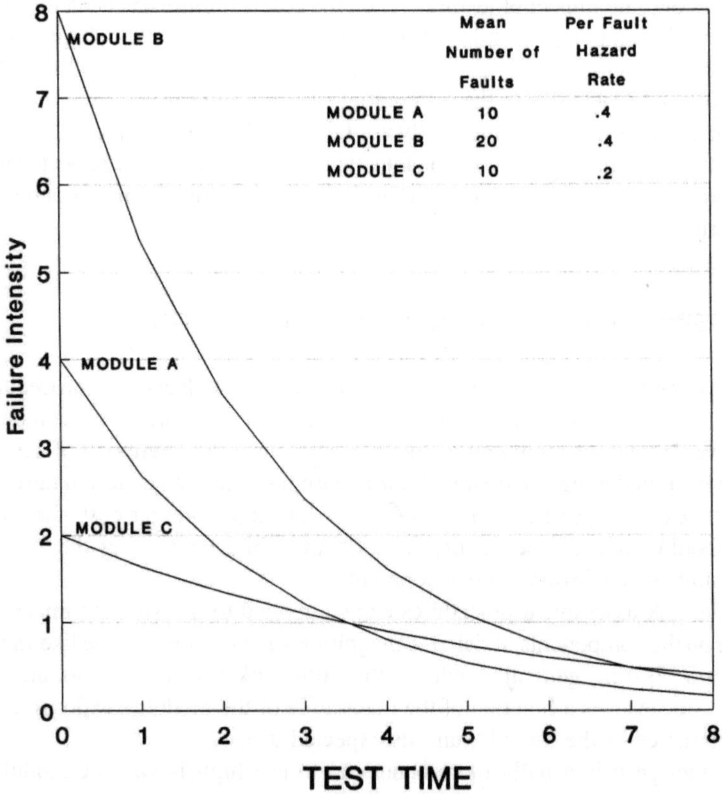

Figure 9.1. Failure intensity as a function of test time.

affecting the reduction in the expected number of failures. The frequency of operational use of a module must be considered to determine the resulting impact on risk of a change in failure intensity. Although an expenditure of test time can cause a substantial reduction in module failure intensity, the magnitude of the benefit is a function of the degree of use of that module. Fig. 9.2 depicts the impact of operational use on the risk profile of two modules. Although both modules have equivalent exposure and failure intensity profiles, testing the more frequently used module has more significant impact on risk.

Figure 9.3 illustrates several risk profiles and shows how test effort affects risk. The risk assessment methods provide these profiles and demonstrate the benefit of additional testing. Unique exposure of each module is first estimated. Reduction in the expected number of operational failures is then measured with a software reliability model that includes an estimate of the expected operational

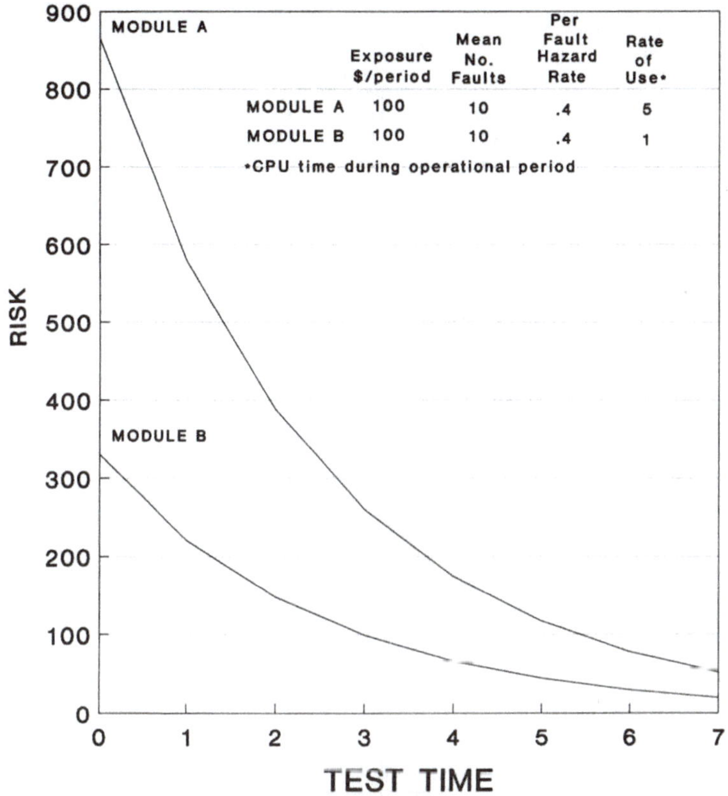

Figure 9.2. Impact of operational use on risk.

use of the individual modules. Thence, the impact of additional testing time on risk is evaluated.

9.4. A DECISION MODEL TO DETERMINE OPTIMUM TEST TIME

A decision model has been developed that determines how much test time a module should receive to maximize net benefit from testing. While traditional testing strategies measure testing benefit only in terms of the number of faults uncovered, the new testing strategy measures benefits of testing in terms of the economic impact of faults.

The net benefit from testing is measured as the risk reduction resulting from testing the module minus the cost of testing:

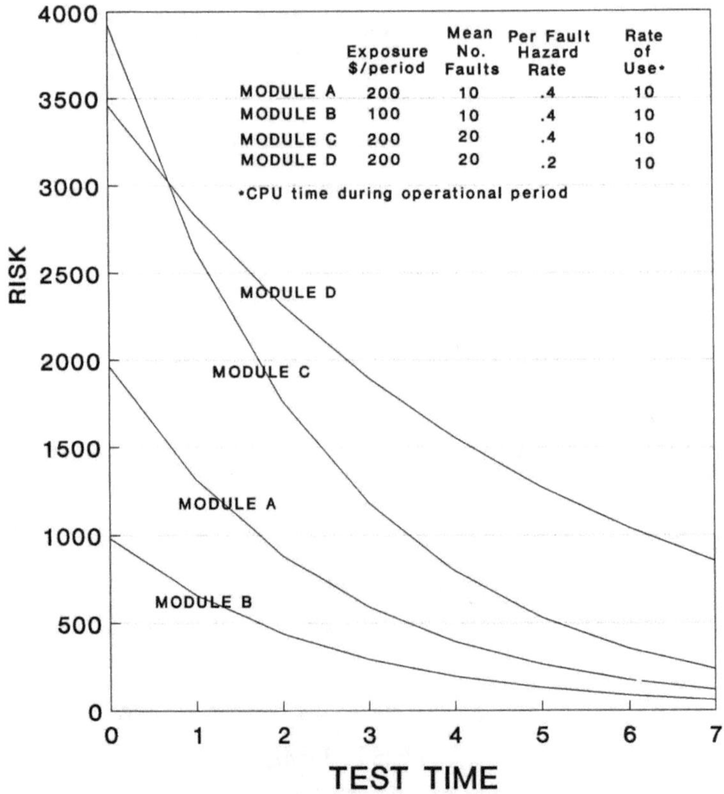

Figure 9.3. Risk profiles.

$$\mathrm{NB}(t_T) = R(T,t_T) - \mathrm{TC}(t_T) \tag{9.1}$$

where $\mathrm{NB}(t_T)$ = the net benefit from testing module for time t_T, $R(T,t_T)$ = the change in failure risk during operational time T when the module is tested for time t_T, and $\mathrm{TC}(t_T)$ = total cost of testing for time t_T.

The benefit from testing is measured by the magnitude of the resulting reduction in operational risk due to testing. No benefit is assumed from early release of poorly tested software. If there is some benefit to releasing software early, because of competitive pressures or the need to meet deadlines or replace existing, error-prone systems, then the benefit from testing is reduced by an estimate of the economic impact of early release.

A module is tested for time t_T, measured in CPU time. The reduction in risk can then be measured as

$$R(T,t_T) = X(T)\mu\{1 - \exp(-\theta t_0(T)) + \exp[-\theta(t_T + t_0(T)] - \exp(-\theta t_T)\} \quad (9.2)$$

where

$X(T)$ = expected exposure due to failure resulting from faults in the module during operational time T

μ = mean number of faults in the module

θ = per fault hazard rate

$t_0(T)$ = execution time of a module during operational time period T

Note that t_0 and t_T are measured in execution or CPU time, while T is measured in calendar time.

The cost of testing includes the costs of both machine and personnel time to find and fix errors. This includes test planning and development as well as the costs incurred in running test cases and analyzing results. These costs are assumed to increase linearly with the amount of testing time. In addition, the costs to prepare failure reports, find and remove faults, and re-test, insuring that faults no longer exist, are directly related to the number of failures. It is assumed that the cost of testing is a function only of the time spent testing and the number of failures and is independent of the characteristics of the program.* Total costs can then be expressed as follows:

$$\mathrm{TC}(t_T) = K_1\mu[1 - \exp(-\theta t_T)] + K_2 t_T \quad (9.3)$$

where

K_1 = cost per failure (machine time and personnel time)

K_2 = cost per CPU time spent testing

Unit costs can generally be obtained from historical test information. Costs should include expenditures for both failure identification and correction. Failure identification involves testing, determining what failures have occurred, and documenting these failures. Failure correction includes fault identification, finding the fault that caused the failure, and fault correction, which includes testing and documenting the correction. Both failure identification and correction require the expenditure of machine and personnel time. Estimates of average machine and personnel time expended for each failure and unit of execution time can be collected from similar completed projects, or a Delphi survey could be used (Musa *et al.*, 1987). Additionally, average machine and personnel costs can be obtained from historical records. Since environmental considerations, such as the test team's skill level and the use of debugging aids or

*Fault location may affect the time required to detect errors (Gibson and Senn, 1989; Sheppard *et al.*, 1979). If the debugging time can be shown to be a function of some characteristics of the software, such as complexity or size, this information could be incorporated in equation (9.3).

test tools, may affect the expenditure of resources, it is preferable to use historical information obtained in a similar environment.

The amount of time spent testing that maximizes the net benefit from testing can be derived by substituting equations (9.2) and (9.3) into equation (9.1) and then differentiating equation (9.1). The optimum amount of test time is

$$t_\tau^* = -\frac{1}{\theta}\ln\frac{K_2}{(\theta\mu)\{X(T)[1 - \exp(-\theta t_o(T))] - K_1\}} \tag{9.4}$$

Note that an optimum value for t_τ^* exists only if

$$X(T)[1 - \exp(-\theta t_o(T))] > K_1 \quad \text{and}$$
$$(\theta\mu)\{X(T)[1 - \exp(-\theta t_o(T))] - K_1\} > K_2.$$

In other words, module testing is cost effective only if failure risk exceeds at least the cost of finding and fixing the average number of faults in the module plus the cost to run the software until it fails (e.g., $R > K_2\theta^{-1} + \mu K_1$). These boundaries determine parameter threshold levels for cost-effective testing.

9.5. APPLICATION OF THE OPTIMUM TEST TIME MODEL

Risk information developed for modules in the CLS will be used to demonstrate the application of this model. First, the following assumptions were made:

- Commercial loan software has a five-year life.
- The present value of monthly exposure remains constant.
- Expected monthly use remains constant.
- Unit costs are \$965 per failure and \$28 per CPU minute of testing.*
- Exposure is a linear function, i.e., exposure for k time units is estimated as $kX(T)$ where $X(T)$ is exposure per time period T, which in this case was one month.

The latter assumption yields upper limits for optimal test time since exposure is expected to be smaller if faults are corrected before k time periods. This problem will be addressed in the future by estimating exposure limits during the entire operational period.

The impact of testing on net benefit was investigated for each of the

*Unit cost estimates are based on data from other software development projects since data was unavailable for this application. This data assumed personnel cost including labor and overhead = \$75/hour and computer cost = \$500/CPU hour. Failure identification and correction effort were assumed to require 5.5 person hours/failure and 1.1 CPU hour/failure plus 2.43 CPU hour/CPU hour and 5.91 person hours/CPU hour (Musa *et al.*, 1987).

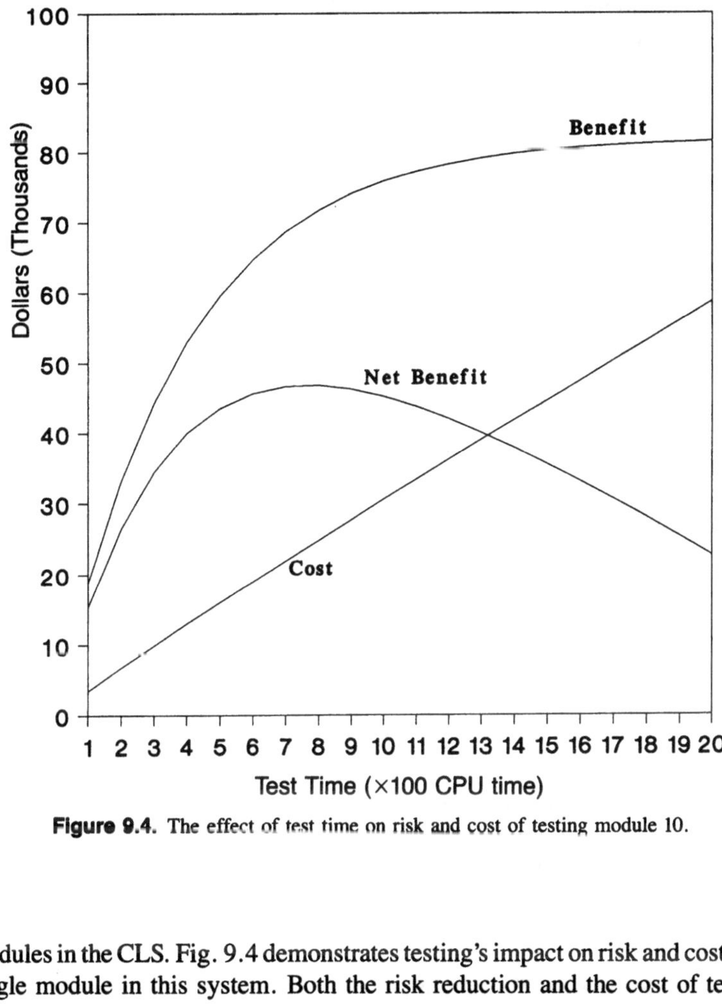

Figure 9.4. The effect of test time on risk and cost of testing module 10.

modules in the CLS. Fig. 9.4 demonstrates testing's impact on risk and cost for a single module in this system. Both the risk reduction and the cost of testing increase as testing time increases. The net benefit from testing this module increases until approximately 767 CPU units of testing have been expended. Thereafter, the cost of debugging increasingly reduces the benefit from testing; in short, the net benefit decreases.

Table 9.1 illustrates results of the model's application to several modules in the CLS. Modules 2300, 2400, and 3500 require a significant amount of testing compared to the other modules. These modules had extremely high failure risk throughout the project's five-year life. On the other hand, the net benefit from additional testing of several other modules, such as 164, 1040, and 1150, was not high enough to justify additional testing given the costs involved.

Table 9.1. Optimal Test Time for CLS Modules

Module	Optimal test time (CPU time)
10	767
21	497
111	0
164	0
1040	0
1070	1115
1150	0
2300	3892
2400	4268
2450	1714
3500	3721
4600	0

The model's usefulness is a function of the accuracy of parameter estimates. Sensitivity analysis is appropriate to examine the impact of estimate variations. Parameter boundary values were investigated to determine levels at which testing (not initially indicated) becomes cost effective. The impact on optimum test time from changing individual parameters was also investigated.

Boundary-value analysis determines the threshold level, the minimum value of an input parameter such that testing is cost effective. Results are provided in Table 9.2 for several modules whose parameters did not initially suggest that additional testing time was warranted. For example, application of the optimum test time model indicated that module 1040 did not warrant additional testing. (Optimal test time shown in Table 9.1 is 0.) Suppose the unit cost to test module 1040 were reduced to $27.70/CPU minute. This is its

Table 9.2. Parameter Threshold Levels

	Computer cost ($ per CPU minute)		Exposure ($/month)		Use (CPU time)		Faults (number)	
Module	Threshold	% change	Threshold	% change	Threshold	% change	Threshold	% change
164	2.29	−92	4610	[a]	3.82	[a]	8.35	[a]
1040	27.70	−1	1300	+1	10.35	+1.5	.69	+1
1150	23.20	−17	2128	+18	1.43	+19	3.5	+20
4600	9.90	−65	80	+60	22.4	[a]	53.2	[a]

[a]Change exceeds 100%.

Table 9.3. Effect on Optimum Test Time of Doubling Parameters for Module 10

	Optimum test time	Change (%)
Base case	767	—
Cost/failure	753	−2
Cost/CPU time	501	−35
Use	986	+28
Exposure	1041	+36
Mean no faults	1034	+35
Per fault rate	626	−18

threshold value; at this level, it becomes effective to test the module. Since testing cost is currently estimated at $28/CPU min., this translates into a 1% change in the cost of testing time required for cost-effective testing to be indicated. Similarly, if module 1040's exposure were $1300/month instead of $1287/month (an increase of 1%) testing would become cost effective. Small decreases in testing cost, or small increases in exposure, use, or number of faults would indicate the need to test module 1040. However, the parameters in module 164 must change significantly before testing module 164 becomes cost effective. This information supplements testing decisions.

Sensitivity analyses were also performed to analyze individual parameter variations. Table 9.3 provides the impact on testing time for one module when each parameter is individually doubled. Doubling the cost per failure has a relatively minor effect on optimum test time compared to doubling the unit cost per CPU time. Doubling the unit cost per CPU time decreases the optimal test time by an amount equivalent to the increase in test time that would be indicated by doubling either exposure or average number of faults. This information can guide testing based on the degree of confidence in the accuracy of the parameter estimates.

REFERENCES

Adrion, W. R., M. A. Branstad, and J. Cherniavsky, "Validation, Verification and Testing of Computer Software," *Computing Surveys* **14**(2), (June 1982), 159–192.

Brown, D., S. Maghsoodloo, and W. Deason, "A Cost Model for Determining the Optimal Number of Software Test Cases," *IEEE Trans. Software Engrg*. **SE-15**(2), (February 1989), 218–221.

Chusko, T., "Test Data Selection and Quality Estimation based on the Concept of Essential Branches for Path Testing," *IEEE Trans. Software Engrg*. **SE-13**(5), (May 1987), 509–517.

Dalal, S. R. and C. L. Mallows, "When Should One Stop Testing Software?" *J. Amer. Statist. Assoc*. **83**(403), (September 1988), 872–879.

Forman, E. and N. Singpurwalla, "An Empirical Stopping Rule for Debugging and Testing Computer Software," *J. Amer. Statist. Assoc.* **72**(360), (December 1977), 750–757.

Gibsen, V. and T. Senn, "System Structure and Software Maintenance Performance," *Comm. ACM* **32**(3), (March 1989), 347–358.

Goodenough, J. B. and S. L. Gerhart, "Toward a Theory of Testing: Data Selection Criteria," in *Current Trends in Programming Methodology: Volume I Program Validation* (R. T. Yeh, ed.), Englewood Cliffs, NJ: Prentice-Hall, 1977, pp. 44–79.

Howden, W. E., "Reliability of the Path Analysis Testing Strategy," *IEEE Trans. Software Engrg.* **SE-2**(3), (September 1976), 208–215.

——"A Functional Approach to Program Testing and Analysis," *IEEE Trans. Software Engrg.* **SE-12**(10), (November 1986), 997–1005.

Huang, J. C., "Error Detection through Program Testing," *Current Trends in Programming Methodology: Volume II, Program Validation* (R. T. Yeh, ed.), Englewood Cliffs, NJ: Prentice-Hall, 1977, pp. 16–43.

Koch, H. and P. Kubat, "Optimal Release Time of Computer Software," *IEEE Trans. Software Engrg.* **SE-9**(3), (May 1983), 323–327.

Kruger, G., "Project Management Using Software Reliability Growth Models," *Hewlett-Packard J.* **39**(3), (June 1988), 30–35.

Kubat, P. and H. S. Koch, "Managing Test Procedures to Achieve Reliable Software," *IEEE Trans. Reliability* **R-32**(3), (August 1983), 299–303.

Musa, J. D., A. Iannino, and K. Okumoto, *Software Reliability: Measurement, Prediction, Application*, New York: McGraw-Hill, 1987.

Myers, G. J., *The Art of Software Testing*, New York: Wiley, 1979.

Okumoto, K. and A. Goel, "Optimum Release Time for Software Systems Based on Reliability and Cost Criteria," *J. Systems and Software* **1**(4), (1980), 315–318.

Prather, R. and J. Myers, "The Path Prefix Software Testing Strategy," *IEEE Trans. Software Engrg.* **SE-13**(7), (July 1987), 761–766.

Redwine, Jr., S., "An Engineering Approach to Software Test Data Design," *IEEE Trans. Software Engrg.* **SE-9**(2), (March 1983), 191–200.

Richardson, D. J. and L. A. Clarke, "Partition Analysis: A Method Combining Testing and Verification," *IEEE Trans. Software Engrg*, **SE-11**(12), (December 1985), 1477–1490.

Ross, S., "Software Reliability: The Stopping Rule Problem," *IEEE Trans. Software Engrg.* **SE-11**(12), (December 1985), 1472–1476.

Schneidewind, N., "Application of Program Graphs and Complexity Analysis to Software Development and Testing," *IEEE Trans. Reliability* **R-28**(3), (August 1979), 192–198.

Sheppard, S., B. Curtis, P. Milliman, and T. Love, "Modern Coding Practices and Programmer Performance," *Computer* **12**(12), (December 1979), 41–49.

Yourdon, E. and L. Constantine, *Structured Design: Fundamentals of a Discipline of Computer Program and Systems Design*, Englewood Cliffs, NJ: Prentice-Hall, 1979.

Zelkowitz, M. V., "Perspectives on Software Engineering," *ACM Computing Surveys* **10**(2), (June 1978), 197–216.

Chapter 10

Software Maintenance

Software maintenance consumes 60–80% of most companies' software budgets (Freedman and Weinberg, 1982; Parikh 1982), the largest single item contributing to high software costs (Yau and Tsai, 1986). U.S. corporations now spend $30 billion annually on software maintenance and, by 1995, the process of fixing and upgrading aging applications software programs will employ 90% of all software resources (Moad, 1990). New code is added faster than old code is discarded, increasing the maintainable systems base. Moreover, growth in system size averages 10% per year (Swanson and Beath, 1990) and maintenance expenditures generally increase as systems age. Large multinational corporations require a 15% increase in programming staff every year just to meet growing maintenance needs (Jones, 1986). And the introduction of fourth-generation languages has not curbed the growth in maintenance requirements (Chapin, 1984; Lehner, 1990; Parikh, 1986).

The recent plea for more software maintenance research is not surprising in light of these trends, coupled with the fact that the amount of research in software maintenance has been minimal as compared to that in software development and testing (Schneidewind, 1987). Research efforts recently have begun to focus on developing improved maintenance practices and design approaches enhancing maintainability, as well as maintenance management policies whose objective is to integrate design and maintenance functions and provide guidelines for inspections and walkthroughs that reduce "side effects" (unanticipated and undesired effects of maintenance).

A need also exists for research that provides guidelines for management policies dealing with growing backlogs of both development and maintenance. Managers must balance increasing maintenance requirements with development efforts; otherwise, maintenance could consume nearly all information-systems resources. In fact, some organizations, such as The Federal Home Loan Bank (the agency that regulates the thrift industry), are so overwhelmed with maintenance that they no longer have the time or resources to develop new applications (Moad, 1990). Strategic use of the maintenance function requires improved methods for managing resources. Managers require information to help determine where to focus maintenance efforts when resources are limited. Moreover, tools are needed to determine strategically how and when to respond to software problems.

This chapter's objective is to describe how the measurement of software failure risk aids the management of risk as a system is used. It demonstrates how software failure risk assessment helps maintenance managers make the following decisions:

- What is the most cost-effective allocation of limited resources to the maintenance of large systems?
- Should faults be fixed immediately, or should fault corrections be incorporated in a new system release?
- Should software simply be fixed, or should it be redesigned and redeveloped?
- How can failure risk be minimized when software is adapted to new requirements?

The chapter describes decisions faced by the software maintenance manager and traditional types of information used to make these decisions. How software failure risk measures can guide maintenance strategies will be discussed along with applications to the case studies introduced in Part II.

10.1. BACKGROUND

Most maintenance is perfective (55%) rather than corrective (20%) or adaptive (25%) (Lientz and Swanson, 1980). Perfective maintenance is performed to enhance performance, maintainability, or execution efficiency. Whereas corrective maintenance identifies and corrects software, performance, and implementation failures, adaptive maintenance conforms software to new data requirements or processing environments in order to minimize functionality risk that arises when the environment changes.

High levels of perfective maintenance exist because managers judge that the cost of perfecting software is justified by the anticipated improvements resulting from perfection rather than merely correction. There is little theory to guide these judgments. Moreover, there is little theory to guide decisions about the allocation of effort. Fix-and-improve reviews* have been suggested, particularly for those portions of the system with the greatest maintenance cost (Freedman and Weinberg, 1982). Maintenance cost, however, does not measure future expected loss due to failure, only historical cost of fixing the software.

The addition of new capabilities must be justified by the cost of such maintenance and its impact on functionality risk. In practice, experienced judgments incorporate subjective assessments of software failure risk to determine not only the appropriate type of maintenance but where efforts should be focused (Parikh, 1986; Vallabhaneni, 1987). But there is little theoretical support for these assessments.

Maintenance management decisions involve trade-offs between costs and benefits. While maintenance costs can generally be estimated from historical records, comparable measurement of the benefits of maintenance is more difficult. First, maintenance can create code more easily maintainable in the future. This can be measured by decreased expected future maintenance costs. Second, maintenance can add functionality to a system, with benefits estimated in terms of the expected impact on future operations. Finally, maintenance can reduce or eliminate the possibility of future failure.† Benefits accruing from reduced failure likelihood have been, perhaps, the most difficult factor to estimate.

Prior maintenance research has not explicitly considered the consequences, or the potential magnitude of exposure due to faults in the software. Researchers have considered the impact of maintenance strategies on the number of defects or software reliability (Adams, 1984; Baker, 1988). This research implicitly assumes that all errors have the same consequences. Although failure cost has been considered when computing reliability dependent cost (Musa *et al.*, 1987), prior research has not addressed the measurement of failure cost or impact. An individual software module's failure risk should be compared with the cost of repairing or replacing that module to determine the most cost-effective maintenance strategy.

10.2. ALLOCATION OF MAINTENANCE RESOURCES

Competing demands for programmer time are among the most severe problems in maintenance, second only to level of demand (Lientz, 1983).

*These reviews attempt to leave the code better than it was originally, not only fixing the code but "cultivating" it as well (Freedman and Weinberg, 1982).

†Poor maintenance can also increase the probability of failure.

Continued growth in the size of application-systems portfolios, despite limitations on the size of information-systems organizations, will only exacerbate this problem. Limited financial assets and limited availability of personnel will continue to confine resources. Research has begun to study how work can be organized to carry out the joint tasks of maintenance and development. Alternative bases for systems staff organization have been investigated (Swanson and Beath, 1990). Although improved organization can enhance performance, it will not eliminate the problem. There are simply too many requirements for information systems staffs to handle. Methods are needed to improve productivity and manage the allocation of effort to available resources.

The observation that 80% of maintenance efforts are directed at only 20% of the code has lead to the development of one method for allocating maintenance efforts: "worst-first" maintenance focuses on the worst code, or the code upon which most maintenance effort has historically been expended (Weinberg, 1982). This allocation assumes that past maintenance efforts are indicative of future maintenance requirements, an assumption that is often valid. Nevertheless, as functionality changes and software is fixed, prior poor performance may no longer predict future problems. Moreover, maintenance cost does *not* include the cost or expected loss due to failure, which may be higher in a section of the code that has not previously been maintained.

Evidence drawn from the case studies presented in Part II suggests that high-failure-risk modules account for only a small portion of the software. In the CLS, 89% of the modules had negligible failure risk prior to use (less than $1/month) and 98% of the modules had estimated failure risk less than $100/month. In fact, only three of the modules, representing 2% of all modules analyzed, demonstrated substantial failure risk prior to their use. This proportion increased to only 4% (six modules) after the system was operated for eight months at the savings and loan institution. In the funds-transfer system, failure risk was minimal throughout; only five modules had failure risk greater than $0.20/day, with only 30% of all modules exhibiting failure risk greater than $0.01/day. Finally, only 10% of the payables processing modules had failure risk exceeding $1.00/month.

The Pareto principle may be more effectively applied to failure risk as opposed to past maintenance cost. The ability to measure module failure risk provides the capability to perform "high-risk first" maintenance. When resources are limited, portions of the software that exhibit the highest failure risk should be primary maintenance candidates. Modules may exhibit high failure risk because they have high failure likelihood, often corresponding with modules that historically had the highest maintenance cost. Modules with low failure likelihood, however, may exhibit extremely high exposure, warranting expenditure of maintenance efforts even though they may have failed infrequently. On the other hand, some modules that traditionally had high maintenance costs may have little exposure. Focusing maintenance efforts on these modules may be keeping personnel from performing high-benefit development or maintenance activities with more significant potential payoff.

Failure risk assessments should be periodically updated as a system is used. Exposure changes as system and module use change. New estimates of failure likelihood may be developed as faults leading to failures are found and corrected. Revised estimates can redirect maintenance efforts, providing information regarding when and where to perform maintenance.

Evaluation of the economic impact of maintenance has another advantage: the failure risk assessment can serve as a motivational factor. Maintenance has typically not been considered a "valuable" career opportunity, because programmers feel that they are not advancing with new technology (Parikh, 1986). When compared with new application development, improvements are less visible because the impact of code revisions is not easily measured. Maintenance tasks can appear boring and thankless when maintainers are not cognizant of their importance. Information regarding the economic significance of the failures whose likelihood is reduced during maintenance can provide motivation for maintenance.

To demonstrate how failure risk can guide maintenance, Table 10.1 (condensed from Table 5.13) reviews the reevaluation of failure risk after operation of the CLS. Module 2300 (financial posting) and module 2400 (billing extract) had the highest failure risk of all modules. When maintenance resources are limited, efforts should focus on these two modules rather than, for example, module 111 (payoff inquiry) or module 10 (online interface). Moreover, the measurable significance to the savings and loan institution that results from reducing the failure risk of modules 2300 and 2400 might inspire the maintainer to improve and perfect this portion of the software. During eight months of operation at the savings and loan institution, the number of faults found in the

Table 10.1. Failure Risk Assessments

		Estimated risk ($/month)	
Module	Description	Prior to use	After 8 months
10	Online	27	22
111	Payoff inquiry	0	0
162	Turndown inquiry	0	0
1150	Validation and update	7	135
2300	Financial posting	1157	1404
2400	Billing extract	2370	1248
2450	Billing print	54	406
3500	Report extract	781	406

modules that print bills (2450) and validate and update data files (1150) significantly increased the failure risk in these modules as compared to initial estimates. It is suggested that these modules be carefully reviewed. "Fix-and-improve" or perfective maintenance is indicated.

10.3. IMMEDIATE VERSUS SCHEDULED MAINTENANCE

Managers generally have two responses to operational software failure: either the faulty software that led to the failure is repaired immediately or repairs are postponed. Scheduled maintenance defers changes until a predetermined time when a group of corrections are installed together rather than being repaired when each maintenance request is received (Lindhorst, 1982). Scheduled maintenance is frequently used when software is purchased. Buyers wait until a new release or series of releases is supplied by the software vendor to correct any problems. Sometimes, even when changes are supplied, users are reluctant to install them because of anticipated problems. For example, users of IBM software products periodically receive Program Temporary Fixes (PTFs). The PTF typically incorporate fixes for all significant errors found in the product within the last two months. Some users install all PTFs preventively, some install only selected PTFs, and others just kept PTFs as an immediate source for fixes should the need arise. Finally, some install PTFs only after waiting to see if other users encounter new design errors (Adams, 1984).

Users are frequently more aware of the costs and risk of fixes than they are persuaded of their benefits because it is difficult to demonstrate benefits in terms of the hypothetical events that they hopefully avert (Adams, 1984). The benefit from fixing errors immediately is the decreased failure risk during the time period until maintenance is scheduled. It may, however, cost more to implement a change immediately because resources are needed to prepare, disseminate, and install corrections. In addition, there is the added risk of introducing additional faults. Moreover, scheduling maintenance has several benefits, not easily quantifiable, including consolidation of requests, programmer job enrichment, forcing user departments to think more about requested changes, periodic application evaluation, elimination of the "squeaky wheel syndrome," programmer back-up, better planning, and recognition that data processing change requests are as important as user requests (Lindhorst, 1982). In addition, design errors may be more obvious when the corrections are implemented together. These benefits of scheduled maintenance must be balanced against the decreased failure risk resulting from immediate repairs. Several researchers developed models that consider the impact of scheduled maintenance on reliability or reduction in rate of problems (Adams, 1984; Baker, 1988). However, since reliability does not incorporate the economic consequence of failure, it does not measure the true benefit of the repair.

Failure risk assessment provides guidelines to determine whether to fix faults immediately or wait and schedule all system maintenance, possibly with the installation of a new release. If the additional cost to fix a module immediately is less than the operational failure risk, then the maintenance manager should consider fixing it immediately. Of course, additional nonquantifiable benefits from scheduled maintenance, referred to above, should be weighed and considered in the decision. On the other hand, scheduled maintenance is desirable if the operational failure risk is less than the additional cost to immediately implement the changes.

For example, assume that the cost of an immediate field repair of module 2450 of the CLS after eight months of operation would cost $300 more than waiting until installation of a release scheduled two months later. Since the estimated failure risk of this module is $406 per month, the savings and loan can decrease average failure risk by repairing the module immediately. Of course, this decrease in failure risk should be evaluated against other benefits from deferring the changes until the new release. On the other hand, suppose that the savings and loan institution estimated the additional cost to immediately fix module 1150 at $300. Failure risk of module 1150 is only $135 per month and would not justify the cost of immediate repair.

Of course, the failure risk assessments represent average failure risk arising from all faults in a module. Actual failure risk reduction will not be equal to average failure risk, but to actual loss that results from the failure to fix the software, adjusted for the failure risk introduced by new software. The failure risk assessments can, however, provide guidelines to determine whether immediate repairs should be considered.

10.4. PERFECTIVE VERSUS CORRECTIVE MAINTENANCE

Maintenance managers have often chosen to perfect software rather than simply correct it. Several characteristics of application software have traditionally suggested the need to redesign software. These include (Vallabhaneni, 1987):

- Frequent system failures
- Code more than seven to ten years old
- Overly complex program structure and logic
- Code written for outdated hardware
- Running in emulation mode

- Very large modules or unit subroutines
- Excessive resource requirements
- Hard-coded parameters that are subject to change
- Difficulty in keeping maintainers
- Seriously deficient documentation
- Missing or incomplete design specifications

These factors affect performance, maintainability, and often the reliability of the software. The decision to perfect software involves an implicit tradeoff between the costs to perfect and the anticipated benefits. The latter include not only the decrease in future maintenance and performance costs, but the decrease in operational failure risk.

Perfecting software can reduce the likelihood of failure by providing software with fewer faults or reduced probability of failures causing faults. "Perfected" software may meet the specifications more closely and/or be structured to minimize errors. For example, modules can be redesigned so that high-exposure functions are isolated in smaller, less complex, and thoroughly tested modules with reduced failure likelihood.

Perfective maintenance can also reduce future maintenance costs when more easily maintainable software is developed. Improved code structure and proper documentation can reduce future maintenance efforts.

Perfective maintenance, however, is frequently more costly than corrective maintenance, because it involves redesign, redevelopment, and retesting of the software. An exception exists if existing software is so poorly written that it is impossible to correct without introducing new faults.

For example, consider module 1150 of the CLS. Assume that corrective maintenance for this module (after eight months operation) costs $100. Suppose redesign of the software would cost $1000. The question is whether expenditure of the additional $900 is warranted. The failure risk of module 1150 is $1535/month for the next year of operation. In addition, the expected cost to fix a fault is $100. Since the expected number of failures during the next year is 0.85, the expected cost to fix the software is $85. Thus, the total operational cost in the next year is $1620. If the software is perfected, however, the failure risk is estimated to be only $200 during the next year, because high-exposure functions will be segregated in small, well-structured modules. Since the perfected software will be more easily maintainable, the cost to fix the software is estimated to be only $20 per failure. The expected number of failures in the new modules during the next year is 0.6. Thus, the operational cost of the perfected software is $212. The additional cost is $900, while the reduction in operational cost for just one year is $1408, implying that the benefits of perfective maintenance support the additional cost.

The impact of various design structures can be analyzed to determine the resulting contribution to failure risk. Attention to the failure risk assessment of the new design not only shows whether the perfective maintenance is warranted but also indicates how maintenance can decrease failure risk. In particular, isolation of high-exposure functions in small, well-written, and structured modules can reduce failure risk.

10.5. ENHANCEMENTS

Maintenance can involve adding new system functionality. Systems can become functionally inappropriate when environments change. Moreover, when a software product proves useful, people try to apply it in new cases that are often at the edge of or beyond its original domain (Brooks, 1987). While new features and applications add benefits, they also introduce new failure risk. Software failure risk assessment provides the ability to evaluate the impact of changes on both exposure and failure likelihood.

External risks must first be identified when new capabilities are proposed. How these new functions will be incorporated in the external use of the system must be reviewed in order to determine exposure. Changes to operating procedures can be indicated when measuring the exposure of these new functions, helping to minimize failure risk arising from such maintenance.

Design alternatives for integrating these new functions must be carefully considered. The effects of maintenance changes can be very costly, as demonstrated by the AT&T breakdown that stemmed from an improvement in the original telephone switching system undertaken in order to reduce the time between dialing and ringing from 20 seconds to 4 seconds (Elmer-Dewitt, 1990). Risks can be identified only by carefully reviewing the dependencies in the software system. By focusing on hazards introduced with the new functions, the system can be reverse-engineered to consider all software modules contributing to the hazard. This may help identify potential side effects before they occur. Structural exposure assessment identifies the alternative impacts on failure risk of various designs. Evaluation of alternative design strategies can aid in failure risk minimization. Finally, failure risk assessment can measure the failure risk of proposed new software, and the risk can then be compared with the benefits derived from the new functionality in order to evaluate the cost effectiveness of proposed maintenance.

To illustrate, consider the funds-transfer system discussed in Chapter 6. The bank operations center installed this system to process wire transfers for four banks. Suppose that one year later further bank consolidation occurs, new banks are incorporated, and a new bank divisional structure is established. The system must now be revised. The first task should be to consider the change's impact on external processing: How will the new banks communicate with the operations center? How will their inclusion affect the external hazards and exposure? The second task is to design the system changes in order to minimize exposure, both external to the software and within the software itself. Various designs should be considered. For example, separate modules might be added that would process transfers for these new banks, or existing modules could be changed. Failure risks of these alternative designs should be evaluated and compared. Moreover, this risk evaluation process helps eliminate side effects.

Consider next the voucher-processing system described in Chapter 7. The system incorporates special inventory processing for several transactions that are entered by accounts payable personnel, item quantities and LIFO codes are maintained in inventory records. Field locations do not enter and record this information. If this capability were added in the future, it would be necessary to evaluate the risks associated with recording this information in the field. External field use would be compared with internal accounts payable use in order to identify external exposure. The failure risk of design changes proposed for the existing data-entry modules would be reviewed in order to determine the impact of this maintenance on failure risk.

REFERENCES

Adams, E. N., "Optimizing Preventive Service of Software Products," *IBM J. Systems Develop.* **28**(1), (January 1984), 2–14.

Baker, C. T., "Effects of Field Service on Software Reliability," *IEEE Trans. Software Engrg.* **SE-14**(2), (February 1988), 254–258.

Brooks, F., "No Silver Bullet: Essence and Accidents of Software Engineering," *IEEE Computer*, April, 1987, pp. 10–19.

Chapin, N., "Software Maintenance with Fourth-Generation Languages," *Software Engrg. Notes* **9**(1), (January 1984), 41–42.

Elmer-Dewitt, P., "Ghost in the Machine," *Time*, January 29, 1990, pp. 58–59.

Freedman, D. P. and G. M. Weinberg, "Maintenance Reviews," in *Techniques of Program and System Maintenance* (G. Parikh, ed.), Cambridge, MA: Winthrop, 1982, pp. 53–55.

Jones, C., *Programming Productivity*, New York: McGraw-Hill, 1986.

Lehner, F., "Cost Comparison for the Development and Maintenance of Application Systems in 3rd and 4th Generation Languages," *Information and Management*, 1990, pp. 131–141.

Lientz, B. P., "Issues in Software Maintenance," *Computing Surveys* **15**(3), (September 1983), 271–278.

Lientz, B. P. and E. B. Swanson, *Software Maintenance Management*, Reading, MA: Addison-Wesley, 1980.

Lindhorst, W. M., "Scheduled Program Maintenance," in *Techniques of Program and System Maintenance* (G. Parikh, ed.) Cambridge, MA: Winthrop, 1982, pp. 129–132.

Moad, J., "Maintaining the Competitive Edge," *Datamation* February 15, 1990, pp. 61–66.

Musa, J. D., A. Iannino, and K. Okumoto, *Software Reliability: Measurement, Prediction, Application*, New York: McGraw-Hill, 1987.

Parikh, G., *The Guide to Software Maintenance*, Cambridge, MA: Winthrop, 1982.

Parikh, G., *Handbook of Software Maintenance*, New York: Wiley, 1986.

Schneidewind, N. F., "The State of Software Maintenance," *IEEE Trans. Software Engrg.* **SE-13**(3), (March 1987), 303–310.

Swanson, E. B. and C. M. Beath, "Departmentalization in Software Development and Maintenance," *Comm. ACM* **33**(6), (June, 1990), 658–667.

Vallabhaneni, S. R., *Auditing the Maintenance of Software*, Englewood Cliffs, NJ: Prentice-Hall, 1987.

Weinberg, G. M., "Worst-First Maintenance," in *Techniques of Program and System Maintenance* (G. Parikh, ed.), Cambridge, MA: Winthrop, 1982.

Yau, S.S. and T. J. Tsai, "A Survey of Software Design Techniques," *IEEE Trans. Software Engrg.* **SE-12**(6), (June 1986), 713–721.

Chapter 11

Software Purchase

No longer do companies develop customized systems for every application. Software purchase has become an attractive alternative to inhouse software development. It not only provides economies of scale, but often reduces development risks. The failure risk assessment methodology can be used to manage the acquisition and implementation of purchased software.

Software development increasingly requires highly specialized skills, difficult for information systems departments to find and maintain. Many specialized software companies have grown to meet these demands. In addition, information systems departments are faced with increasing demands for new development as well as growing maintenance requirements. This contributes to the desirability of purchased software, particularly if the purchased software can provide the basic features necessary for the application: "Why reinvent the wheel?" Although bought software may imperfectly address business needs, developing software inhouse may be too costly, and in many cases may increase the time required to make the application operational and useful. It may be more cost effective to refine purchased software to meet unique requirements.

Software purchase alters the risk profile of an information systems project (Clemons *et al.*, 1990). It can reduce some components of risk, such as attempting to produce a system that cannot be developed with existing personnel or technology. It also introduces new risks. Users of purchased software are not involved in internal design reviews where potential operational problems can be identified and risk managed as the software is developed. Since companies often rely on paper exercises, customer testimonials, and vendor-supplied documentation to make purchase decisions (Gershkoff, 1990), the customer may not be cognizant of all changes required to operate the system in the new environment. Tailoring a generic system to fit a specific environment can introduce new risks. Furthermore, purchasing a generic system rather than developing a customized one may entail the loss of some functionality, limiting the system's usefulness. Finally, the purchase of software brings about a new dependence on an outside vendor for future support.

This chapter discusses the impact of software purchase on the components of risk in systems implementation. It describes how the acquisition and implementation of purchased software can be managed in order to minimize software failure risk. The traditional approach to decisions regarding the purchase and implementation of a new software system is demonstrated by describing how the savings and loan institution in Chapter 5 acquired the CLS presented there. How risk measurements could have aided this process is also discussed.

11.1. SOFTWARE ACQUISITION RISK

Generally, the purchase of software reduces one component of project risk, the risk that a project can be completed on time and within budget. It is frequently more difficult to plan and subsequently meet a schedule for a complete development effort than for the installation of a developed system. However, a second component of project risk, the risk that the project results in a system with adequate performance and quality assurance, may not be reduced simply by purchasing a developed system. Moreover, the need to tailor a generic application to a specific location may render a company even more vulnerable to incorrect operation than if the software were developed inhouse.

Functionality risk can be reduced if users truly understand how a system will operate. In the past, purchased software provided more opportunity to preview system operation than inhouse development did. However, prototyping now provides this capability for inhouse development as well. Functionality risk also decreases when software addresses all user requirements. When a generic software package is purchased, it often does not meet specific user requirements. If the system is not altered to address these requirements, users may have to live with a system that does not meet their specific needs, increasing functionality risk.

Financial risk can be reduced with purchased software. While it is often difficult to estimate the cost of software development, the initial cost of the purchased software is known. Cost estimation is limited to the effort needed to install the system in the new environment. The latter can be more accurately estimated, however, only if the customer truly understands the customization and integration requirements.

Technical risk, the risk that the development will go beyond what is technically possible, is generally reduced by purchasing systems from developers with specialized expertise. Political and internal risk may increase with purchased software if members of the internal systems development group perceive the acquisition of purchased software as a threat to their livelihood.

Finally, environmental and competitive risk can also increase with outsourcing of software development. An organization can lose the competitive advantage to be gained by offering one's own system. For example, American Airlines gained a clear advantage in the airline industry by its inhouse development of the SABRE reservation system. This system not only provided American with the capability of giving preferential booking to their own flights, but provided important competitive information for pricing and service action (McFarlan, 1984).

The acquisition of software also introduces risk associated with the purchase transaction, including both the risk of appropriable rent and the loss of resource control (Clemons and Row, 1990). Purchased software is generally maintained by a vendor who frequently supplies periodic new releases to buyers and corrects problems as they arise. Risk from appropriable rents (Klein *et al.*, 1978) occurs when a vendor attempts to opportunistically renegotiate a contract by either increasing the cost of maintenance or refusing to provide maintenance. Since buyers often allow required technical skills to atrophy, they may lose the ability to perform maintenance inhouse, also losing control of resources. Since there is often a high switching cost to convert to another system, the relationship can result in substantial transaction risk.

When making the decision to buy software, it is necessary to trade off the impact of the transaction on all the components of risk. Even if purchase appears beneficial, it will still pose risk. In particular, it can present operational software failure risk because of an inability either to provide necessary functionality or to operate correctly, as a result of inadequate development procedures. Operational failure risk can be minimized by managing the acquisition and implementation of the purchased software with specific methods to identify and measure these risks.

The selection of a software system should include an evaluation of the operational failure risk of a potential system in the customer's environment, in addition to the traditional functional assessment of the proposed system's capabilities. The risk assessment methodology forces a company to explicitly consider the operational use of the system and accompanying changes in its environment before it acquires the system. Risks, identified early, can be used when selecting among competing products as well as when installing the software.

Installation often requires customization, followed by testing in the new environment. Software risk assessment can guide the allocation of testing effort, insuring that the customer's high-risk system components are identified and thoroughly tested before use. Training procedures that focus on the high-risk functions identified for the customer's installation can be designed for the new environment.

11.2. BUYING SOFTWARE

Buying a software system involves selection of software that not only meets user requirements but can be implemented with minimal risk. Decisions necessary to acquire and implement a system are described below, along with a discussion of how formal methods to measure risk can guide these decisions.

A purchased system's functional capabilities must be analyzed in the context of the business environment in which it will operate. If the software does not meet a large number of the requirements, the customization and integration may require almost the level of effort needed to develop the system internally (Gerskhoff, 1990). Existing installations of the software should be analyzed for compatibility with the company's existing installation. The operating requirements should be reviewed, either insuring that they fit the existing technology or verifying that the technology can be expanded to accommodate the software.

Formal methods, such as scoring models or weighted ratings, can be used to choose among competing software systems. These methods focus on what the proposed system can do, whether it meets user requirements, and how it can improve the organization's capabilities. The decision to acquire a software package must also be based upon an understanding of the risks incurred by the use of the new software. In addition to considering how the system will function, the purchaser should focus on what can go wrong when using the proposed system. Changes in the company's operations and environment can be risky if not properly anticipated. Analyzing the transitions that may accommodate the installation of the software is much more difficult than analyzing its ability to meet existing requirements, but failure to do so is the source of perhaps the greatest risk. Formal methods for evaluating external risk can aid this process.

Installation planning follows software acquisition. If the software is to replace an existing system, the company has several installation options. The system can be installed in parallel with the existing system, or it can simply replace the old system, a "cold turkey" installation of the new system. In some cases, a small pilot application of the new system may be feasible. The latter may be particularly attractive for a new system performing completely new functions.

Installation decisions should reflect the cost and risk of failure. A parallel system is costly and difficult to maintain, and there are often difficulties in determining what the output should be compared with, because the new system may provide more accurate results. However, the cold turkey installation of an acquisition can place the company in an unacceptable position of risk if the system does not work correctly. Testing is especially critical for this mode of implementation. The small pilot application may not create the environmental changes necessary to test the risk of failure of the complete system.

Since software can have latent errors, a key consideration is the length of time to either run a pilot or parallel system or to test the new installation before users begin to rely on the output. This decision should consider the cost of continued testing and schedule delays as well as the failure risk. If the risk of failure exceeds the cost, continued testing would be warranted. However, portions of the software with minimal failure risk may not justify the cost of additional testing or maintenance of parallel operations. Risk assessment can be used to focus testing efforts on portions of the system that pose the greatest risk in the customer's environment.

Improper user training can contribute to operational failure risk. Purchased systems are generally supplied with user documentation that must be tailored to provide training in the customer's environment. External operational procedures must be developed to minimize external risks. The software risk assessment can be used to develop user training procedures that focus on high-risk components of the system. In addition, it can provide information to indicate external procedures that can minimize the exposure associated with these components.

11.3. BACKGROUND: ACQUIRING THE CLS

Traditional implementation of purchased software will be described by providing the background for the savings and loan's acquisition and implementation of the CLS whose risk was assessed in Chapter 5.

Prior to the early 1980s, all savings and loan institutions were restricted in their lending to fixed-rate, long-term home mortgages, funded by short-term deposits. In 1983, deregulation provided an environment for savings and loans to adjust their traditional business by broadening their product lines to include shorter-maturity loans.

This savings and loan established its commercial business lending department in 1984, acquiring a basic information system to keep track of its simply structured loans. Within the next several years, the savings and loan expanded quickly through an aggressive acquisition policy and entrance into new markets. Rapid growth taxed the capabilities of the loan information system. Furthermore, changes in the external environment required changes in the information systems. The savings and loan recognized the need to implement an enhanced system.

The initial acquisition task, determining what was required in the new system, was assigned to a group of approximately ten people, consisting of main office and field personnel and system developers. The task force developed a list of requirements in the following six areas:

- Loan accounting and operations
- Loan structures
- Collateral recordkeeping
- Audit and security controls
- Management reporting
- Remote inquiry capabilities

For example, loan accounting and operations requirements included ease of new loan establishment, low number of screens, ability to carry over common account information, complete edit verification on all input items, flexible billing schedules, and multiple transaction options.

The task force proceeded to develop a questionnaire addressing these requirements. The task force identified six commercially available software products. All of the systems were from companies with at least fifteen years in the business and with more than fifty technical support people; four systems had at least twenty-five installations each. The systems ranged in age from new (less than one month) to seventeen years old. The number of programs in these systems ranged from 200 to 800. Using their questionnaires as the basis for telephone interviews, the task force obtained information regarding each of the items on their requirements list. Each system received a rating on each of the requirements. In addition, a summary of the major strengths and weaknesses of each of the systems was prepared.

Based on the results of the ratings, the group recommended the system that was acquired and whose risk is evaluated in Chapter 5. This system met almost all the requirements; the cost of acquiring this system and customizing it to fit their needs was less than the cost of internal development.

The savings and loan made a very careful, thorough investigation of how the proposed system would meet the identified requirements. The formalized analysis concentrated on specific requirements and how the system would meet these requirements. Although informally considered, there was no formal analysis of the risk of each of the systems or explicit consideration of what could go wrong when each system would be used at the savings and loan. The purchase decision could have been augmented with information gained from external risk identification, as will be discussed below.

This system was implemented at the savings and loan in 1987. Test procedures and training plans were developed during implementation planning.

The system was tested during a three-month implementation period, followed by a planned one-month parallel operation with the existing system. Due to problems that arose during the first month of parallel operation, management approved a second month of parallel testing, after which the system became totally operational. During the first eight months of operation, 34 problems were uncovered, requiring corrections to 21 modules in the system.

Training programs were developed for both loan office and main office personnel. Loan office personnel were provided with training in setting up specific types of loans and responding to customer inquiries. The acquired system offered many additional capabilities (e.g., alternative loan structures) that the savings and loan did not plan to use immediately. Information regarding these features was provided to the loan officers in manuals. Main office personnel were instructed in data entry and verification procedures; exception handling was outlined in data entry manuals.

11.4. IMPROVING SOFTWARE ACQUISITION DECISIONS WITH RISK ASSESSMENT

Risk assessment forces explicit consideration of the external use of the proposed system and its associated risks, considerations that can supplement an analysis of a system's capability of meeting functional requirements. This explicit analysis of operational use and hazards is the most significant contribution of the risk assessment procedures to the purchase of software.

The decision to acquire the CLS could have incorporated information from the external risk assessment of all proposed systems. Procedures used by loan officers, note tellers, and loan control personnel varied with each proposed system, depending upon its functional capabilities. Variations in audit reports and inquiry screens provided by the systems contribute to differences in external risk. Different features offered by the proposed systems change the external processing and hence the external exposure. The assessment of external risk for each proposed software system demonstrates its risk in the new environment.

For example, consider the hazard of *overadvancing committed dollars*, which means that customers receive loan advances exceeding the legal lending limit. Since commitments are made at various levels of an organization, linkages are required so that total commitments can be monitored. Accident sequences and failure modes for each of the proposed systems demonstrated differences in exposure to this hazard. For example, one of the systems considered required much extra manual work on the part of the loan officer to identify these linkages. An alternative system used participations, affiliations, and indirect liabilities to establish these linkages, requiring additional officer training. A third system had pointers across organization levels, which posed different external risks due to the different manual processing functions required to support these linkages.

Next, consider the hazards of *not producing bills* and *invalid accruals*. Differences in processing features among the various proposed systems affected external processing requirements for producing bills. Several systems that were considered required billing defaults to be set manually, while others included different types of automatic defaults, each with its own associated risks. While some systems had fixed payment frequencies, others had overlapping schedules which would affect the billing cycle and external processing. Some systems calculated customer billed amount; one billed only the payment amount on a note record; another billed a percentage of outstanding balance. The external risk assessment forced consideration of how these differences affected external processing and resulted in differences in external risk.

External risk assessment, by focusing on what can go wrong, requires consideration of how the environment will change. This savings and loan planned to begin direct posting to its general ledger at some time in the future. The various procedures required by each system to accomplish this task were analyzed to determine which would minimize external exposure due to the identified hazard of *misposting of transactions to general ledger*.

As loan officers gain experience with the system, they may attempt to use previously untried functions, causing them to access certain portions of the system invalidly. They might establish more complex loan structures, increasing the hazard of *invalid interest accruals*. The loan officers might not be as familiar with procedures to set up these loans, and these more complex structures might involve previously unused code. Procedures needed for training and use of these features were evaluated for each system. External accident sequences and failure modes for each of the systems identified differences in external risk due to these hazards.

11.5. IMPROVING SYSTEM IMPLEMENTATION DECISIONS WITH RISK ASSESSMENT

How should a new system be installed? Where should test effort be focused? How much testing is needed? What type of training procedures are needed? These questions must be addressed when implementing a purchased system. The risk assessment methodology could have been used to address these questions when the CLS was implemented.

The type of implementation—parallel, pilot, cold turkey—is a function of the type of system, the cost of installation, and the risk of failure. In all cases, testing is required since the system is operating in a new environment. Usually, this testing is black-box or functional, rather than white-box or structural. The decision to stop testing is made when the manager feels that the functions have been adequately tested or the deadline for new system use arrives. Module risk assessment can be used to allow the project manager to structurally test the system so that portions of the system that have the greatest risk of failure in this new environment receive adequate testing as discussed, in Chapter 9.

The ability to reliably use formal risk assessment methods early in the testing effort depends on the availability of data. If adequate historical failure information is available, early testing efforts can be guided by the risk assessment. In the absence of this information, more generic failure likelihood data can be used initially, but the results need to be validated in the specific environment. (This was the case with the funds system.) Furthermore, in instances where purchased software is supplied without technical systems documentation, specific risk estimates may be difficult to obtain. Nevertheless, external risk assessment may still be used to rank modules or system functions based on exposure. Future research needs to focus on the ways to use risk to manage the implementation of purchased software in the absence of complete failure and/or systems data.

Training procedures can be developed using risk assessments. Modules with the greatest risk of failure must be monitored most closely. Therefore, output from these modules must be most stringently reviewed. Procedures for reviewing audit reports should insure that the results of processing within these modules are evaluated most carefully.

REFERENCES

Clemons, E. K. and M. C. Row, "Information Technology and Industrial Cooperation," Working Paper, Department of Decision Sciences, Wharton School, University of Pennsylvania, 1990.

Clemons, E. K., B. W. Weber, and D. Brennen, "Components of Risk in Strategic IT Programs: Implications and Risk Management," *Proc. Conf. Strategic Information Architectures*, June 22, 1990, University of Pennsylvania, Philadelphia.

Gershkoff, I., "The Make or Buy Game," *Datamation*, February 15, 1990, pp. 73–77.

Klein, B., R. G. Crawford, and A. A. Alchian, "Vertical Integration, Appropriable Rents, and the Competitive Contracting Process," *J. Law and Business* **21**(2), (October 1978), 297–326.

McFarlan, F. W., "Information Technology Changes the Way You Compete," *Harvard Business Rev.*, (May-June 1984), pp. 98–103.

Appendixes

Appendix A

Fault Prediction Methods

Software failure risk assessment methodology uses module size to predict the number of faults prior to test. "It has long been assumed that the size of a program has the most effect on the number of inherent faults it contains" (Musa *et al.*, 1987). But size accounts for only 50–60% of the variation in the number of faults (Musa *et al.*, 1987). The accuracy of the risk assessments could be increased if fault predictability could be improved. The objective of this appendix is to explore existing fault prediction research to provide direction for future studies that can improve the accuracy of risk estimates.

A description of how software faults are introduced provides the foundation for a taxonomy of the literature. This classification clarifies often unstated assumptions regarding the choice of predictor variables. Moreover, it highlights relationships among the studies and serves as a vehicle for critical evaluation of that research. The taxonomy suggests inadequacies in theory and deficiencies in current knowledge of software faults.

This review suggests several future research topics. Characteristics of early development products (requirements specifications, design documents, and prototypes) should be considered for predicting software faults. Task or problem complexity measures may predict faults resulting from omitted requirements and code. While several code metrics exist, more theoretical research is necessary to justify and improve their use in fault prediction.

A.1. SOFTWARE FAULT INTRODUCTION

Software fault prediction methodology should be grounded in theory that describes the relationship between an independent variable and the injection of faults in software. This requires an understanding of how faults are introduced into software.

Software faults results from errors in the process of developing a software product in order to meet specific user needs. They are manifested by incorrect or incomplete code that causes system failure—operation of the software in a manner that does not meet users' needs. While faults can be introduced throughout the software life cycle, they are frequently not discovered until code is tested or used.

Faults can be introduced as requirements are developed, when requirements are translated into a software design or prototype, when the code is written and tested, or as the software is used (see Fig. A.1). A transformation occurs during each phase when the developer translates an input such as a problem description or design document into its respective product. When an error occurs, a fault in that product results. This fault is caused by either

- incorrect or incomplete input, or
- errors in the transformation, the task of translating the input into the product.

For example, design document faults result from either incomplete or incorrect specifications or from incorrect translation of these specifications to that design.

A.2. FAULT PREDICTION TAXONOMY

The number of faults in code can be estimated by analyzing either products of the life cycle (shown as rectangles in Fig. A.1) or the process involved in developing these products (arrows in Fig. A.1). In either case, the analysis can be predictive or inferential. Whereas *predictive* variables are characteristics of processes or products that explain why more (fewer) faults will be introduced in later stages of development or use, *inferential* variables explain why more (fewer) errors have already occurred in the development cycle. The taxonomy in Table A.1 incorporates some fault prediction variables.

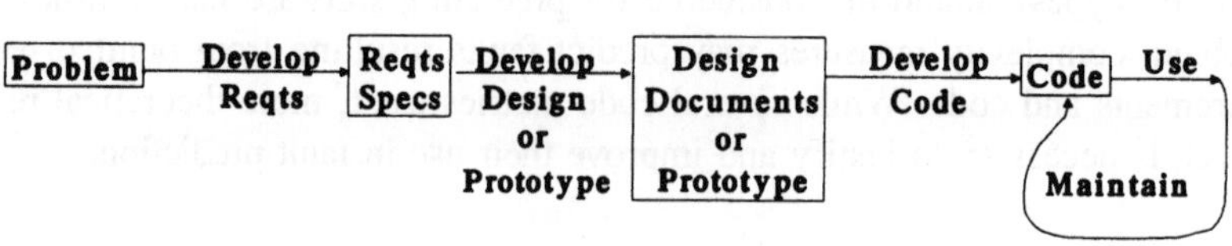

Figure A.1. Software development process and products.

Table A.1. Taxonomy of Software Fault Prediction Variables

	Predictive	Inferential
Product	Quantity design documents	Code size
	Extensiveness of specifications	Code complexity
	Complexity of design	Design complexity
	Input variablility	
Process	Design errors	Developer skill
	Requirements changes	Use of structured methods
		Development team organization
		Deadline pressures

Product predictive variables are problem or product characteristics that cause future errors or failures. For example, it is hypothesized that extensive requirements specifications lead to fewer code faults because there is little opportunity to omit requirements. More complex design documents are hypothesized to cause more coding errors due to comprehension difficulties. Code measures can also be predictive measures: complexity and diversity of code input may lead to more errors when using that code.

Product inferential variables are product characteristics that result if errors were introduced when developing that product. For example, it is often assumed that longer code has more faults because more opportunities existed to introduce them. Characteristics of development products that precede the code, such as requirements specifications, design documents, and prototypes, may indicate that they themselves have more faults. It is generally assumed that these faults subsequently translate into code faults.*

Process predictive variables are process characteristics that cause future errors. The most common predictive measures of future errors are counts of requirements changes and design errors. More changes or design errors are assumed to indicate that more errors will continue to be made.

Process inferential variables are characteristics of the translation process, usually measured during or after development rather than in advance.† These studies look at the *who*, *what*, *when*, *why*, and *how* of software development:

- *Who* performed the development process? Did programmer or designer skill affect errors?

*Sometimes experienced developers recognize and correct these errors before the software is produced.

†These measures would be predictive if they were estimated before development occurs. However, this would require complete knowledge of an unchanging environment, a rare situation in software development.

- *What* steps did the developer take? Did the use of development techniques such as stepwise refinement, iterative development, a life cycle approach, or structured programming affect errors?
- *How* was development performed? Did organizational factors such as the impact of the team approach, the use of reviews, and the grouping of individuals significantly affect the number of errors?
- *Why* was development performed as it was? Was there a match between tasks and approach or between tasks and assigned skill levels? Did this match affect the number of errors?
- *When* was development carried out? How much time was allotted to the tasks? Were there time pressures? Did these factors significantly affect the number of errors?

A.3. SUMMARY OF RESEARCH RESULTS

Key software fault prediction studies are classified in Table A.2. Most are product inferential studies; the vast majority of these used code inferential measures because the code is the most readily available software development product—the product tested to find faults. Furthermore, objective measures of code characteristics are often available, measurable with automated tools. This research assumes that a characteristic of the code is indicative of the degree of error-proneness of the process involved in generating that code. It therefore assumes two specific relationships: between code and process and between process and fault introduction.

Substantially less research has focused on measuring characteristics of products of the software development life cycle prior to the code to either infer the existence of errors in these documents or to predict future sources of error when translating these documents into code.

Although many studies have proposed improved software development techniques, fault predictions incorporate process variables less often than product variables. First, process predictive studies rely on the assumption that the development environment remains constant—an assumption rarely met. Second, empirical measurement difficulties with process variables make inference difficult. Whereas the significance of individual and environmental factors and the importance of certain design and programming techniques are often expounded, only a few studies have attempted to measure the impact of these factors on the number of software faults.

A.3.1. Product Predictive Studies

Existing studies have typically analyzed design document characteristics (See Table A.3). For example, minimal design documentation means that the

Table A.2. Classification of Studies

	Predictive	Inferential
Product	Yin and Winchester, 1978 Takahashi and Kamayachi, 1989	Akiyama, 1971 Gannon and Horning, 1975 Klobert, 1977 Schneidewind, 1979 Schneidewind and Hoffman, 1979 Feuer and Fowlkes, 1979 Ottenstein, 1979 Dunsmore and Gannon, 1980 Lipow, 1982 Basili and Hutchens, 1983 Basili and Perricone, 1984 Gaffney, 1984 Gremillon, 1984 Shen *et al.*, 1985 Basili and Patnaik, 1986 Card *et al.*, 1986 Harrison and Cook, 1986 Selby and Porter, 1988 Takahashi and Kamayachi, 1989
Process	Lipow and Thayer, 1977 Yu *et al.*, 1988 Takahashi and Kamayachi, 1989	Basili and Reiter, 1981 Basili and Hutchens, 1983 Basili and Perricone, 1984 Card *et al.*, 1986 Selby *et al.*, 1987 Card *et al.*, 1987 Selby and Porter, 1988 Takahashi and Kamayachi, 1989

development of code is more error prone (Takahashi and Kamayachi, 1989). Measures of design complexity predict more errors will be made when translating this more complex design into code (Yin and Winchester, 1978).

Studies of requirements specifications or prototype features to predict faults are lacking. In addition, study of characteristics of the code to predict whether more faults will be made when using that code (rather than to infer that more faults were made when developing the code) are also lacking.

Table A.3. Product Predictive Studies

Authors	Independent variables
Yin and Winchester, 1978	Network complexity
Takahashi and Kamayachi, 1989	Number of pages of program design documents

A.3.2. Product Inferential Studies

Product inferential studies have generally concentrated on relating the number of faults to either code size or complexity (Table A.4). Many researchers have reported that larger programs tend to have more errors than smaller ones, both during the development process (Basili and Hutchens, 1983; Gaffney, 1984; Lipow, 1982; Shen *et al.*, 1985; Takahashi and Kamayachi, 1989) and during maintenance (Feuer and Fowlkes, 1979; Gremillion, 1984), suggesting that errors be normalized by measuring fault density or errors per thousand lines of code. Standard fault densities could then estimate the number of errors in software based upon size. The implicit assumption here—that fault density is independent of size—has been supported by the results of Akiyama (1971), Card *et al.* (1986), and Takahashi and Kamayachi (1989). However, Feuer and Fowlkes (1979), Gaffney (1984), and Lipow (1982) reported higher fault densities in larger programs, whereas Basili and Perricone (1984), Ottenstein (1979), and Shen *et al.* (1985) reported higher fault densities in smaller modules. The nature of the relationship between size and the number of faults has not been well established.

Table A.4. Product Inferential Studies

Authors	Independent variable	Stage of fault detection
Takahashi and Kamayachi, 1989	Size	Code inspection, unit testing
Selby and Porter, 1988	Size, complexity, style	Total development
Card *et al.*, 1986	Size, complexity	Total development
Harrison and Cook, 1986	Programming style	System testing
Basili and Patnaik, 1986	Size	System testing
Shen *et al.*, 1985	Complexity, size	After unit testing
Basili and Perricone, 1984	Size, complexity	All phases
Gaffney, 1984	Size, complexity	All phases
Gremillon, 1984	Size	Repair only
Basili and Hutchens, 1983	Complexity	All changes
Lipow, 1982	Complexity	All changes
Dunsmore and Gannon, 1980	Programming language constructs	Throughout process
Schneidewind, 1979	Complexity	After first successful compile
Schneidewind and Hoffman, 1979	Complexity	After first successful compile
Feuer and Fowlkes, 1979	Size, complexity	Maintenance
Ottenstein, 1979	Complexity	Beginning of testing
Klobert, 1977	Complexity	After initial module tests
Gannon and Horning, 1975	Languages	Throughout process
Akiyama, 1971	Complexity	Includes unit test

Similar results exist for error prediction studies based on code complexity. The most common variable used to measure code complexity, the cyclomatic number, or the number of basic paths that, when taken in combination, generate every possible path (McCabe, 1976), has been shown to correlate with the number of lines of code (Basili and Hutchens, 1983; Basili and Perricone, 1984; Feuer and Fowlkes, 1979; Gaffney, 1984; Gremillion, 1984). Most researchers have concluded that size is a better single predictor of the number of faults than complexity (Basili and Hutchens, 1983; Feuer and Fowlkes, 1979; Gaffney, 1984, Gremillion, 1984). Schneidewind (1979), Schneidewind and Hoffman (1979), and Shen *et al.* (1985) have shown that complexity measures could identify modules most likely to contain errors, but the relationship is not expressible as a mathematical function, a claim contested by Basili and Perricone (1984). The ability to detect errors has been shown to decrease with complexity (Green *et al.*, 1976) so it is possible that complexity can predict the number of faults that remain after testing rather than the total number of inherent faults prior to test.

Although code size and complexity are used most frequently, several other characteristics have also been studied, including Halstead's software science metrics and language and style characteristics. The notion that the number of errors is a function of the level of the language (Gannon, 1977; Gannon and Horning, 1975; Lipow, 1982) has been contested (Gaffney, 1984). Evidence that style characteristics, such as data communication and nesting depth, are correlated with errors (Dunsmore and Gannon, 1980) has not been substantiated (Feuer and Fowlkes, 1979; Gremillion, 1984; Harrison and Cook, 1986). One study empirically analyzed errors by type of statement—e.g., allocation, assignment, or input/output (Youngs, 1981)—but the use of this information to predict faults has not been addressed.

A.3.3. Process Predictive Studies

Process predictive studies do not consider individual project or program characteristics that affect the number of errors, but instead assume that the number of software faults can be predicted directly from the number of faults discovered or changes required early in the development process (see Table A.5). These errors or changes are generally assumed to indicate either erroneous understanding of a problem or volatile requirements expected to translate to more faults. The underlying assumption is similar to Myers's testing principle:

> The probability of the existence of more errors in a section of a program is proportional to the number of errors already found in that section. (Myers 1979)

Table A.5. Process Predictive Studies

Authors	Independent variable
Takahashi and Kamayachi, 1989	Frequency of Program specification change
Yu *et al.*, 1988	Number of defects during design review, code inspection
Lipow and Thayer, 1977	Number of design problem reports

A.3.4. Process Inferential Studies

Process inferential studies estimate the number of faults in software by inferring a relationship between a characteristic of the development process and its propensity to cause errors. Although much effort has been exerted to suggest ways to improve software development, and much research suggesting that several techniques reduce errors, there has been little attempt to predict errors based on these methods. Studies that address the basic process questions—who, what, how, why and when?—will be described below (see Table A.6).

A.3.4.1. Who Develops the Software?

The individual programmer's experience, talent and constitution have been suggested as factors affecting errors (Endres, 1975). The significance of variability in programming performance has been supported by Brooks (1977), Vessey (1986), and Weinberg (1971). However the nature of the relationship

Table A.6. Process Inferential Studies

Authors	Type	Variables
Takahashi and Kamayachi, 1989	Who?	Number years programming experience
	What?	Level of technology
Selby and Porter, 1988	When?	Design/code effort
Selby *et al.*, 1987	Who?	Programming language experience
	When?	Design, code effort
Card *et al.*, 1987	Who?	General, application experience
	What?	Level of technology
	When?	Design schedule
	How?	Programmer teams
Card *et al.*, 1986	What?	Software reuse
Basili and Perricone, 1984	What?	Code reuse
Basili and Hutchens, 1983	Who?	Programmer
	How?	Individual versus teams
	What?	Disciplined versus *ad hoc*
Basili and Reiter, 1979	What?	Disciplined methodology
	How?	Size of team

between individual programmer performance and the number of faults has not been established. Brown and Lipow (1975), Card *et al.* (1987), and Takahashi and Kamayachi (1989) have reported that more experienced developers produce code with fewer faults, a claim not substantiated by Selby *et al.* (1987) or Vessey and Weber (1984). Youngs (1981) reported that both beginners and advanced programmers had approximately the same number of errors on the first runs of all programs. Experienced programmers reportedly find more faults (Basili and Selby, 1987; Youngs, 1981); hence, programmer ability, like complexity, might measure the number of faults remaining after rather than before testing.

Although the emphasis has been on programmer skill, Adelson (1985) found large differences in design skill between novices and experts. The number of software faults may well depend upon the designer's experience, but empirical studies to demonstrate this relationship are lacking.

A.3.4.2. What Techniques Are Used?

Software development research has focused on developing methodologies that aid in the analysis of requirements and the design of new systems (Basili and Perricone, 1984; Boar, 1984; Card *et al.*, 1986; DeMarco, 1979; Gane and Sarson, 1979; Hamilton and Zeldin, 1976; Jackson, 1975; Myers, 1975; Nauman and Jenkins, 1982; Orr, 1977; Ross, 1977; Teicherow and Hershey, 1977; Yourdon and Constantine, 1979). The variety of tools and techniques provided by these methods enables the software developer to define more clearly how a system is supposed to operate. Although these methodologies claim to provide more reliable software, few studies measured the relationship between their use and the number of faults (Basili and Perricone, 1984; Card *et al.*, 1986).

A.3.4.3. How Is Software Developed?

Research supports the establishment of organizational schemes to improve development (Brooks, 1982; Weinberg, 1971): the *how* of development. Minimizing the number of individuals has been suggested as one factor that impacts system integrity (Brooks, 1982, Zelkowitz, 1978). In addition, the use of design and code reviews, quality assurance techniques, and the team approach improve the development process (Brooks, 1982; Weinberg, 1971). Empirical studies support the notion that the way a system is developed affects its fault rate (Basili and Reiter, 1979; Card *et al.*, 1987; Selby *et al.*, 1987).

A.3.4.4. Why Are Development Techniques Used?

Researchers have suggested that the *why* of the development process (why does development proceed in a certain manner?) affects the introduction of faults. Vessey and Weber (1983) suggest that complexity can be effectively reduced by matching the designers' problem-solving processes with methods, tools, and techniques designed to aid them in their tasks. A design tool's helpfulness depends upon the designer's experience with the object and domain of design (Adelson and Soloway, 1985). One factor that may increase reliability is a match between task and approach and between task and assigned skill level (Vessey, 1986). However, the impact of the *why* of development on the introduction of faults has not been studied.

A.3.4.5. When Is Software Developed?

Evidence suggests that projects produced under severe time limitations may have more faults (Brooks, 1982). Nevertheless, one study did not find that design schedule (related weight of design in the development process as measured by percent of total development schedule) affected errors (Card *et al.*, 1987). More empirical work is required to investigate whether the *when* of software development can predict software faults.

A.4. DISCUSSION OF LITERATURE: IMPLICATIONS FOR FUTURE RESEARCH

Studies using code inferential variables do not provide conclusive evidence of a relationship between these characteristics and the introduction of errors in the development process. Moreover, these variables are insufficient when measuring problem complexity and requirements or design omissions. Finally, since the discovery of many software failures depends on how the software is used, code use (predictive) may more adequately address the true likelihood of finding faults than does analysis of code structure (inferential).

Research has also not substantiated the usefulness of various software development methods: Do they reduce the number of errors to be found during the test phase, or do they make it easier to find errors during this phase? Key process variables, particularly the "why" of software development, have not been studied.

A.4.1. Code Inferential Variables

Theoretical support for using code inferential variables to predict software faults has been contested. Moreover, these variables do not account for process variability. More cognitive studies are necessary to truly understand the nature of error infusion.

The theory supporting the use of code inferential variables assumes that memory limitation derives from simple stimuli or sensory recognition (Halstead, 1977). This contention has been disputed with the argument that programming parameters come from long-term memory (Brooks, 1977; Coulter, 1983; Curtis, 1980), suggesting that limitations of human programming ability vary in proportion to the programmer's experience and talents in order to accommodate long-term memory. Furthermore, other process factors, such as greater care exercised when coding larger modules (Basili and Perricone, 1984; Shen *et al.*, 1985), are not reflected in product metrics. This may explain the often contradictory results of the studies based upon size.

These predictions might be improved if individual performance were studied. Process variability would be reduced if individuals were to use similar development methods and operate in similar environments from one project to another.

A.4.2. Problem Complexity Measurement

Metrics such as control complexity do not capture all aspects of problem complexity. Furthermore, code control complexity focuses on the effect of complexity, not the cause. In fact, control complexity may be high due to the existence of a large number of error recovery features, resulting in fewer faults causing failure. Studies should focus on developing measures of problem and requirements complexity. Function points (Albrecht, 1979) or measures of external complexity (Lee *et al.*, 1988) are possible candidates.

A.4.3. Requirements and Design Documents

Studies evaluating the sources of errors (Basili and Perricone, 1984; Boehm *et al.*, 1975; Endres, 1975; Glass, 1981; Hamilton and Zeldin, 1976; Rubey *et al.*, 1975) have reported that requirements and design errors may account for at least one-half of all software errors. These studies suggest that measures of requirements and design quality might be helpful in estimating the number of faults. Furthermore, studies have shown that over one-third of all software failures result from errors of omission (Basili and Perricone, 1984; Glass, 1981; Rubey *et al.*, 1975). Code inference measures can predict errors of omission only if it is assumed that longer and more complex code results when developers omit more code; but, if requirements were not omitted, the code might very well be longer! Analysis of the design process or products could be helpful for predicting omissions. Requirements and design document metrics can supplement code metrics to develop improved estimates.

One possibility for predicting errors of omission is to develop a target relationship between problem complexity and product size. If actual size relative to estimated size is too large, too much complexity could lead to errors. If actual size relative to estimated size is too small, omissions might be indicated. Basic theoretical research linking size, number of faults, and problem complexity is needed.

A.4.4. Code Predictive Measures

Code metrics to predict faults have generally been inferential. The propensity to produce failure may depend more on how the code is used (or tested) than on the complexity or size of the code produced. In fact, one explanation for the larger number of defects occasionally found in smaller modules is that these errors are more apparent (Basili and Perricone, 1984; Shen *et al.*, 1985). Thus, an interesting area of study is the development and use of code predictive metrics that would measure the different ways in which either the software could be used (number of different inputs) or the environment might change.

A.4.5. Process Variables

More cognitive research is needed to determine how error introduction is related to software development. Understanding why the development task is performed in a certain manner and whether proper skills are used could enhance prediction ability. The problem here is not only to determine the critical factors but also how to objectively measure them.

Although there has been a lot of anecdotal evidence suggesting development practices that improve software, research must distinguish between practices that decrease the error rate and those that simply facilitate finding faults. This is difficult because there are many interdependent factors. Furthermore, many factors, such as skill and organization, are difficult to measure objectively. The use of historical fault information collected for individuals can minimize the need to measure and compare process variables.

A.4.6. Process Predictive Studies

Process predictive studies assume that history will repeat itself; i.e., more early errors implies more faults in the software. However, if very thorough testing occurs in the design stage, more errors should be uncovered early in the process, decreasing, rather than increasing, the number of faults found later. One study has recently analyzed the ratio of changes to the amount of effort in order to indicate design progress (Chmura *et al.*, 1990). This approach may also be useful for error prediction. The ratio of changes relative to a metric describing design difficulty could be a potential predictive variable.

A.5. CONCLUSIONS

Although there has been a substantial amount of research in the prediction of software failures, there is still much room for improvement. Future research agendas in software fault prediction should include the following tasks:

- To develop and relate problem complexity metrics to faults.
- To develop requirements and design quality metrics to either infer errors in these documents/programs or predict the causes of future errors, including errors of omission.
- To use different predictor variables for faults of different type and source, e.g., requirements omissions, code omissions, design misinterpretations.
- To develop metrics on an individual basis rather than a general basis in order to reflect similar process characteristics.
- To study the impact of process variables on the number of initial errors before and after testing.
- To develop code metrics that predict difficulty when using code rather than developing it.
- To provide theoretical support for existing and new metrics.

REFERENCES

Adelson, B. and E. Soloway, "The Role of Domain Experience in Software Design," *IEEE Trans. Software Engrg*. **SE-11**(11), (November 1985), 1351–1360.

Akiyama, F., "An Example of Software System Debugging," *Proc. IFIP Congress 71* (August 23–28, 1971), Ljubljana, Yugoslavia, Amsterdam: North Holland, pp. 353–359.

Albrecht, A., "Measuring Application Development Productivity," *Proc. Joint SHARE/GUIDE/IBM Application Development Sympos.*, (October, 1979), Chicago.

Basili, V. and D. Hutchens, "An Empirical Study of a Syntactic Complexity Family, *IEEE Trans. Software Engrg*. **SE-9**(6), (November 1983), 664–672.

Basili, V. and D. Patnaik, "A Study on Fault Prediction and Reliability Assessment in the SEL Environment," Technical Report TR-1699, *NASA Collected Software Engineering Papers: Volume IV*, November, 1986, 4.1–4.27.

Basili, V. and B. Perricone, "Software Errors and Complexity: An Empirical Investigation," *Comm. ACM* **27**(1), (January 1984), 42–52.

Basili, V. and R. Reiter, "An Investigation of Human Factors in Software Development," *Computer* **12**, (December 1979), 21–28.

——"A Controlled Experiment Quantitatively Comparing Software Development Approaches," *IEEE Trans. Software Engrg*. **SE-7**(3), (May 1981), 299–320.

Basili, V. and R. Selby, "Comparing the Effectiveness of Software Testing Strategies," *IEEE Trans. Software Engrg*. **SE-13**(12), (December 1987), 1278–1296.

Boar, B., *Application Prototyping*, New York: Wiley, 1984.

Boehm, B., R. McClean, and D. Urfrig, "Some Experiences with Automated Aids to the Design of Large Scale Reliable Software," in *Proc. Internat. Conf. Reliable Software*, (April 1975), Los Angeles, New York: ACM, 1975, pp. 105–113.

Brooks, F., *The Mythical Man-Month*, Reading, MA: Addison-Wesley, 1982.

Brooks, R., "Towards a Theory of the Cognitive Processes in Computer Programming," *Internat. J. Man-Machine Stud*. **9**, (1977) 737–751.

Brown, J. and M. Lipow, "Testing for Software Reliability," *Proc. 1975 Internat. Conf. Reliable Software*, (April, 1975), Los Angeles, New York: ACM, pp. 518–527.

Card, D., V. Church, and W. Agresti, "An Empirical Study of Software Design Practices," *IEEE Trans. Software Engrg*. **SE-12**(2), (February 1986), 264–271.

Card, D., F. McGarry, and G. Page, "Evaluating Software Engineering Technologies," *IEEE Trans. Software Engrg.* **SE-13**(7), (July 1987), 845–851.

Chmura, L. J., A. F. Norcio, and T. J. Wicinski, "Evaluating Software Design Processes by Analyzing Change Data over Time," *IEEE Trans. Software Engrg.* **SE-16**(7), (July 1990), 729–740.

Coulter, N., "Software Science and Cognitive Psychology," *IEEE Trans. Software Engrg.* **SE-9**(2), (March 1983), 166–171.

Curtis, B., "Measurement and Experimentation in Software Engineering," *Proc. IEEE* **68**(9), (September 1980), 1144–1157.

DeMarco, T., *Structured Analysis and System Specifications*, Englewood Cliffs, NJ: Prentice-Hall, 1979.

Dunsmore, H. and J. Gannon, "Analysis of the Effects of Programming Factors on Programming Effort," *J. Systems and Software* **1**, (1980), 141–153.

Endres, A., "An Analysis of Errors and Their Causes in System Programs," *IEEE Trans. Software Engrg.* **SE-1**(2), (June 1975), 140–149.

Feuer, A. and E. Fowlkes, "Some Results from an Empirical Study of Computer Software," *Proc. Fourth Internat. Conf. on Software Engrg.* (September 17-19, 1979), Munich, Germany, New York: IEEE, pp. 351–355.

Gaffney, J., "Estimating the Number of Faults in Code," *IEEE Trans. Software Engrg.* **SE-10**(4), (July 1984), 459–464.

Gane, C. and T. Sarson, *Structured Systems Analysis: Tools and Techniques*, Englewood Cliffs, NJ: Prentice-Hall, 1979.

Gannon, J., "An Experimental Evaluation of Data Type Conventions," *Comm. ACM* **20**(8), (1977), 584–595.

Gannon, J. and J. Horning, "Language Design for Programming Reliability," *IEEE Trans. Software Engrg.* **SE-1**(2), (June 1975), 179–191.

Glass, R., "Persistent Software Errors," *IEEE Trans. Software Engrg.* **SE-7**(2), (March 1981), 162–168.

Green, T., N. Schneidewind, G. Howard, and R. Pariseau, "Program Structures, Complexity and Error Characteristics," *Proc. Sympos. Computer Software Engrg.*, (April 20–22, 1976), Polytechnic Institute of New York, New York: Halstead, pp. 139–154.

Gremillion, L., "Determinants of Program Repair Maintenance Requirements," *Comm. ACM* **27**(8), (August 1984), 626–632.

Halstead, M. H., *Elements of Software Science*, New York: North American Elsevier, 1977.

Hamilton, M. and S. Zeldin, "Higher Order Software—A Methodology for Defining Software," *IEEE Trans. Software Engrg.* **SE-2**(1), (March 1976), 9–32.

Harrison, W. and C. Cook, "A Note on the Berry-Meekings Style Metric," *Comm. ACM* **29**(2), (February 1986), 123–125.

Jackson, J., *Principles of Program Design*, London: Academic Press, 1975.

Klobert, R., "Calculation of Error Proneness of Computer Programs," *Proc. AIAA/NASA/IEEE/ACM Computers in Aerospace Conf.*, (October 31–Nov. 2, 1977), Los Angeles, 422–426.

Lee, K., T. Dillon, and K. Forward, "Software Complexity and its Impact on Software Reliability," *IEEE Trans. Software Engrg.* **SE-14**(11), (November 1988), 1645–1655.

Lipow, M., "Number of Faults per Line of Code," *IEEE Trans. Software Engrg.* **SE-8**(4), (July 1982), 437–439.

Lipow, M. and T. Thayer, "Prediction of Software Failures", *Proc. Reliability and Maintainability Sympos.*, (1977), Philadelphia, New York: IEEE, pp. 489–494.

McCabe, T., "A Complexity Measure," *IEEE Trans. Software Engrg.* **SE-2**(4), (December 1976), 308–320.

Musa, J. D., A. Iannino, and K. Okumoto, *Software Reliability: Measurement, Prediction, Application*, New York: McGraw-Hill, 1987.

Myers, G., *Reliable Software Through Composite Design*, New York: Van Nostrand and Reinhold, 1975.

——, *The Art of Software Testing*, New York: Wiley, 1979.

Neumann, J. and M. Jenkins, "Prototyping: The New Paradigm for Systems Development," *MIS Quarterly*, September, 1982, pp. 29–44.

Orr, K., *Structured Systems Development*, New York: Yourdon Press, 1977.

Ottenstein, L., "Quantitative Estimates of Debugging Requirements," *IEEE Trans. Software Engrg.* **SE-5**(5), (September 1979), 504–514.

Ross, D., "Structured Analysis for Requirements Definition," *IEEE Trans. Software Engrg.* **SE-3**(1), (January 1977), 6–16.

Rubey, R., J. Dana, and P. Biche, "Quantitative Aspects of Software Validation," *IEEE Trans. Software Engrg.* **SE-1**(2), (June 1975), 150–155.

Schneidewind, N., "Application of Program Graphs and Complexity Analysis to Software Development and Testing," *IEEE Trans. Reliability* **R-28**(3), (August 1979), 192–198.

Schneidewind, N. and H. Hoffmann, "An Experiment in Software Error Data Collection and Analysis," *IEEE Trans. Software Engrg.* **SE-5**(3), (May 1979), 276–286.

Selby, R. and A. Porter, "Learning from Examples: Generation and Evaluation of Decision Trees for Software Resource Analysis," *IEEE Trans. Software Engrg.* **SE-14**(12), (December 1988), 1743–1756.

Selby, R., V. Basili, and F. Baker, "Cleanroom Software Development: An Empirical Evaluation," *IEEE Trans. Software Engrg.* **SE-13**(9), (September 1987), 1027–1037.

Shen, V., T. Yu, S. Thebaut, and L. Paulsen, "Identifying Error-Prone Software—An Empirical Study", *IEEE Trans. Software Engrg.* **SE-11**(4), (April 1985), 317–323.

Takahashi, M and Y. Kamayachi, "An Empirical Study of a Model for Program Error Prediction," *IEEE Trans. Software Engrg.* **SE-15**(1), (January 1989), 82–86.

Teicherow, D. and E. Hershey, "PLA/PSA: A Computer-Aided Technique for Structured Documentation and Analysis of Information Processing Systems," *IEEE Trans. Software Engrg.* **SE-3**(1), (January 1977), 41–48.

Vessey, I., "Strategies for Research into Systems Development: A Cognitive Perspective," Working Paper, University of Pittsburgh, 1986.

Vessey, I. and R. Weber, "Some Factors Affecting Program Repair Maintenance: An Empirical Study," *Comm. ACM* **26**(2), (February 1983), 128–134.

——"Research on Structured Programming: An Empiricist's Evaluation," *IEEE Trans. Software Engrg.* **SE-10**(4), (July 1984), 397–407.

Weinberg, G. M., *The Psychology of Computer Programming*, Van Nostrand Reinhold, New York, 1971.

Yin, B. H. and J. Winchester, "The Establishment and Use of Measures to Evaluate the Quality of Software Designs," *Proceedings of the ACM Software Quality and Assurance Workshop*, (November 1978), San Diego: ACM, pp. 45–52.

Yourdon, E. and L. Constantine, *Structured Design: Fundamentals of a Discipline of Computer Program and Systems Design*, Englewood Cliffs, NJ: Prentice-Hall, 1979.

Youngs, E., "Human Errors in Programming," in *IEEE Tutorial: Human Factors in Software Development* (B. Curtis, ed.) New York: IEEE, 1981, pp. 383–392.

Yu, T., V. Shen, and H. Dunsmore, "An Analysis of Several Software Defect Models," *IEEE Trans. Software Engrg.* **SE-14**(9), (September 1988), 1261–1270.

Zelkowitz, M., "Perspectives on Software Engineering," *Computing Surveys* **10**(2), (June 1978), 197–216.

Appendix B

Mathematical Derivations

B.1. BAYESIAN ESTIMATORS

B.1.1. Prior Distributions

$$f(\mu) = \frac{b^a \mu^{a-1} e^{-b\mu}}{\Gamma(a)} \tag{B.1}$$

$$f(\theta) = \frac{d^c \theta^{c-1} e^{-d\theta}}{\Gamma(b)} \tag{B.2}$$

B.1.2. Likelihood Function and Derivation

Assume a module is tested until time t_e and n failures are observed at times $t_1, t_2, \ldots, t_n$, where $t_n < t_e$. Let $\{t_1, t_2, \ldots, t_n, t_e\} = S$.

$$p(S/\mu, \theta) = \frac{(\mu\theta)^n \exp[-\theta \Sigma t_i] \exp[-\mu(1 - e^{-\theta t_e})]}{n!}, \tag{B.3}$$

where n = number of faults found during execution time t_e; t_i = execution time of module at time of failure; S = set of failure times $t_1, \ldots, t_n$, plus execution time; t_e = amount of time module has executed; θ = per fault hazard rate.

Derivation:

$$P(S/N,\theta) = \binom{N}{n}\left(\prod_{i=1}^{n}\theta e^{-\theta t_i}\right)\left(\prod_{i=1}^{N-n} e^{-\theta t_e}\right) \tag{B.4}$$

$$p(S/N,\theta) = \binom{N}{n}\theta^n \exp\left\{-\theta\left[\sum_{i=1}^{n} t_i + (N-n)t_e\right]\right\} \tag{B.5}$$

Since N has a Poisson distribution,

$$p(S,N/\mu,\theta) = \sum_{N=n}^{\infty}\frac{N!}{(N-n)!n!}\theta^n e^{-\theta[\Sigma t_i+(N-n)t_e]}(\mu^N e^{-\mu}/N!) \tag{B.6}$$

$$p(S,N/\mu,\theta) = \theta^n e^{-\theta\Sigma t_i}e^{-\mu}\sum_{N=n}^{\infty}\frac{\mu^N}{n!(N-n)!}e^{-\theta(N-n)t_e} \tag{B.7}$$

$$p(S,N/\mu,\theta) = \frac{\theta^n e^{-\theta\Sigma t_i}e^{-\mu}}{n!}\sum_{N=0}^{\infty}\frac{\mu^{n+N}}{N!}e^{-\theta N t_e} \tag{B.8}$$

$$p(S,N/\mu,\theta) = \frac{(\mu\theta)^n e^{-\theta\Sigma t_i}e^{-\mu}}{n!}\sum_{N=0}^{\infty}\frac{[\mu e^{-\theta t_e}]^N}{N!} \tag{B.9}$$

$$p(S,N/\mu,\theta) = \frac{(\mu\theta)^n e^{-\theta\Sigma t_i}e^{-\mu}}{n!}\exp(\mu e^{-\theta t_e}) \tag{B.10}$$

$$p(S,N/\mu,\theta) = \frac{(\mu\theta)^n e^{-\theta\Sigma t_i}}{n!}\exp[-\mu(1-e^{-\theta t_e})] \tag{B.11}$$

It is interesting to note that t_i, n, and t_e are sufficient statistics to estimate the likelihood function. The individual t_i are not necessary because of the assumption of exponential (memoryless) time to failure.

B.1.3. Joint Posterior Distribution

$$f(\mu,\theta/S) \propto f(S/\mu,\theta)f(\mu)f(\theta) \tag{B.12}$$

$$f(\mu,\theta/S) \propto \frac{(\mu\theta)^n e^{-\theta\Sigma t_i}\exp[-\mu(1-e^{-\theta t_e})]}{n!}\frac{b^a\mu^{a-1}e^{-b\mu}}{\Gamma(a)}\frac{d^c\theta^{c-1}e^{-d\theta}}{\Gamma(c)} \tag{B.13}$$

$$F(\mu,\theta/S) \propto \frac{b^a d^c}{n!\Gamma(a)\Gamma(c)}\mu^{n+a-1}\theta^{n+c-1}e^{-\theta(\Sigma t_i+d)}e^{-\mu b}\exp[-\mu(1-e^{-\theta t_e})] \tag{B.14}$$

B.1.4. Posterior Marginal Distributions and Derivations

$$f(\mu/S) \propto \int_0^{\infty} f(\mu,\theta/S)\,d\theta \tag{B.15}$$

$$f(\mu/S) \propto \frac{b^a d^c \mu^{n+a-1} e^{-\mu(b+1)}}{n!\Gamma(a)\Gamma(c)} \sum_{j=0}^{\infty} \frac{\mu^j}{j!} \frac{(n+c-1)!}{[jt_e + \Sigma t_i + d]^{n+c}} \tag{B.16}$$

$$f(\theta/S) \propto \int_0^\infty f(\mu, \theta/S)\, d\mu \tag{B.17}$$

$$f(\theta/S) \propto \frac{b^a d^c \theta^{n+c-1} e^{-\theta(\Sigma t_i + d)}}{n!\Gamma(a)\Gamma(c)} \frac{(n+a-1)!}{[(1-e^{-\theta t_e}) + b]^{n+a}} \tag{B.18}$$

Derivations:

$$f(\mu/S) \propto \int_0^\infty f(\mu, \theta/S)\, d\theta \tag{B.19}$$

$$f(\mu/S) \propto \frac{b^a d^c \mu^{n+a-1} e^{-\mu(b+1)}}{n!\Gamma(a)\Gamma(c)} \int_0^\infty \theta^{n+c-1} e^{-\theta(\Sigma t_i + d)} \exp(\mu e^{-\theta t_e}) d\theta \tag{B.20}$$

Now,

$$\exp(\mu e^{-\theta t_e}) = \sum_{j=0}^{\infty} (1/j!)[\mu e^{-\theta t_e}]^j = \sum_{j=0}^{\infty} \frac{\mu^j}{j!} e^{-\theta j t_e} \tag{B.21}$$

So

$$f(\mu/S) \propto \frac{b^a d^c \mu^{n+a-1} e^{-\mu(b+1)}}{n!\Gamma(a)\Gamma(c)} \int_0^\infty \theta^{n+c-1} \sum_{j=0}^{\infty} \frac{\mu^j}{j!} e^{-\theta[jt_e + \Sigma t_i + d]}\, d\theta \tag{B.22}$$

$$f(\mu/S) \propto \frac{b^a d^c \mu^{n+a-1} e^{-\mu(b+1)}}{n!\Gamma(a)\Gamma(c)} \sum_{j=0}^{\infty} \frac{\mu^j}{j!} \int_0^\infty \theta^{n+c-1} \mathrm{e}^{-\theta[jt_e + \Sigma t_i + d]}\, d\theta \tag{B.23}$$

Since

$$\int_0^\infty x^n e^{-ax}\, dx = \frac{n!}{a^{n+1}}, \tag{B.24}$$

$$f(\mu/S) \propto \frac{b^a d^c \mu^{n+a-1} e^{-\mu(b+1)}}{n!\Gamma(a)\Gamma(c)} \sum_{j=0}^{\infty} \frac{\mu^j}{j!} \frac{(n+c-1)!}{[jt_e + \Sigma t_i + d]^{n+c}} \tag{B.25}$$

$$f(\theta/S) \propto \int_0^\infty f(\mu, \theta/S)\, d\mu \tag{B.26}$$

$$f(\theta/S) \propto \frac{b^a d^c \theta^{n+c-1} e^{-\theta(\sum t_i + d)}}{n!\Gamma(a)\Gamma(c)} \int_0^\infty \mu^{n+a-1} \exp[-\mu(1 - e^{-\theta t_e}) + b]\, d\mu \tag{B.27}$$

Now since

$$\int_0^\infty x^n e^{-ax}\, dx = \frac{n!}{a^{n+1}} \tag{B.28}$$

$$f(\theta/S) \propto \frac{b^a d^c \theta^{n+c-1} e^{-\theta(\Sigma t_i + d)}}{n!\Gamma(a)\Gamma(c)} \frac{(n+a-1)!}{[1 - e^{-\theta t_e} + b]^{n+a}} \tag{B.29}$$

B.1.5. Estimators

The mean estimators of μ and θ are as follows:

$$E(\mu) = \int_0^\infty \mu f(\mu/S)\, d\mu \tag{B.30}$$

$$E(\mu) = \int_0^\infty \frac{\dfrac{b^a d^c \mu^{n+a} e^{-\mu(b+1)}}{n!\Gamma(a)\Gamma(c)} \sum_{j=0}^{\infty} \dfrac{\mu^j}{j!} \dfrac{(n+c-1)!}{(jt_e + \Sigma t_i + d)^{n+c}}}{\displaystyle\int_0^\infty \left[\frac{b^a d^c \mu^{n+a-1} e^{-\mu(b+1)}}{n!\Gamma(a)\Gamma(c)} \sum_{j=0}^{\infty} \frac{\mu^j}{j!} \frac{(n+c-1)!}{(jt_e + \Sigma t_i + d)^{n+c}} \right] d\mu} d\mu \tag{B.31}$$

$$E(\theta) = \int_0^\infty \theta f(\theta/S)\, d\theta \tag{B.32}$$

$$E(\theta) = \int_0^\infty \frac{\dfrac{b^a d^c \theta^{n+c} e^{-\theta(\Sigma t_i + d)}}{n!\Gamma(a)\Gamma(c)} \dfrac{(n+a-1)!}{(1 - e^{-\theta t_e} + b)^{n+a}}}{\displaystyle\int_0^\infty \left[\frac{b^a d^c \theta^{n+c-1} e^{-\theta(\Sigma t_i + d)}}{n!\Gamma(a)\Gamma(c)} \frac{(n+a-1)!}{(1 - e^{-\theta t_e} + b)^{n+a}} \right] d\theta} d\theta \tag{B.33}$$

The mean estimator of $e^{-\theta t}$ is $e^{-\theta t} f(\theta/S)\, d\theta$ (Mood *et al.*, 1974).

B.2. PRIOR DISTRIBUTION OF NUMBER OF FAULTS

Proof: If N is Poisson with mean μ, and μ has a Γ distribution with parameters a and b, then the distribution of N is negative binomial.

$$f(N/a, b) = \int_0^\infty \frac{e^{-\mu}\mu^N}{N!} \frac{b^a \mu^{a-1} e^{-b\mu}}{\Gamma(a)} d\mu \tag{B.34}$$

$$f(N/a, b) = \frac{b^a}{N!(a-1)!} \int_0^\infty e^{-\mu(b+1)} \mu^{N+a-1}\, d\mu \tag{B.35}$$

Since

$$\int_0^\infty x^n e^{-ax}\, dx = \frac{n!}{a^{n+1}} \tag{B.36}$$

$$f(N/a, b) = \frac{b^a}{N!(a-1)!} \frac{(N+a-1)!}{(b+1)^{N+a}} = \frac{(N+a-1)!}{(N!)(a-1)!} \left(\frac{b}{b+1}\right)^a \left(\frac{1}{b+1}\right)^N \tag{B.37}$$

This is a negative binomial distribution with parameters a and $b/(b+1)$.

REFERENCE

Mood, A., F. Graybill, and D. Boes, *Introduction to the Theory of Statistics*, New York: McGraw-Hill, 1974.

Appendix C

Hazard Consequence Assessment

Assumptions and Calculations

C.1. COMMERICAL LOAN SYSTEM

Hazard	Assumptions	Consequence ($/month)
Not producing bills	Average monthly bills = $26.7 million. Probability that loan output control will not recognize bills are missing = 0.10. Probability that customer will not alert savings and loan that bills are missing = 0.10.	267,000
Invalid interest	Average monthly interest = $2.4 million. Probability that customer will not alert savings and loan of missing interest = 0.10. Probability that accrual schedule is not entered = 0.10. Overcharges in interest result in customer service problems.	29,000

Hazard	Assumptions	Consequence ($/month)
	Expected undercharges in interest on 50% of accounts at 2%/year.	
Invalid fees	Fees charged on 10% of accounts amounting to 1% of loan. Probability that customer will not alert savings and loan if fees are invalid = 0.10. Additional processing costs for fixing fees.	3,000
Incorrect tracking of payments, disbursements	Overbill 50% resulting in loss of goodwill and additional processing costs. Underbill 50% of time. Probability that loan control does not recognize billing errors = 0.01. Probability customer does not notify savings and loan = 0.2.	5,300
Invalid access	Probability that savings and loan does not recognize invalid access with fraudulent information = 0.001, resulting in loss of average loan of $170,000. Clerical processing costs to fix invalid information: 20 hours @ $25/hour.	700
Overadvance commitments	Probability of exceeding legal lending limit = 0.01. Fines for exceeding legal lending = 1% of average loan. Clerical costs to fix customer accounts: 15 hours @ $25/hour.	400
Insufficient collateral	Probability that customer defaults with insufficient collateral on loan of $170,000 = 0.005.	850
Misposting to general ledger	Clerical costs of $25/hour for 10 hours/week.	1,000
Customer service problems	Goodwill loss due to customer dissatisfaction estimated at 0.01% of average monthly billings. Clerical costs of $25/hour for 13 hours.	3,000

Hazard	Assumptions	Consequence ($/month)
Not managing collateral documentation	Negotiable securities 50% of which have periodic coupons, comprise 40% of collateral. Interest can be lost for one month at 10%/year. Includes late fees and clerical costs to fix of $230.	600
Additional clerical support	8 hours/week @ $25/hour.	800
Invalid government reports	Clerical effort to correct: 10 hours/week @ $25/hour.	1,000

C.2. FUNDS-TRANSFER SECURITY SYSTEM

Hazard	Assumptions	Consequence ($/day)
Outgoing wires not sent	Average daily outgoing wires = $2 million. Liability is equal to 90 days' interest @ 10%/year. Probability that personnel do not realize wires were not sent = 0.001. Probability of loss of interest if wires are not sent = 0.2. Clerical cost to send wires: 1 hour @ $25/hour.	35
Incoming wire not received	Average daily incoming wires = $2 million. Liability is equal to 90 days' interest @ 10%/year. Probability that personnel do not realize wires were not received = 0.005. (Note: This is greater than for outgoing wires because there are fewer external checks.)	75

Hazard	Assumptions	Consequence ($/day)
	Probability of loss of interest if wires are not received = .2. Clerical cost to obtain information: 1 hour @ $25/hour.	
Outgoing wires sent but not posted	Clerical costs to adjust: 1 hour @ $25/hour. No other liabilities, since amounts are checked against general ledger.	25
Incoming wires received but not posted	Clerical costs to adjust: 1 hour @ $25/hour. No other liabilities, since amounts are checked against general ledger.	25
Wires sent with insufficient funds	Average daily wires = $2 million. Probability that customer initiates wire with insuffıcent funds = 0.01. Funds are sufficient for one half of average wire. Liability is equal to 90 days' interest @ 10%/year. Probability that customer borrows money = 0.1. Clerical costs to adjust: 1 hour @ $25/hour.	50
Post outgoing wires to wrong account	Average daily wires = $2 million. Interest is charged for 90 days @ 10%/year. Probability that personnel do not realize the problem exists = 0.005. Probability that customer does not recognize the problem and loan originator incurs loss = 0.2. Probability that invalid recipient could not repay immediately = 0.001. Clerical costs to adjust: 1 hour @ $25/hour.	
Post incoming wires to wrong account	Average daily wires = $2 million. Interest is charged for 90 days @ 10%/year. Probability that wire room personnel do not realize problem = 0.01.	125

Hazard	Assumptions	Consequence ($/day)
	Probability that customer does not recognize problem and loan originator incurs loss = 0.2. Probability that invalid recipient could not repay immediately = 0.001. Clerical costs to adjust: 1 hour @ $25/hour.	
Outgoing wires posted from wrong account	Average daily wires = $2 million. Interest is charged for 90 days @ 10%/year. Probability that customer does not have sufficient funds = 0.001. Clerical costs to adjust: 1 hour @ $25/hour.	75
Fees not charged	Fees are charged on outgoing loans only. Average fees/day = $700. Probability that personnel do not realize problem = 0.01. Clerical costs to adjust: 1 hour @ $25/hour.	32
Incorrect amount wired	Average daily wires = $2 million. Liability is equal to 90 days interest @ 10%/year. Probability that personnel do not realize amount is incorrect = 0.001. Probability of loss of interest = 0.2. Clerical cost to adjust wires: 1 hour @ $25/hour.	35
Incorrect amount received	Average daily incoming wires = $2 million. Liability is equal to 90 days' interest @ 10%/year. Probability that personnel do not realize amount is incorrect. Probability of loss of interest = 0.2. Clerical cost to adjust: 1 hour @ $25/hour.	75
Outgoing wires duplicated	Average daily outgoing wires = $2 million.	35

Hazard	Assumptions	Consequence ($/day)
	Liability is equal to 90 days' interest @ 10%/year. Probability that personnel do not realize duplicate wires were sent = 0.001. Probability of loss of interest = 0.2. Clerical cost to adjust: 1 hour @ $25/hour.	
Unauthorized receipts	Average daily outgoing wires = $2 million. Probability that problem is not realized = 0.0001.	200
Customer service problems	Value of lost business = 0.001% of average wire business per day, $4 million.	40
Extra clerical work	One extra hour per day @ $25/hour.	25

C.3. PAYABLES PROCESSING SYSTEM

Hazard: Do not pay vendor by due date

Assumptions

Late charge penalty = 1.6%/month.
Penalty assessed for one month.
External probability is the probability that a payment is late if software fails.
External probability for standard processing (check requests, patent fees, generic payments) is 0.0001, very low because payment terms are generally net 30 days, allowing sufficient time to accommodate unanticipated problems.
Blanket orders have higher external probability than standard processing because they can be delayed by a discrepancy when the blanket order value is overridden.
Local invoices have higher external probability because approvals can be delayed.
Utility payments have higher external probability than standard processing because of dependence on software for late bill notification.

Calculations

Liability = $ Value of transactions × 0.016
External exposure = Liability × External probability

Results

	External probability	Monthly value ($)	External exposure ($)
Check requests	0.0001	1,430,100	2.29
Blanket orders	0.0010	1,606,500	25.70
Patent fees	0.0001	28,000	0.05
Generic payments	0.0001	43,500	0.07
Local invoices	0.0010	1,714,800	27.44
Utility payments	0.0010	136,045,200	2176.82

Hazard: Pay wrong amount

Assumptions

Equal chance of overpayment or underpayment.

Error involves either transposed digits (899 instead of 989) or slipped digits (9000 instead of 900). Expected underpayment was estimated at 50% of a voucher's value, whereas overpayment was estimated at five times the voucher's value. While slipped digits of more than one place could result in much larger losses, these are expected to be more apparent.

For underpayment, liability is late charge penalty @ 1.6% for one month.

For overpayment, liability is either loss of total amount of overpayment (when no repayment) or interest on overpayment estimated @ 1% per month (when vendor returns overpayment). Average return time is estimated at 3 months.

Probability that overpayment is returned is 0.7.

External probability is the probability that a check is mailed for the wrong amount given software failure.

External probability is low for standard processing because the amount paid is reviewed in Accounts Payable.

External probability is greater for local invoices since these are not verified before they are mailed, but only when approved.

External probability is lowest for utility payments because many are verified by the Energy Department in addition to Accounts Payable.

Calculations

Liability = $ value of transactions × .8065

where 0.8065 =

$$(0.5 \times 0.5 \times 0.016) + (0.5 \times 0.7 \times 0.01 \times 3 \times 5) + (0.5 \times 0.3 \times 5)$$

Underpay — Overpay (returned) — Overpay (not returned)

External exposure = Liability × External probability

Results

	External probability	Monthly value ($)	External exposure ($)
Check requests	0.001	1,430,100	1153.38
Blanket orders	0.001	1,606,500	1295.64
Patent fees	0.001	28,000	22.58
Generic payments	0.001	43,500	35.08
Local invoices	0.005	1,714,800	6914.93
Utility payments	0.0001	136,045,200	10,972.52

Hazard: Charge wrong account numbers

Assumptions

Clerical effort to correct accounts is equal to $3/voucher (12 minutes effort = $15/hour).

Liability exists only if error is found.

Probability that account manager finds errors on local invoices is less than standard processing because s/he had prior opportunity to find error during approval process. If s/he did not recognize the error then, s/he will probably not recognize it later.

There is greater probability that charge distribution errors on large utility bills will be found because of their magnitude as compared to that of other vouchers.

External probability is the probability that account manager finds error.

Calculations

Liability = $3 × Transaction volume

External exposure = Liability × External probability

Results

	External probability	Monthly transactions (Number)	External exposure ($)
Check requests	0.5	4767	7150.50
Blanket orders	0.5	5355	8032.50
Patent fees	0.5	140	210.00
Generic payments	0.5	145	217.50

	External probability	Monthly transactions (Number)	External exposure ($)
Local invoices	0.2	5716	3429.60
Utility payments	0.99	50 (large)	
	0.5	1752 (small)	2776.50

Hazard: Tax information incorrect

Assumptions

There are two types of liabilities, equal probability is assumed for each:

Taxable item may not be coded as taxable, resulting in interest and penalties on the taxes—20% of the value of the taxes, estimated at 6% of the value of the voucher.

Nontaxable item may be coded as taxable, resulting in overpaying taxes. Assume a 6% tax rate.

Applies to all vouchers except patent fees.

External probability is the probability that tax department doesn't recognize error.

External probability is smaller for utility payments because many are reviewed by the Energy Department and tax status is generally known.

Calculations

Liability = \$ value of transactions × 0.036

where $0.036 \times (0.5 \times 0.06 \times 0.2) + (0.5 \times 0.06)$

Taxable Nontaxable

External exposure = Liability × External probability

Results

	External probability	Monthly value ($)	External exposure ($)
Check requests	0.01	1,430,100	514.84
Blanket orders	0.01	1,606,500	578.34
Patent fees			
Generic payments	0.01	43,500	15.66
Local invoices	0.01	1,714,800	617.32
Utility payments	0.0001	136,045,200	489.78

Hazard: Pay wrong vendor

Assumptions

Penalty for not paying on time = 1.6%/month

Assume correct vendor is paid within one month.

Assume wrong vendor returns payment 90% of the time within 3 months. Liability is interest @ 1%/month.

If wrong vendor does not return payment, liability is equal to the value of the voucher.

External probability is the probability that Accounts Payable does not realize wrong vendor is charged.

External probability for this hazard is estimated to be one fifth the external probability of paying the wrong amount. It is felt that personnel who review checks before mailing are more likely to recognize a wrong vendor than a wrong amount.

The external probability is greater for local invoices than standard processing because there is no final verification before payment.

The external probability remains low for utilities because many are verified by the Energy Department.

Calculations

$$\text{Liability} = \$ \text{ value of transactions} \times 0.143$$

$$\text{where } 0.143 = \underset{\text{Late penalty}}{0.016} + \underset{\text{Repay}}{(0.9 \times 3 \times 0.01)} + \underset{\text{Do not repay}}{(0.1 \times 1)}$$

Results

	External probability	Monthly value ($)	External exposure ($)
Check requests	0.0002	1,430,100	40.90
Blanket orders	0.0002	1,606,500	45.95
Patent fees	0.0002	28,000	0.80
Generic payments	0.0002	43,500	1.24
Local invoices	0.0010	1,714,800	245.22
Utility payments	0.00005	136,045,200	972.76

Hazard: Invalid records for hazardous waste

Assumptions

Five percent of all blanket orders and invoices with approval involve hazardous wastes.

Extra clerical effort to find improperly recorded hazardous waste invoices = $10/hazardous waste voucher.

If discovered after 7 years (probability = 0.5), then the potential for a lawsuit is estimated at $1 million with probability = 0.0001. Hence, expected lawsuit penalty is estimated at $50.

No liability is assumed if records are not required.

External probability is the probability that hazardous waste records are needed.

Calculations

Liability = Volume of hazardous waste vouchers × \$10 + expected value of lawsuit

External exposure = Liability × External probability

Results

	External probability	Number of hazardous waste transactions	External exposure (\$)
Blanket orders	0.5	268	1364
Local invoices	0.5	285	1454

Hazard: Invalid inventory records

Assumptions

Clerical effort to adjust invalid inventory records = \$3/inventory voucher.

Liability includes inability to build product because of invalid inventory records, estimated to result in loss of \$50,000 with probability of 0.0001 (\$5).

Inventory records are maintained only for one division of the corporation.

External probability is the probability that error is recognized.

Liability is incurred only if error is recognized.

Calculations

Liability = (Number of inventory transactions × \$3) + \$5

External exposure = Liability × External probability

Results

	External probability	Number of inventory transactions	External exposure (\$)
Check request	0.5	1620	2432.50
Blanket orders	0.5	355	535.00
Patent fees		—	
Generic payments	0.5	145	220.00
Local invoices		—	
Utility payments	0.99	3 (large)	125.86
	0.5	73 (small)	

Hazard: Extra clerical work—low level

Assumptions

Liability involves clerical effort to manually input vouchers.
Inputting voucher requires 6 minutes each ($1.5/voucher @ $15/hour).
Expected effort is equal to two days of processing.
There are twenty working days per month.
Inability to enter data to the system is assumed to require manual entry.

Calculations

External Exposure = Number of monthly vouchers × (2/20) × $1.5

Results

	Number of transactions per month	External exposure ($)
Check requests	4767	715.05
Blanket orders	5355	803.25
Patent fees	140	21.00
Generic payments	145	21.75
Local invoices	5716	857.40
Utility payments	1802	270.30

Hazard: Extra clerical work—high level

Assumptions

Liability involves clerical effort to find and correct invalid information.
Average effort is 20 minutes per voucher ($5/voucher @ $15/hour).
Expected effort equals two days of processing.
There are twenty working days per month.

Calculations

External exposure = Number of monthly vouchers × (2/20) × $5

Results

	Number of transactions per month	External exposure ($)
Check requests	4767	2383.50
Blanket orders	5355	2677.50
Patent fees	140	70.00
Generic payments	145	72.50

	Number of transactions per month	External exposure ($)
Local invoices	5716	2858.00
Utility payments	1802	901.00

Hazard: Duplicate payments

Assumptions

Vendor returns duplicate payment within three months 70% of the time. Liability is equal to interest @ 1%/month.

If vendor does not return duplicate payment, liability equals average value of voucher.

Probability that duplicate is initiated = 0.001

External probability is the product of the probability that a duplicate is initiated and not recognized before sent.

Probability that a local invoice duplicate will not be recognized is lower than for other processing because the approver verifies the invoice online.

Probability that utility duplicate is not recognized is low because of verification in Energy Dept.

Calculations

Liability = \$ value of transactions × 0.321
where 0.321 = (0.7 × 0.01 × 3) + (0.3 × 1)
External exposure = External probability × Liability

Results

	Probability duplicate is not recognized	Monthly value ($)	External exposure ($)
Check requests	0.01	1,430,100	4.59
Blanket orders	0.01	1,686,500	5.15
Patent fees	0.01	28,000	0.09
Generic payments	0.01	43,500	0.14
Local invoices	0.001	1,714,800	0.55
Utility payments	0.005	136,045,200	218.36

Index